sew LINGERIE
Maddie Kulig

Make Size-Inclusive Bras, Panties, Swimwear & More

Everything You Need to Know

stashBOOKS
an imprint of C&T Publishing

Text, photography, and Artwork copyright © 2023 by Marian Madden Kulig

Artwork copyright © 2023 by C&T Publishing, Inc. and Marian Madden Kulig

Publisher: Amy Barrett-Daffin

Creative Director: Gailen Runge

Senior Editor: Roxane Cerda

Editor: Madison Moore

Technical Editor: Debbie Rodgers

Cover/Book Designer: April Mostek

Production Coordinator: Zinnia Heinzmann

Illustrators: Trudy Gardner, Mary Flynn

Photography Coordinator: Rachel Ackley

Photography by Marian Madden Kulig and Katt Wilkins, unless otherwise noted

Published by Stash Books, an imprint of C&T Publishing, Inc., P.O. Box 1456, Lafayette, CA 94549

All rights reserved. No part of this work covered by the copyright hereon may be used in any form or reproduced by any means—graphic, electronic, or mechanical, including photocopying, recording, taping, or information storage and retrieval systems—without written permission from the publisher. The copyrights on individual artworks are retained by the artists as noted in *Sew Lingerie*. These designs may be used to make items for personal use only and may not be used for the purpose of personal profit. Items created to benefit nonprofit groups, or that will be publicly displayed, must be conspicuously labeled with the following credit: "Designs copyright © 2023 by Marian Madden Kulig from the book *Sew Lingerie* from C&T Publishing, Inc." Permission for all other purposes must be requested in writing from C&T Publishing, Inc.

Attention Teachers: C&T Publishing, Inc., encourages the use of our books as texts for teaching. You can find lesson plans for many of our titles at ctpub.com or contact us at ctinfo@ctpub.com.

We take great care to ensure that the information included in our products is accurate and presented in good faith, but no warranty is provided, nor are results guaranteed. Having no control over the choices of materials or procedures used, neither the author nor C&T Publishing, Inc., shall have any liability to any person or entity with respect to any loss or damage caused directly or indirectly by the information contained in this book. For your convenience, we post an up-to-date listing of corrections on our website (ctpub.com). If a correction is not already noted, please contact our customer service department at ctinfo@ctpub.com or P.O. Box 1456, Lafayette, CA 94549.

Trademark (™) and registered trademark (®) names are used throughout this book. Rather than use the symbols with every occurrence of a trademark or registered trademark name, we are using the names only in the editorial fashion and to the benefit of the owner, with no intention of infringement.

Library of Congress Cataloging-in-Publication Data

Names: Kulig, Maddie, 1987- author.

Title: Sew lingerie : make size-inclusive bras, panties, swimwear & more : everything you need to know / Maddie Kulig.

Description: Lafayette, CA : Stash Books, an imprint of C&T Publishing, [2023] | Includes index. | Summary: "In Sew Lingerie, learn the foundations of DIY lingerie, swimwear, and activewear--from the history of lingerie, types of styles, and different fabrics and elastics, to determining your size and making your own garments. Transform your top drawer with affordable, size-inclusive lingerie, swimwear, and activewear that is made just for you"-- Provided by publisher.

Identifiers: LCCN 2023019262 | ISBN 9781644033883 (trade paperback) | ISBN 9781644033289 (ebook)

Subjects: LCSH: Lingerie. | Sport clothes. | Sewing.

Classification: LCC TT670 .K85 2023 | DDC 646.4/204--dc23/eng/20230420

LC record available at https://lccn.loc.gov/2023019262

Printed in the USA

10 9 8 7 6 5 4 3 2

ACKNOWLEDGMENTS

Writing a book has been the most challenging, but also the most rewarding project. When I received an email pitching the idea of a sewing book specifically for lingerie, I hesitated. If you know me, you know that I say yes to any opportunity. Host a Frocktails? Yes, let's do it! Have a retreat in a lodge in the woods? Why not? Fly to Paris for a lingerie trade show? Let's go! But my fingers hovered over the keyboard. Reply? Mark as read? Move to trash? *"Do I know enough?", "Me?", "Can I do this?"* We are all victims of self doubt. 'No' became 'yes' when my husband encouraged me to take on the challenge. He stood by me during every stage of book writing, respecting my time and reminding me how awesome it would be when it was finished. I love you, Ryan. Always have, always will.

Another heartfelt thank you goes to my father, Paul Flanigan. At the ripe age of eighteen and when I had just begun sewing, he encouraged me to start a blog to document what I had made. "You know, this blogging is going to be the next thing." Little did I know that my lil 'ole blog would start as a hobby, then turn into a side business (okay, okay… side hustle) and now has transformed into a life-long career.

To Cora Harrington, lingerie guru who introduced this lingerie sewing nerd to my editor.

To my brothers, James and Gerrit, who still call their sister Maddigans, and have been cheering me on since I first started sewing.

To everyone on the Madalynne team who enables me to be the "Chief Panty Officer" and who shows up every day to help grow the brand: Jenna Smith, Madeline Marvin, Brittney Do, Emma Stevenson, Christine Morozin, Katie Wofford.

A thank you to a fellow bra maker, Jennifer Fairbanks, of Porcelynne Supplies, who has been helping Madalynne for many years, and was pivotal in the creation of this book.

To my two former bosses, Terri Mizelle-Allen and Grace Pirolli, who believed in this college dropout, and gave me a chance to work at one of the biggest fashion retailers. Both set a great example for how to run my own team and set people up for success.

Finally, to you—you who have been a part of my journey since I started my blog, Madalynne, in 2006.

CONTENTS

Introduction 6
  Lingerie Through Time 6
  Body Positivity 9

Getting to Know Lingerie 10
  Types of Lingerie 11
  Lingerie Style Terms 13
  Lingerie Component Terms 18

Tools and Materials 24
  Main Fabrics 25
  Lining Fabrics 27
  Swim Fabrics 28
  Activewear Fabrics 29
  Elastics, Notions, and Underwires 32
  Tools 36

Techniques 40
- Measurements and Sizing 41
- Working with Delicate Fabrics 45
- Making a Toile 47
- Evaluating Fit 48
- Cutting Fabric 50
- Sewing Elastic 52
- Stitch Length 53
- Finishing Seams 53
- Piecing Lace Together 55

Adjusting Patterns 56
- Pattern Making Terms 57
- Common Bra Pattern Alterations 58
- Adjusting Patterns Without Cup Sizes 68
- Adjusting Bra Patterns for Different Underwires 68
- Common Panty Pattern Alterations 70
- Fix Wedgies 74

Panty Projects 76
- Barker Panty 78
- Millie Panty 82
- Ross Panty 86

Bra Projects 94
- Brooklyn Bralette 96
- Margo Bralette 104
- Ryann Bralette 114
- Rey Underwire Bra 124
- Kennedy Sports Bralette 136

Swim Projects 144
- Henrietta One Piece 146
- Hallie Bikini 150

Godiva Underwire Bodysuit 158

Nursing and Mastectomy Bras 168

About the Author 174

Index 175

INTRODUCTION

MY HOBBY, TURNED OBSESSION, turned passionate career started before I sewed my first pair of panties in 2012. Since I can remember, I've been transfixed with lacey, slinky underthings—bras, panties, slips, chemises, negligees. *Gimme, gimme, gimme—I wanted it all!* However, as a petite person with a teeny tiny ribcage and barely A cups, I struggled to find anything that fit, and it felt embarrassing shopping in the pre-teen section. Frustrated, I had the same thought that every sewist does: *"I can make that!"*

So began my journey to make lingerie. Not just for me, but for all people. This book is a culmination of more than ten years of researching, learning, teaching, and fitting thousands of people. The goal of this book is to remove any intimidation you feel surrounding me-made lingerie, and break down terms, construction steps, and pattern making into easy-to-follow concepts. I hope that when you finish reading this book, you will have not only the tools and knowledge, but the confidence and courage to dive into DIY lingerie.

Lingerie Through Time

In just over a century, lingerie has transformed—from restrictive corsets that cinched the waist in, pushed the bust forward, and thrust the derriere backwards, to supportive garments that not only compliment a person's shape, but also their lifestyle.

1914

Mary Phelps patented the "Brassiere"—a device that was lightweight and soft. The modern bra was born.

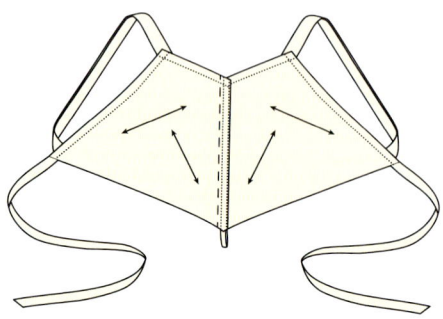

1920s

Young flappers chose lighter and airier fabrics, such as cotton, crepe de chine, shantung, pongee, and rayon.

6   SEW LINGERIE

1941

The first torpedo, or bullet bra, which is a bra that has conical shaped cups was designed by Perma-Lift.

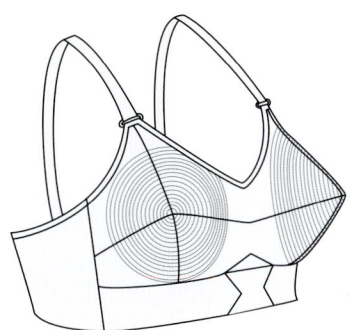

1964

In 1964, the push up bra was invented when Wonderbra released the Dream Lift Model 1300, which was composed of a three-part bra cup, precision angled back, underwires, removable pads (referred to as "cookies"), rigid straps and back support.

1968

Although no bras were actually burned, the anti-bra movement heated-up with the 1968 Miss America Pageant in Atlantic City when contestants began throwing feminine products including bras, hairspray, makeup, girdles, corsets, and false eyelashes into the trash.

1977

The first sports bra, the Jogbra broke down barriers women had long faced in sports.

In 1977, Roy Raymond started Victoria's Secret as a place where men could feel comfortable shopping for women.

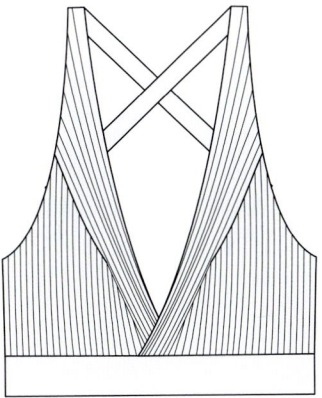

1995

The first Victoria's Secret Fashion Show was launched a few days before Valentine's Day in 1995.

2014

In 2014, American Eagle's loungewear and lingerie line, Aerie, launched its #AerieREAL campaign with a mission to eliminate retouching and accept beauty without revisions.

2018

In 2018, music and fashion icon, Rihanna, launched Savage X Fenty, disrupting the lingerie industry with affordable price points and wide size range.

INTRODUCTION

Lingerie Today

In just over a century, lingerie has been worn in so many different ways, and sometimes not at all. Today, the world is seeking more options in terms of sizing, comfort, diversity, functionality, and sustainability.

The impact of Instagram on the lingerie industry cannot be overlooked either. The social media giant has flipped our perception and definition of beauty by helping make it commonplace for users to post and share images of themselves in lingerie. It has also became a powerful platform to stand up for equality, such as the #freethenipple movement. Only female nipples are banned on Instagram, and people posting the hashtag are standing up against objectifying and censoring breasts and nipples.

Body Positivity

"Love the skin you're in"—it's a message and hashtag that is thrown around ubiquitously today, but that wasn't always the case. It wasn't long ago that only slender bodies deemed socially acceptable were portrayed in the media. There are still many improvements to make around inclusivity, but we have come a long way since the late 1960s. Today, fat, non-white, queer, disabled, and other marginalized groups are depicted as independent, successful, sexy, smart, capable, and—importantly—as loving themselves unapologetically for who they are. But, like all movements, body positivity can fall prey to exclusivity and shame.

One part of the current wave of the body positivity movement began ten years ago as an Instagram hashtag (#bodypositivity) posted by people in the fat acceptance movement—a group consisting mostly of fat and ethnic minorities who praised self love of visibly fat bodies.

It quickly became popular on other social media channels, and businesses and brands took note, using it as a marketing opportunity. Though it started with good intentions, it has been co-opted and created its own standard of what's pretty. Unfortunately, this results in people who are a different size or are a different ethnicity being excluded from the conversation, even though they were the ones who started it.

Recently, body neutrality has grown in popularity over body positivity. While body positivity promotes people to love their bodies no matter their physical appearance, neutrality focuses on the body as a vessel that is neither positive nor negative.

Promoting a diverse range of people and bodies is crucial to the creation of this book. By uplifting marginalized voices and spotlighting all kinds of people, we are working to move forward and help encourage confidence in one's own body. We must push advertisers, businesses, and brands to continue doing their part across the board—portraying a diverse range of people in their campaigns, employing a diverse set of people, stocking plus sizes and creating complete size charts—all while not marketing their efforts as "revolutionary" or "game-changing," words that continue to alienate and other people of different sizes, abilities, or needs. Change is happening slowly, and we must continue pushing for a world where all bodies are treated equitably.

GETTING TO KNOW LINGERIE

This chapter is a great primer for all of the types, terms, and styles of lingerie that you may see in this book, or hear out in the world as you start sewing. Use this chapter as a knowledge base to refer back to as needed.

TYPES OF LINGERIE, *page 11*

LINGERIE STYLE TERMS, *page 13*

LINGERIE COMPONENT TERMS, *page 18*

10 SEW LINGERIE

Types of Lingerie

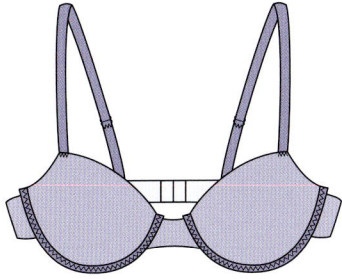

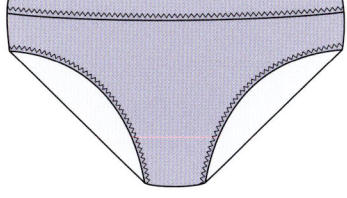

BRA

A bra, short for brassiere, is an undergarment worn to support the breasts. Bras vary widely in use, style, and design.

PANTY

A pair of panties, short for underpants, is an undergarment that covers the body from the waist to the upper thighs. The name for this garment can vary from country to country; they are sometimes called pants, undies, or knickers. Like bras, panties can vary widely in style and design.

BODYSUIT

A bodysuit is a bra and panty combined into one piece. What differentiates a bodysuit from a leotard or a swimsuit is that it has a snap opening at the gusset, or crotch (which can be eliminated if it is not comfortable for the wearer).

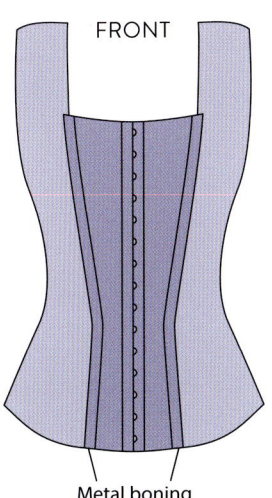

FRONT

Metal boning at seamlines

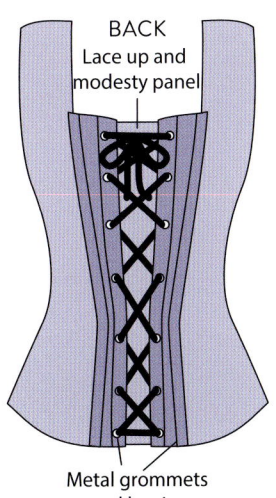

BACK
Lace up and modesty panel

Metal grommets and boning

CORSET

A corset is a tight fitting undergarment primarily worn to cinch the waist and/or fill out the hips. It usually consists of plastic or metal boning and hooks or lacing in the back. Corsets can be used for back support as well.

GETTING TO KNOW LINGERIE

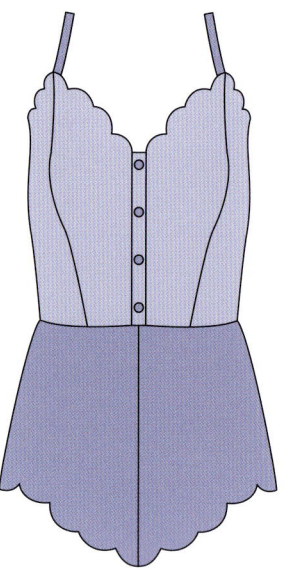

TEDDY

A teddy is a camisole and panty combined into one piece. It is similar to a bodysuit, but is usually looser.

CHEMISE

Translating to "shirt" in French, a chemise or slip is a night dress. It usually ends between the mid-thigh and knee, but it can be long as well. A chemise has other names, including a nightie.

BABYDOLL

A chemise and a babydoll look similar—they're both short, sleeveless, and can be found in a variety of fabrics—but there are key differences. A babydoll ends just below the panties instead of extending down the leg. Some babydolls end above the panty line so they can be sold with panties as a set. Chemises also usually have a slimmer fit, especially around the hips, while babydolls usually have fabric that is gathered underneath the breasts that flares out around the waist and hips.

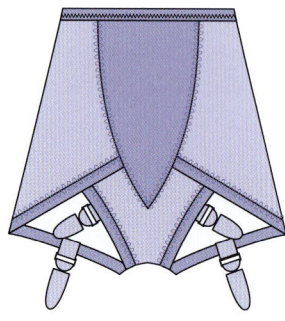
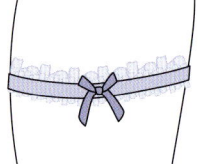

GIRDLE

A girdle is a form-fitting undergarment that is meant to create a smooth fit and appearance around the torso and sometimes in the legs. A girdle can be worn for medical reasons, but is usually worn underneath special occasion, form-fitting garments (like a wedding dress) or garments made of sheer fabrics. They are often worn to avoid visible panty lines (VPLs) or indentations due to skin or fat.

GARTER

Most often worn by brides, a garter is a band of fabric worn around the thigh. It can be worn alone, or it can be hooked onto stockings to ensure that they stay in place.

SEW LINGERIE

Lingerie Style Terms

Bra Types

Bra Component Terms (page 18) will help to clarify all the descriptions in this section.

FULL CUP
A full cup bra covers the breast tissue entirely.

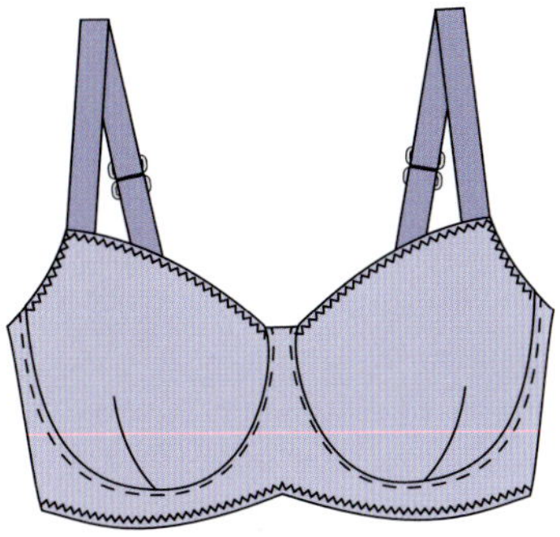

DARTED CUP
A bra with darted cups has bust darts which usually begin at the wire seam line and end ½" (13mm) from the fullest part of the cup. There can be one dart or multiple darts. The more darts, the more volume the bra cup can accommodate.

BRALETTE
There are many factors that differentiate a bra from a bralette, but the key difference is that a bralette does not have an underwire. If made with the correct fabrics and elastics, bralettes can be just as supportive as underwire bras. While a bra is mostly a foundation garment, bralettes have a fashion element to them.

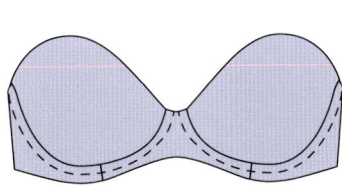

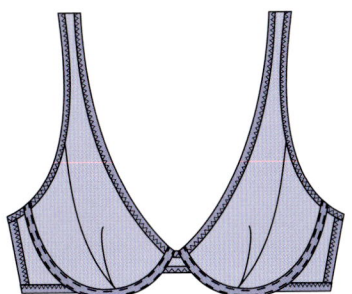

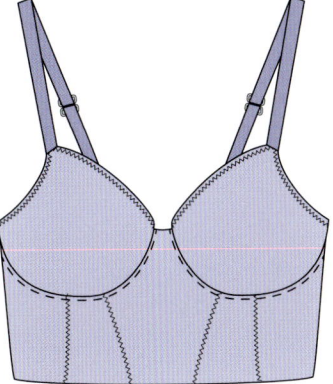

STRAPLESS
Just as the name suggests, a strapless bra does not have straps. Strapless bras usually rely on a wider band, longer underwires, and silicone elastic to stay in place.

PLUNGE
A plunge bra neckline extends down to a gore that sits lower on the chest wall. This results in more visible cleavage. Plunge bras are a great option for blouses or dresses with low necklines.

LONGLINE
A longline bra extends from the bra cups down towards the waist. Since 80% of a bra's support comes from the band, a longline bra can offer more support.

GETTING TO KNOW LINGERIE

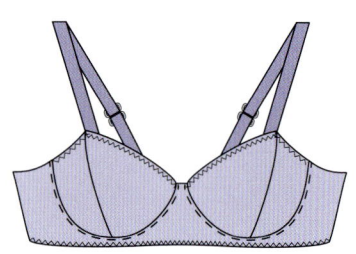

DEMI

A demi bra covers half to three-quarters of the breast, creating more cleavage.

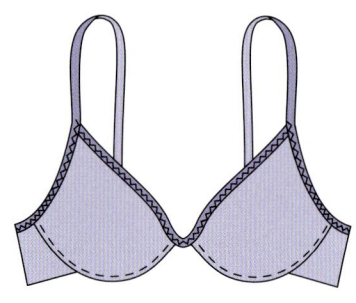

BUSTIER

A bustier bra is similar to a longline bra in that both extend down towards the waist, but a bustier usually has boning with paneling. A bustier also pushes the breasts up to create cleavage.

MOLDED/CONTOUR

Molded cup bras have pre-shaped bra cups without seams that create a natural, smooth, rounded shape, ideal for wearing underneath tight fitting clothing.

PUSH UP

A push up bra is a bra that creates cleavage by using padding inside the lower cups to push the breasts upwards.

BALCONETTE

A balconette, or balcony bra, is a bra with a completely horizontal neckline. The cups are usually low cut and the straps are usually set wide. Meaning "little balcony", some people claim the name comes from the idea that the bra cannot be seen if someone was looking down from a balcony.

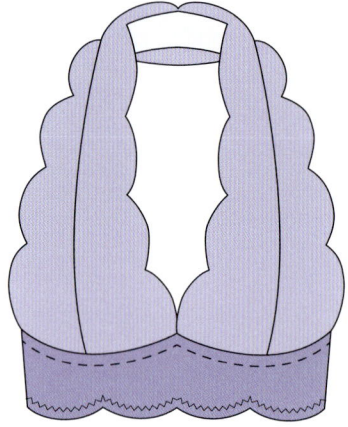

HALTER

A halter bra is a bra in which the straps wrap around the neck. Halter bras are a great option for backless tops and dresses. A halter is not a great option for full busted people since the weight of the breasts is pulling down on the neck.

Breast Terms

Cleavage: Technically, cleavage means the hollow, or space, in between breasts. It has taken on a new meaning, and generally refers to a neckline that emphasizes décolletage (the upper portion of the breast).

Lift: Lift refers to how much a bra pushes or directs the breast tissue upwards.

Chest wall: Chest wall is a bra making term for the ribcage.

SEW LINGERIE

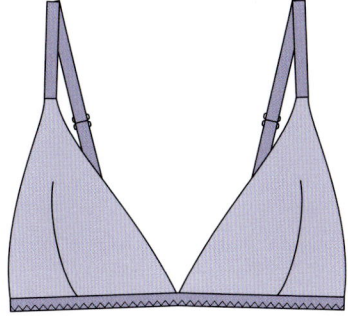

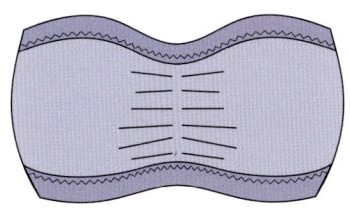

PEEK-A-BOO

A peek-a-boo bra is a bra with open areas, or all of the bra cup is open, so breasts and/or nipples are exposed.

TRIANGLE

A triangle bra is a bra with triangle shaped cups.

BANDEAU

A bandeau bra usually has material wrapping around the torso in one piece. Bandeau bras can have cups, but most often do not. Some people, including transgender men, wear bandeau bras to bind their breasts in place and create the appearance of a flat chest.

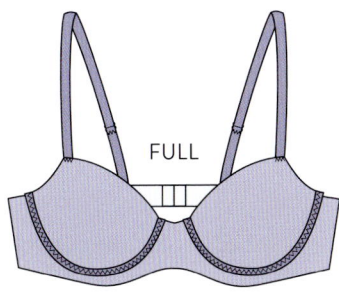

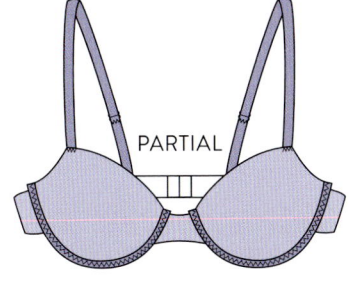

SPORTS

A sports bra is a more supportive style usually worn during exercise. Its main purpose is to reduce or eliminate breast movement.

LOUNGE

A lounge bra is a type of bra that is less supportive and meant for leisure activities like working from home or running errands.

UNDERWIRE BRA

A bra with cups supported by a wire called an underwire. Most underwire bras fall into two categories:

Full Band: The cups of the bra are sewn into the frame of the bra.

Partial Band: The bra does not have a frame, and the band and the bridge are separate pieces.

Breast Root: Breast root is the crease or fold underneath the breasts where the breast tissue comes away from the chest wall. This is where an underwire should sit in order to properly carry and support the weight of the breasts.

GETTING TO KNOW LINGERIE

Panty Types

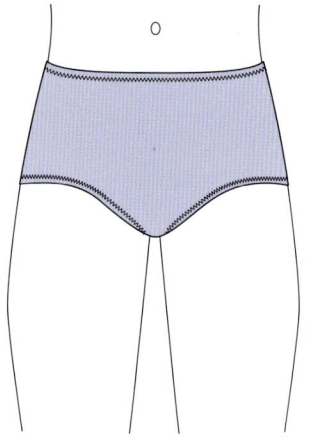

BRIEF
Briefs are a classic, everyday panty that are usually low cut and full coverage in the rear.

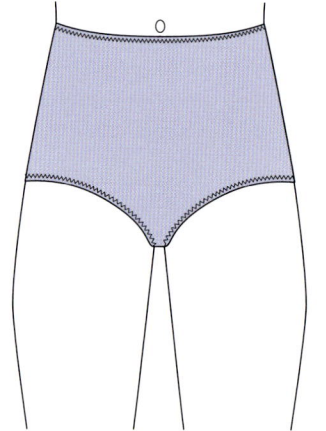

HIGH-RISE
High-rise briefs are similar to a standard brief in that they offer full coverage, but they sit higher on the waist.

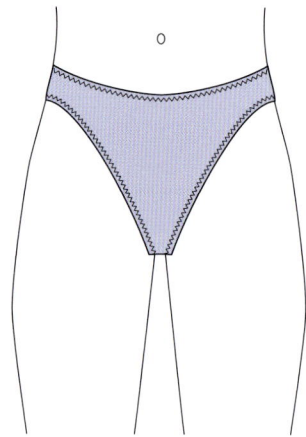

FRENCH CUT
French cut panties sit high on the waist like a high-rise brief, and they also have leg openings that hit higher on the hip/waist.

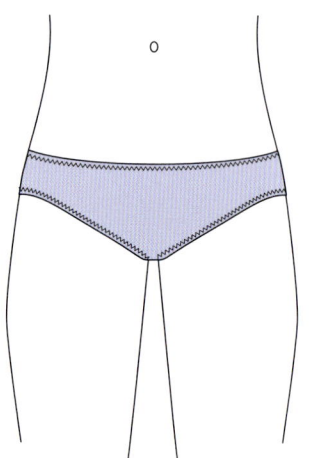

BIKINI
Bikinis are similar to briefs but provide less coverage of the rear.

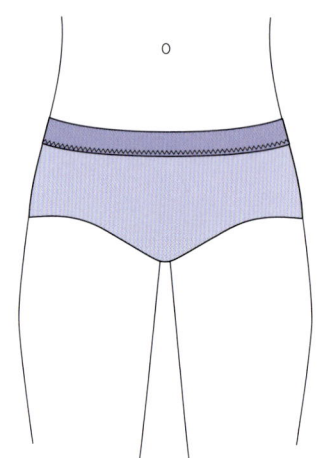

BOYSHORT
Boyshorts offer full front and back coverage, with the leg openings ending just below the top of the thigh. Boyshorts resemble men's underwear (hence the name) and offer extra modesty under a skirt or dress.

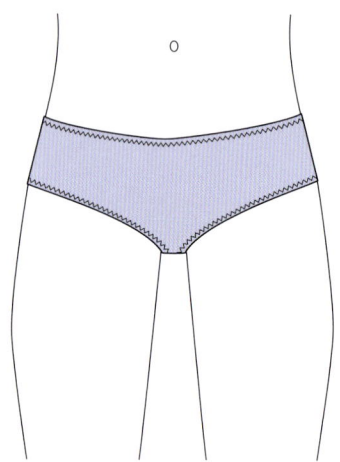

HIP HUGGER/HIPSTER
Hip huggers sit on the hips and have low-cut leg openings, offering slightly more coverage on the legline than a bikini and slightly less than a boyshort.

16 SEW LINGERIE

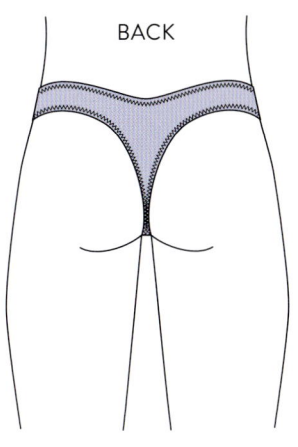
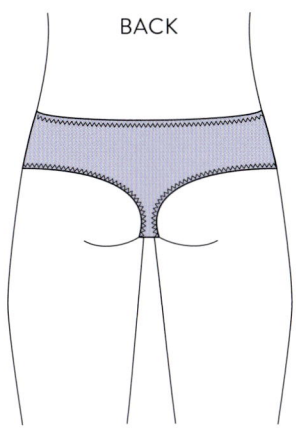
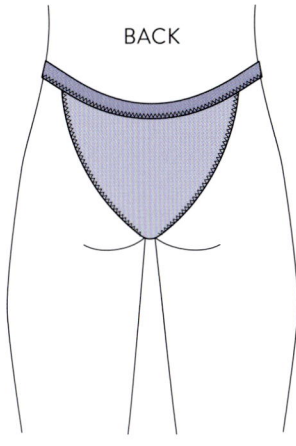

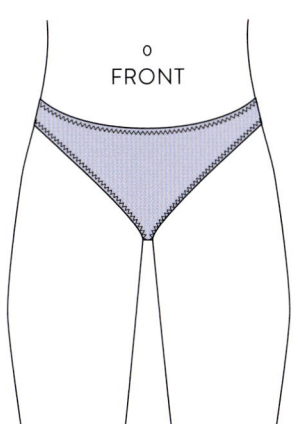
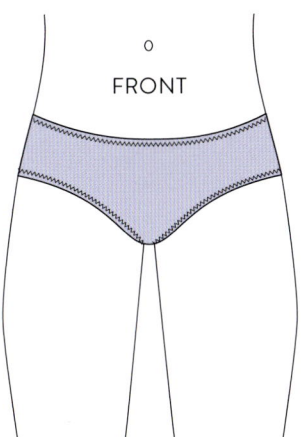
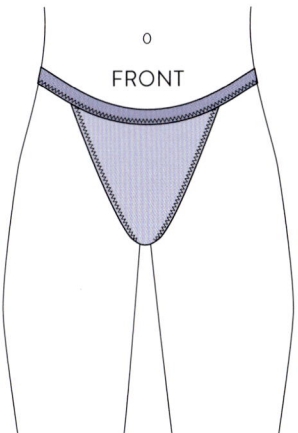

THONG

Thongs offer no rear coverage by laying between the butt cheeks and are meant to be worn underneath pants and skirts to eliminate VPLs.

CHEEKY

Cheeky panties are between a classic brief and a thong. They are usually low cut and offer some back coverage, with just a little butt cheek peeking through.

TANGA

A tanga is between a bikini and a thong, and has wide elastic or fabric connecting the front to the back at the sides.

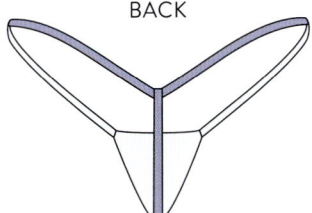
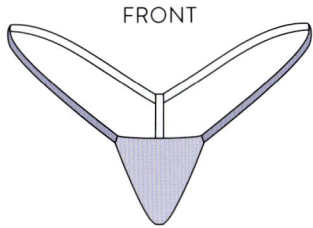

G-STRING

A G-string has the least amount of coverage. Similar to a thong, a g-string is meant to eliminate VPLs by having a single string or elastic in the back.

GETTING TO KNOW LINGERIE

Lingerie Component Terms

Lingerie, especially bras, can be very complex garments. Wing, gore, hook and eye—a bra can contain many pieces, each playing an integral part in achieving the proper support. Understanding the anatomy of a bra and its purpose will make you a better lingerie sewist and help you find what style works best for your body.

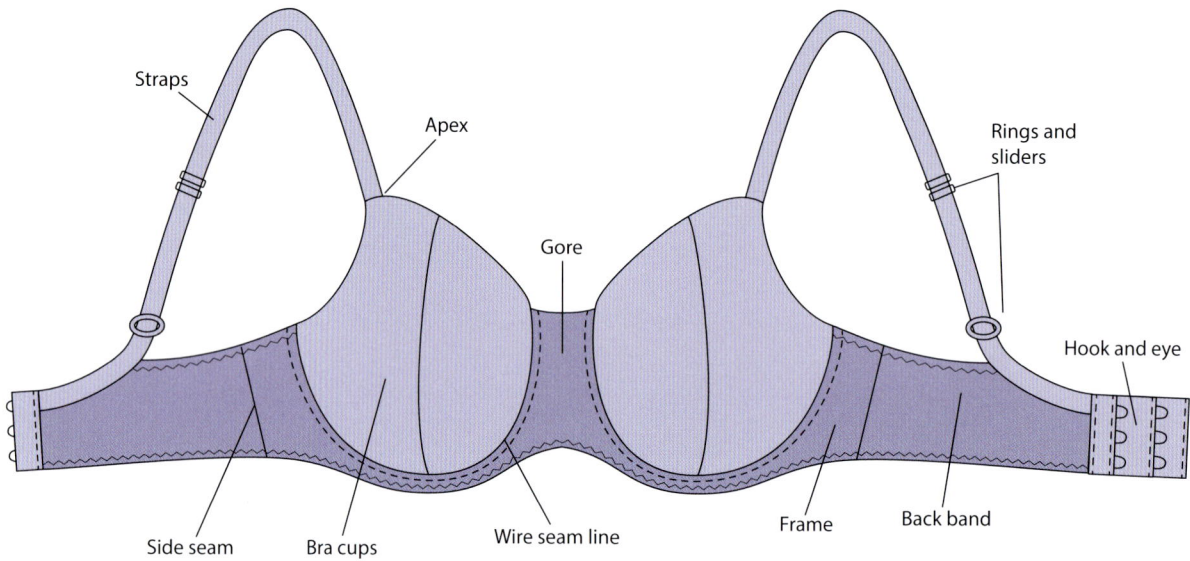

Bra Components

Cups

Bra cups cover, hold and shape the breasts. The shapes of bra cups vary depending on fashion trends, the desired look, and desired support. Nowadays, most bra cups are a round, natural shape. The silhouette of a bra cup plays a big part in its style. Bra cups can have a single cup that holds both breasts, such as a sports bra or bandeau bra, or a bra can have two, three, or four sections. The more seams or sections a bra cup has, the more volume it can support.

Bra cup seams can be vertical, horizontal, diagonal, or a combination. The type of seaming can be used to achieve different levels of support. They can also be seamless, lined, or unlined. If a bra has an underwire, the underwire is part of the cup and is encased in channeling sewn to the wire seam line. The wire seam line is the seam that connects the bra cups to the gore, frame or band.

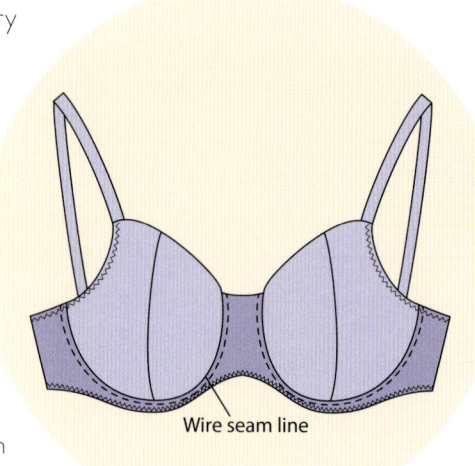

SEW LINGERIE

HORIZONTAL SEAMED CUP

A horizontal cup seam starts and ends in the wire seam.

Upper cup: The upper cup, also called the top cup, is the part of the cup above the horizontal seam line. If you have breasts that are different sizes or shapes, an upper cup made with stretch fabrics can help achieve a symmetrical fit because the stretch can accommodate the differences within the same bra.

Lower cup: The lower cup, also called the bottom cup, is the part of the cup below the horizontal seam line. It is essential to providing lift. The lower cup can be reinforced with lining, have padding, or be made of a firm material, all of which provide additional lift.

Side cup (power bar): Power bars are panels that are most often paired with a horizontal seamed cup to push the breast tissue towards the center front. This creates a push up effect. They also provide some additional support and lift.

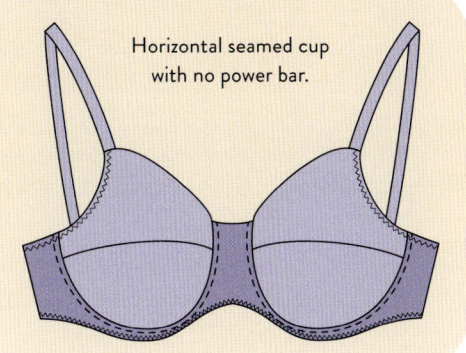

Horizontal seamed cup with no power bar.

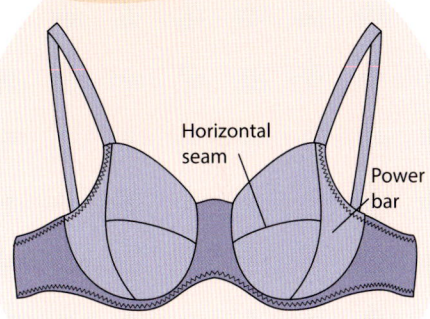

Horizontal seam
Power bar

VERTICAL SEAMED CUP

A vertical cup seam starts in the wire seam line and ends in the neckline.

Center front cup: The cup closest to the center front.

Side cup: The cup closest to the underarm. Just like a power bar, side cups can be used to push the breast tissue towards the center front to create a push up effect.

Middle cup: In the case where the cup has two or more vertical seams, the middle cup(s) are in between the center front and side cups. The more seams a bra cup has, the more volume it can accommodate, so having a middle cup(s) is recommended for people with larger cup sizes.

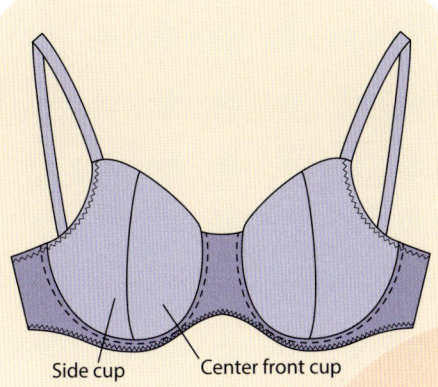

Side cup
Center front cup

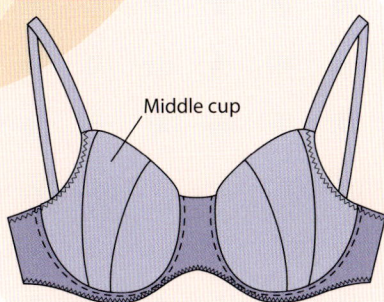

Middle cup

GETTING TO KNOW LINGERIE 19

DIAGONAL SEAMED CUP

A diagonal seam starts in the underarm and ends in the wire seam line. Diagonal seamed cups are most often used in combination with a vertical seam that splits the lower cup into two sections. The diagonal seam and the vertical seam on the lower cup work together to provide lift, add support, and center the breast tissue.

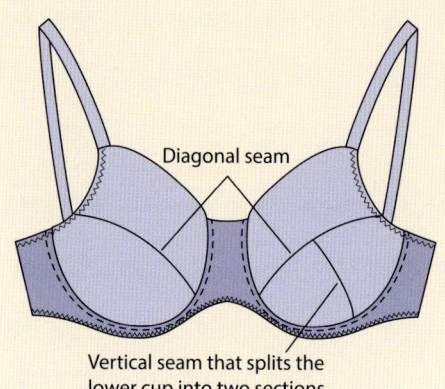

DARTED CUP

A darted cup has one or more darts that are most often placed on the wire seam line. Darted cups are best for small cup sizes (A–D) since darts can only accommodate so much volume. Above a D cup, it is best to choose a seamed cup. For visual reference, see Darted Cup (page 13).

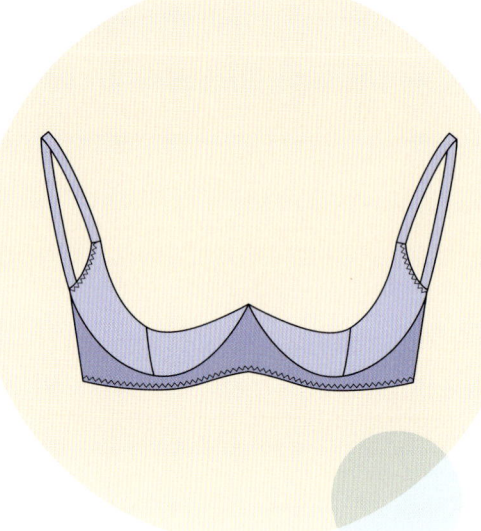

QUARTER CUP

Just as the name suggests, a quarter cup is a bra cup with only a quarter of the fabric of a full coverage bra. The fabric stops below the nipple, and is often molded. Quarter cups without another bra cup are generally made for aesthetic reasons. If a quarter cup is combined with a seamed bra cup, it can provide a lot of lift.

MOLDED CUP

A molded cup, also called a contour cup, is made of a layer of padding that has been pre-shaped to be smooth and round. Molded cups are a great choice for wearing underneath t-shirts, but this construction has limitations. Because the cup is pre-shaped, breasts are forced into a certain shape.

The material of a molded cup can only hold so much weight, so it is not a good choice for very large cup sizes. This is why most very large cup sizes are seamed. For the home sewist, molded cups can be achieved by sewing polylaminate foam together. There will still be a seam, but it is the closest handmade way to get the look of a molded cup. For visual reference, see Molded/Contour (page 14).

Gore (Bridge)

The bridge, or gore, is the piece in between the bra cups at the center front that provides separation between the breasts. The gore should lay flat, or tack, against the chest wall. If the gore does not tack to the chest wall, that is a key indicator that the bra cups do not have enough volume. If the gore is digging in, that is a key indicator the bra cups need less volume.

Different gore widths and depths determine how exposed the breasts are. The higher the gore, the more coverage a bra will have. The lower the gore, the less coverage a bra will have, and thus more breast tissue will be exposed.

> **WIDE OR NARROW BREASTS**
> Take the two finger test to determine if you have wide or narrow set breasts. If you can fit two fingers in between your breasts, then you have wide set breasts. If you can't fit two fingers in between your breasts, then you have normal or narrow set breasts. This isn't exact, but it can be used as a general guideline. If you are wide set, then you can wear bras with different gore widths comfortably. It is more challenging to find the right gore if you are narrow set because there is less space, if any, to accommodate a gore. In most cases, a bra with a gore that is lower will work better for people with narrow set breasts since the gore will be sitting on the chest wall just below where the breasts meet.

Frame (Cradle)

Together with the gore, the frame is responsible for the majority of a bra's support. In some cases, the gore, frame, and back band are considered one piece and just called the band. But in this book, they are separated into different components. The frame is the portion of the bra directly underneath the bra cups. In a partial band bra, there is no frame, only a gore and back band.

GETTING TO KNOW LINGERIE

Back Band (Wing)

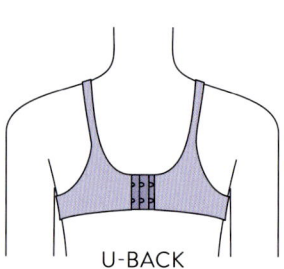
U-BACK

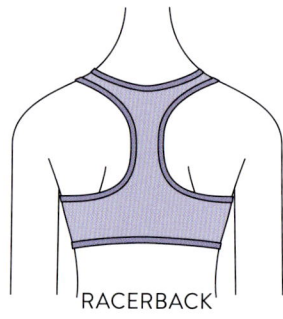
RACERBACK

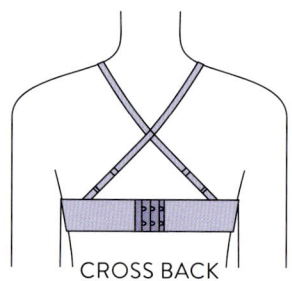
CROSS BACK

The back band, also referred to as the wing, is the back portion of a bra. Back bands can be made of many different types of materials, but should almost always have stretch to ensure a comfortable fit. There are instances where a non-stretch material can be used, like for a bra that has a very narrow band or a bra for a small cup size. Back bands can have different cuts, from U-back to racerback, and more. Each type provides a different level of support.

Straps

Shoulder straps vary in width and placement on a bra. Straps are available with or without stretch and with or without padding. Most shoulder straps are adjustable at the back, but there are some that can be adjusted at the front, called boutique straps. There are also non-adjustable shoulder straps.

RINGS AND SLIDERS

Rings and sliders are sewn onto bra straps and allow the wearer to modify or change the length of shoulder straps. Over time, the elasticity of shoulder straps will give, so rings and sliders allow the wearer to make them tighter to maintain a good fit. The width of rings and sliders should be the same width or ⅛" bigger than the width of the shoulder straps.

Hook and Eye

A hook and eye is a fastener sewn to the back of a bra. One side has metal or plastic hooks and the other side has eyes where the hook is fastened. Hooks and eyes are measured by the number of rows and columns they have. The most common are 1 × 3, 2 × 3 or 3 × 3. Hooks and eyes are also available as long strips which are most often used in longline bras, corsets, or bras for very large cup sizes.

The hook should be fastened on the loosest setting when the wearer first wears a bra. As the elasticity of the bra gives over time, the hook should be fastened to the middle setting, and then the tightest setting. If you buy or make a bra and have to immediately put it on the tightest setting in order for it to fit, you should go down a band size.

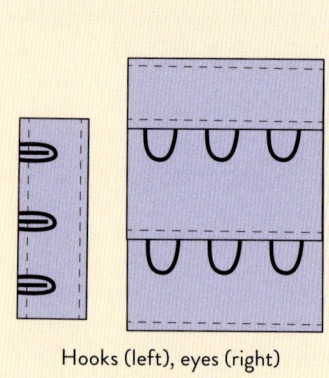
Hooks (left), eyes (right)

SEW LINGERIE

Underwire

Underwires are pivotal, but not essential to providing support. Underwires mimic the shape of the breast root (page 15). Underwires anchor the bra to the torso; the gore on a bra that does not have an underwire will pull away from the body. Underwires are usually narrower than the breast root, which helps the breasts "scoop" into the cup, and "spring open" when worn.

Another key determinant in how much support an underwire will provide is the gauge and material. Underwires can be made of metal, plastic, or silicone and can be coated or uncoated. Underwires can be a thin gauge, which is best for small cups, or heavy gauge, which is best for larger cups. Read more about this notion in Underwire (page 35).

Underwire Channeling

Underwires are inserted into a trim called underwire channeling. It should not be between the channeling and the fabric. Some bras are made with channeling, but without the underwire. This is a great option for people who like the look of an underwire bra, but dislike underwire itself.

Internal Sling

An internal sling is a piece of fabric sewn into the wire seam line that provides additional support. The fabric is usually made of non-stretch material and typically is not more than half the height of the cup itself.

Panty Components

Front
The front is the front part of the panty that covers the stomach and pubis.

Back
The back is the back part of the panty that covers the butt.

Waistband
The waistband is the band around the waist that helps the panty stay in place and contours the waist and hips. The waistband can be made of elastic, lace, or other stretch material.

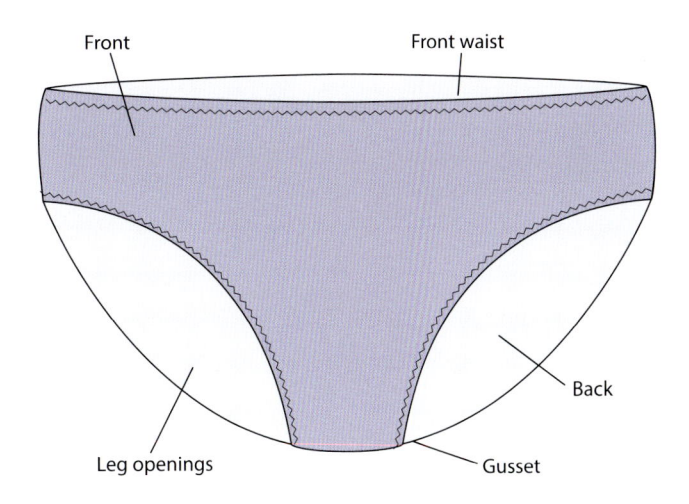

Leg Openings
The leg openings are where the legs are inserted, allowing the wearer to put on or take off the panties.

Gusset
The gusset covers the genital area and is usually lined with an absorbent material like cotton.

GETTING TO KNOW LINGERIE

TOOLS AND MATERIALS

Having the right tools and materials is so important when sewing lingerie, activewear, and swimwear. Let's imagine you have a scalloped lace that has the prettiest, embroidered edge and is the perfect shade of purple. But without the right quality elastic, it will be a pain to sew. No really—the biggest pain in the you know what. Cursing at your machine and fabric will ensue. This chapter will get you acquainted with all the necessary terms, and I'll also share my tips for shopping and scoring the best quality supplies.

Main Fabrics

Main fabrics can be called many different things—fashion, outer—but basically, it means the fabric that is either used the most in a project or the fabric that is seen on the exterior of a finished garment.

A GALLOON LACE True confession, when I first heard the term 'galloon,' I thought it referred to some sort of pirate thing. *Galloon, say what?* It's a fabric term that has a broad meaning, but in the world of bra making, it refers to a type of lace that has one or both edges finished with a decorative, scalloped edge. If both edges are decorative, it is called a double galloon lace.

Galloon laces range in widths, from ½″ (13mm) to over 40″ (101cm). Narrower widths, between ½″ (13mm) and 4″ (10cm) are used most often for panties. Widths between 4″ (10cm) and 11″ (28cm) are used most often for bras. Galloon laces that are 11″ (28cm) or wider are used a lot in bodysuits, but can be used in bras and panties. Galloon laces can be stretch or non stretch.

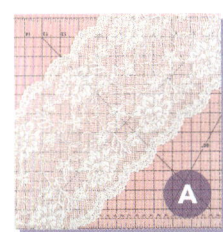

B EMBROIDERED TULLE LACE has an embroidered design that is stitched to a tulle or net base. If the embroidery is stitched on the edge, it is a type of galloon lace. The fabric can be embellished with decorative elements such as beads and ribbons, and it is usually used for higher end or special occasion lingerie. Since it is on a net or tulle base, it is most commonly non stretch.

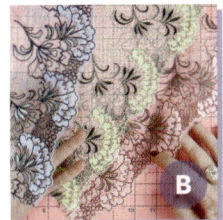

C ALL OVER LACE doesn't have a decorative edge. It can be stretch or non stretch, and it usually comes on a bolt that is 36″ (91cm), 45″ (114cm), or 58″ (147cm) wide. It is easy to find in craft stores and online.

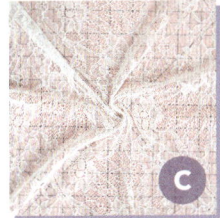

D SPANDEX is what allows fabric to stretch and then recover to its original shape. LYCRA is the trademarked brand name of spandex, also sometimes called elastane. Even though it is technically a fiber, it is often referred to as a fabric. What I love about spandex fabric is that it can be used in lingerie, swimwear and activewear and is easy to find, so you get more bang for your buck!

E SILK is a luxurious fabric that is super strong, breathable, wicks moisture, and is hypoallergenic. Pure silk does not fray like a poly or blended silk, which is important when dealing with ¼″ (6mm) seam allowances in bra making.

TOOLS AND MATERIALS 25

F **STRETCH MESH** is a semi-sheer fabric that can be solid, printed or embellished.

G **STRETCH VELVET** is a soft, luxurious fabric that has a pile: tufts or loops of fibers or yarns that stand up from the base of the fabric. It also has a smooth nap, meaning the texture of the fabric can be aligned in one direction to make the fabric smooth. Stretch velvet can be bulky, so use it in lingerie designs that have minimal seaming.

H **COTTON** is super soft, breathable, washes easily, and doesn't cause many allergic reactions. Many people look for cotton lingerie because lingerie made with synthetic fabric can result in rashes, hives, etc. for wearers with sensitive skin or bodies. But, cotton absorbs and holds onto moisture and loses its shape easily, which is a major downside when using it in lingerie.

I **BAMBOO** is a plant-based alternative to cotton. It is often marketed as a sustainable option since bamboo is one of the fastest growing trees on the planet, but with manufacturing practices, it often isn't very eco-friendly. Bamboo wicks sweat, is extremely soft, has antimicrobial properties, and is absorbent. It is warm in the winter and cool in the summer, just like silk.

J **JERSEY** —a lightweight, stretchy knit—is available in a variety of different fibers: cotton, polyester, rayon, bamboo, and more. Because it is so soft, it is often used in panties, teddies, chemises, and other nightwear. I recommend using supportive lining alongside it for a bra or bralette.

K **DUOPLEX** is a low stretch, knit fabric made of 100% polyester. It does not have much mechanical give—the amount of stretch a fabric has due to the way it is woven—on the cross grain. It has no stretch lengthwise. It usually has one matte side and one shiny side, making it a reversible fabric. Because it is so strong, it can be used for the bra cups, frames, or bridges without having to use a lining.

YES OR NO? SHOULD YOU PREWASH LINGERIE FABRICS

What is prewashing? Washing fabric in the same manner that the finished garment will be washed before sewing is called prewashing. Why is it done? It can reduce shrinking and crocking, which is the rubbing off of color on a fabric when wet or dry, as well as remove starches and other chemicals that were applied during the manufacturing process. Prewashing is recommended for most garment fabrics.

So why would you prewash fabrics for garments but not for lingerie? Well, most synthetics don't shrink. Also, most people don't wash their bras and special occasion lingerie pieces as often as other garments.

Ninety nine percent of the time, I do not prewash lingerie fabrics. But, I would if the fabric felt stiff, or if I was using a natural fiber, like cotton, that might shrink. If you're going to prewash your lingerie fabrics, hand or machine wash on a low/gentle cycle. Use a mild or a lingerie detergent, such as The Laundress' Delicate Wash. If the fabric is stretchy and larger than 1 yard, don't hang it to dry, as it might stretch out.

Lining Fabrics

Linings are not necessary, but they're highly recommended if you want lingerie that can support you throughout the day. We've all seen those pretty little lacy things in lingerie shops that are made of the sheerest fabrics and the skimpiest elastic. Regardless of your size, you wonder, *"How is that going to support this?"* Most of the time, they don't, and are novelty pieces not meant to be worn for more than a few hours. There's a time and place for those pieces in your lingerie drawer. I love pulling them out to feel extra special.

> **WHAT IS GSM?**
>
> GSM stands for grams per square meter, which refers to the weight of a fabric. The higher a fabric's GSM, the thicker and more supportive it is. For example, standard stretch mesh is usually between 60–150 GSM and power net is usually between 220–280 GSM.

However, if you're looking for support, you're going to achieve it with lining fabrics! There are six lining fabrics commonly used, with each providing a different level of support. Lining also provides a soft layer against the skin (some laces can be scratchy), and using the same lining from project to project also allows you to experiment with different main fabrics without altering the fit of the garment.

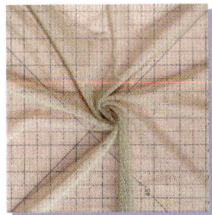

STRETCH MESH Standard stretch mesh is a versatile fabric used as a lining for sizes X-small through medium and A–C cups sizes. It is most often a nylon spandex blend between 60–150 GSM. It's used as a lining for panties or bras that use a stretch fabric as the main fabric.

POWER NET Stretch mesh and power net have the same construction—they're both meshes. Power net, however, is more opaque, has a higher GSM, and offers more support. Most power nets are available in 220–280 GSM and are used for sizes large and above or cup sizes D+.

TOOLS AND MATERIALS 27

A `SHEER CUP LINING` Also known as marquisette, sheer cup lining is a strong, supportive fabric made of 100% nylon. It provides an almost invisible layer of support that can be used underneath stretch and non stretch lace, as well as other delicate fabrics. Because it offers maximum support, it can also be used for the frame and/or bridge.

B `15 DENIER TRICOT` is similar to sheer cup lining in that it provides an almost invisible layer to be used underneath lace, but it instead has mechanical give in the crosswise direction. Tricot fabric is a knit material that has a zigzag effect on the front and a crosswise rib on the back.

C `BRA TULLE` is a type of tulle that is much softer than craft tulle. It has slight mechanical give, making it a great alternative to sheer cup lining or 15 denier tricot. Two layers of bra tulle can be used at the same time (with the grainline in opposite directions) to create a very supportive but extremely soft lining option.

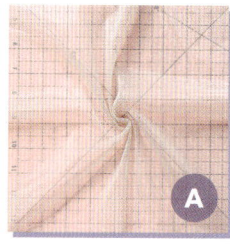
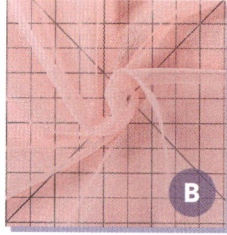
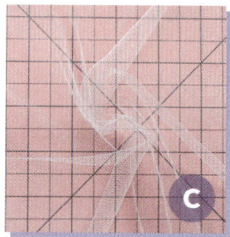

Swim Fabrics

The most common type of swimwear fabrics have spandex. This material is my top, (really, my only) pick for swimwear. Spandex holds its color and is resistant to salt, sun, and chlorine.

Spandex is extremely stretchy, has great recovery, and is often blended with other fibers to help maintain shape and support. LYCRA (a trademarked brand name of spandex) can be inserted into wovens or jerseys, and is used in activewear, swimwear, underwear, hosiery, and pretty much any other garment you can think of.

Another thing to consider is what kind of beach or pool goer you are. If you're not the type to go in the water, you could get away with your fabric not being not chlorine resistant. I recommend staying away from anything that has natural fibers; cotton will absorb and hold water, and some become see through when wet, too.

Polyester or Nylon?

Spandex fabrics are usually made of a polyester or nylon blend. Both are synthetic, but have different properties.

NYLON VS. POLYESTER

NYLON	POLYESTER
Considered a synthetic silk	Stronger yarn than nylon
More prone to pilling	Less prone to pilling
Less hydrophobic (will dry slower than polyester)	More hydrophobic (will dry faster)
Less colorfast (will lose color faster)	More colorfast (will retain color longer)

SCUBA fabric, which is also called neoprene, is a type of swimwear fabric that is entirely waterproof, which makes it an ideal material for wetsuits and other swim gear designed to insulate against wet and cold environments.

PBT, which stands for polybutylene terephthalate, is texturized polyester with natural stretch like spandex. The most important characteristic of PBT is that it is chlorine resistant. It is also resistant to salt water and color fading.

SWIMWEAR LINING FABRICS Use stretch mesh or power net as a lining for swimwear. Both of these fabrics will hold up to salt, sun, and chlorine. Lining made specifically for swimwear exists, but is more difficult to find. If shopping online or in stores, look for "swimsuit lining", which is called helenka in some places.

Activewear Fabrics

> **POLYESTER OR NYLON?**
> The above table that compares polyester and nylon also applies to activewear fabrics.

Moisture wicking: Refers to how well a fabric draws moisture away from the body. A fabric that has wicking abilities allows you to sweat without overheating.

Anti-microbial: Characteristic of fabric that offers protection against bacteria, mold, mildew, and other hazardous microbes. The yarns in the fabric prevent microbes from developing while simultaneously promoting moisture movement, thereby maximizing comfort and extending the life of the fabric.

Quick drying: Fabric that goes from wet to damp in under thirty minutes and dries completely within a few hours.

NYLON SPANDEX Tactel is an INVISTA trademarked nylon fiber. It is light, very cool, and most commonly used for performance underwear (and no panty line underwear), but it can also be used for tops and leggings. It has excellent moisture wicking and quick drying properties.

SPACE DYES are fabrics made with dyed yarns, which create a fun, unique multi-color appearance. These are most commonly used for leggings.

DRI-FIT is a trademark of Nike and has excellent evaporation rate (AKA excellent moisture wicking properties). Dri-fit usually has a little stretch, and is most commonly used in active wear shirts (the shirts that are given away at races like marathons are usually Dri-Fit).

NATURAL FIBERS There are natural options for active wear fabric, but stay away from cotton in all activewear. Cotton is hydrophilic, holds up to 25 times its weight in water, and takes a long time to dry. Cotton socks can lead to nasty blisters.

Bamboo: Bamboo can be manufactured with moisture wicking, antimicrobial or quick drying properties. Read more about Bamboo (page 26).

TENCEL: Similar to bamboo, TENCEL is made from wood pulp. The name TENCEL actually stands for Tenacity and Cellulose combined. It is not only antimicrobial, but it also contains tiny fibrils, or small hairs, that give the fabric a soft texture.

Wool: Wool? Wait, what? This fabric is no longer a staple just for hikers. Wool creates pockets that trap air, so it regulates heat and keeps the body warm. It is also breathable and wicks moisture, making it perfect for any outdoor workout. Bonus: Wool is naturally antimicrobial and can be washed less than polyester and other materials.

Econyl: Econyl is a recycled nylon that is produced from fishing nets, fabric scraps, carpet flooring, and industrial plastic. The nylon is returned to its original state and turned into a fabric that can ultimately be recycled again when the customer is done with the garment.

ACTIVEWEAR LINING FABRICS The same fabrics used to line your lingerie and swimwear can also be used to line your activewear. It's great for stash busting!

CARING FOR ACTIVEWEAR

Has your workout gear ever smelled even after washing? That's because the moisture wicking properties of synthetic fabrics can cause them to repel water when being washed. Add ¼–½ cup of white vinegar or baking soda to the wash. You can also look for special detergent for activewear. Don't use fabric softener on your activewear fabrics; it can prevent detergent from reaching the dirt and remove any special finishing on the fabric. Wash inside out with cold water and lay flat to dry. Do not put active wear fabric in the dryer, especially on high heat.

SEW LINGERIE

DOGS and Fabric Stretchiness

In garment sewing, grainline refers to the direction of the fabric that has the least amount of stretch. In most cases, sewists align patterns with the grainline when cutting them out.

When sewing lingerie, swimwear or activewear, you instead cut patterns along the DOGS, which is short for direction of greatest stretch. It is the direction of the fabric that has the most amount of stretch.

How to Find DOGS

Finding the DOGS in a fabric is actually pretty easy. To find the DOGS, pull lengthwise and crosswise on the fabric. Stretch a little bit inside from the edge of the fabric. Which direction of pulling has more stretch? This is the DOGS.

There is either stretch in one direction, called 2-way stretch, or stretch in all directions, called 4-way stretch. If you're using a 2-way stretch fabric, then make sure that the DOGS on the pattern aligns with the DOGS on *all fabrics* for the project, including the lining. If you're using a 4-way stretch fabric, you can cut in any direction.

How to Find Percentage of Stretch

The easiest way to calculate stretch percentage is to take 10" (25cm) of fabric and stretch it to the point where it naturally wants to rebound. Yes, you can stretch it all the way out, but instead tug at it a few times and measure at the rebound point. If it rebounds around 13" (30cm), then it has 30% stretch (approximately); if it rebounds around 14" (35cm), then it has 40% stretch (approximately); and so on. Calculate the percentage by dividing the length it stretches by the original length of the unstretched piece, then multiply by 100.

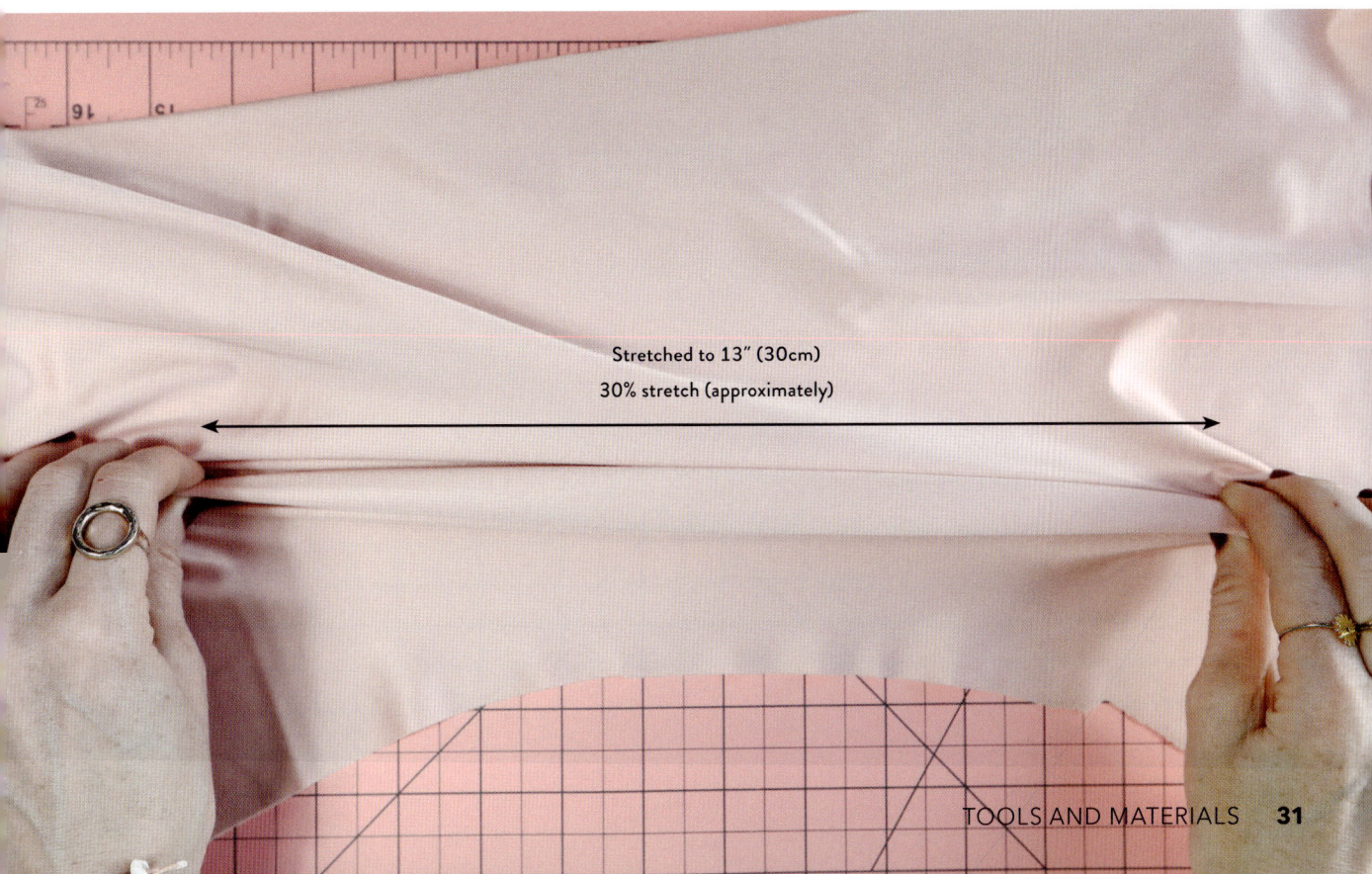

Stretched to 13" (30cm)
30% stretch (approximately)

TOOLS AND MATERIALS 31

Using DOGS for Support

Briefly put, the weight of the breasts in a bra moves in the direction of greatest stretch. Knowing this, you can use the DOGS to add support to your bra. For example, consider a diagonally seamed bra with an upper cup and two lower cups with a vertical seam. If the lower cups have the DOGS going up and down, it will provide lift and create a push up effect.

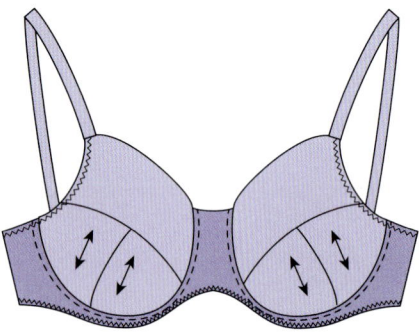

Vertical DOGS in lower cups

Stretch vs. Non Stretch Fabrics

If a bra pattern is designed for stretch fabrics, can you use a non stretch fabric? What about vice versa? Yes and yes! If a pattern was designed for a stretch fabric and you want to use a non stretch fabric, you will most likely have to size up. Make a test bra out of a non stretch fabric similar to your final fabric to assess the fit.

If a pattern was designed for a non stretch and you want to use a stretch fabric, you will most likely have to do the opposite—size down. Again, making a test bra is the easiest way to know how many sizes to go down. Note that the back band *always* needs to be made of stretch fabric.

When it comes to sewing panties, yes, you can use a non stretch fabric. Just like the back band on a bra, the back panel of the panty must be made of stretch fabrics to allow you to move comfortably throughout the day. In most cases, sizing up or down is not necessary.

Elastic, Notions, and Underwires

ELASTICS The majority of bra making involves sewing elastic. There are different types, widths, and weights, and generally speaking, each one serves a purpose and, they are not interchangeable. Many sewists like to "make it work," but when it comes to elastic, avoid this!

A Picot: Picot elastic has one decorative edge and is used in lingerie to finish edges. The design of the decorative edge can vary, but it's typically a row of loops. Widths range from ⅛" (4mm) to over 1" (20mm). Generally, the wider the picot elastic, the more support it offers. Most picot also has one plush side, which feels like a combination of velvet and suede. This is considered the right side and is meant to be worn against the skin and absorb oils and sweat.

B Fold Over: Fold over elastic (FOE) has an indentation down the center and is also used to finish edges in lingerie. Most have one side that is shiny and another that is matte. Widths range from ¼" (6mm) to 1" (20mm) when folded. The shiny side is considered the right side and is meant to be on the exterior of the finished piece.

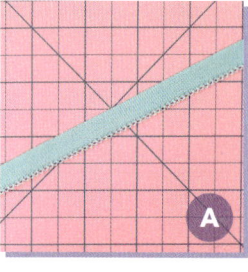
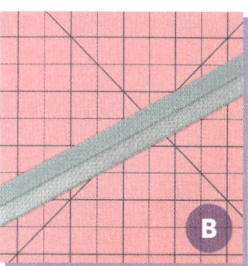

32 SEW LINGERIE

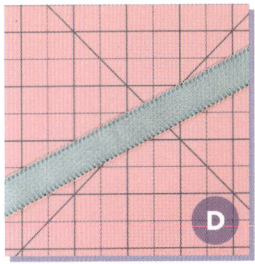
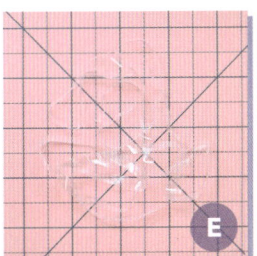
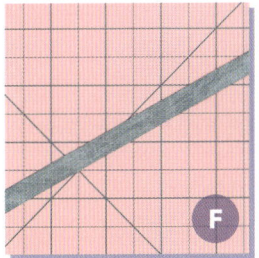
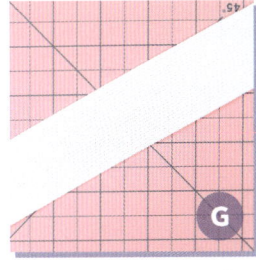
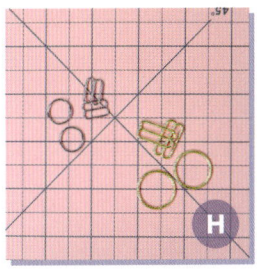

C Wide Band: Wide band elastic is meant for the bottom of a bralette or waistline of a panty. Widths range from ½″ (13mm) to over 3″ (88mm). On a bra or bralette, the wider the band elastic, the more support the band will offer.

D Shoulder Strap: Shoulder strap elastic is meant to be used on the shoulder straps of a bra, but can be used as a decorative element as well, such as on the waistline of a bodysuit. Widths range from ⅛″ (4mm) to over 1″ (20mm). Wider shoulder strap elastic is intended for full busted and plus sizes. Shoulder strap elastic can have a shiny or matte right side.

E Clear: Clear elastic is a film, so it is not knitted or braided like other elastics. It is used in active wear as a stabilizer, and is able to be stretched repeatedly. It is most commonly used inside fold over elastic when fold over elastic is being used as part of strap construction.

F Rubber: Just like clear elastic, rubber elastic is not knitted or braided. It's rubber. It's most commonly used in swimwear to finish edges.

G Knitted: Knitted elastic is most frequently encased inside bands, such as inside a waistband on a legging or inside a bottom band on a sports bralette. The characteristics can vary greatly, from very stiff to super soft.

Swimwear and Activewear Elastic: Rubber, clear, and knitted elastic are used most often on activewear and swimwear, however, fold over, band, and strap elastic can be used as well. Take into account how you'll be wearing the garment as you choose elastic.

H I RINGS, SLIDERS, HOOKS, AND EYES See more information at Rings and Sliders and Hook and Eye (page 22).

J FRONT CLOSURES are sewn onto the front of the bra and allow the bra to be put on and removed from the front. A front closure is especially helpful for people who have limited mobility and cannot put on a hook and eye behind their backs.

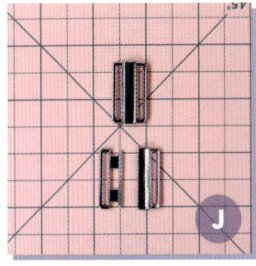

TOOLS AND MATERIALS 33

K **TWILL TAPE** is non stretch tape that is often used in garment sewing. In bra making, it is usually sewn into fold over elastics as part of shoulder strap construction.

L **BONING** is a flat piece of metal or plastic used on the inside of lingerie for shaping and adding support.

M **SNAP CLOSURES** are usually sewn onto the gusset of a bodysuit. See Bodysuit (page 11).

N **G HOOKS** are used in lingerie for removable straps and nursing bralettes, and in swimwear as a closure (like a hook and eye).

O **POLYLAMINATE FOAM** is a layer of foam that is bonded between two layers of fabric on either side. It usually comes in ⅛″ (4mm) or ¼″ (6mm) thickness and is used as an alternative to molded cups. Molded cups only come in one breast shape, but making polylaminate foam cups allows you to make a lightly lined cup that fits your shape exactly.

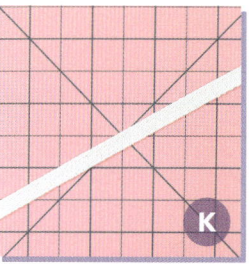
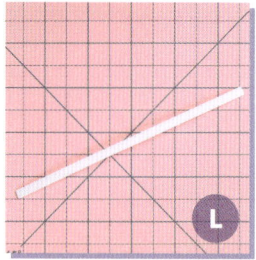
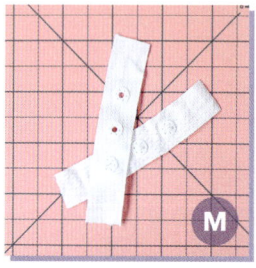
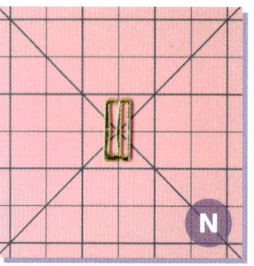
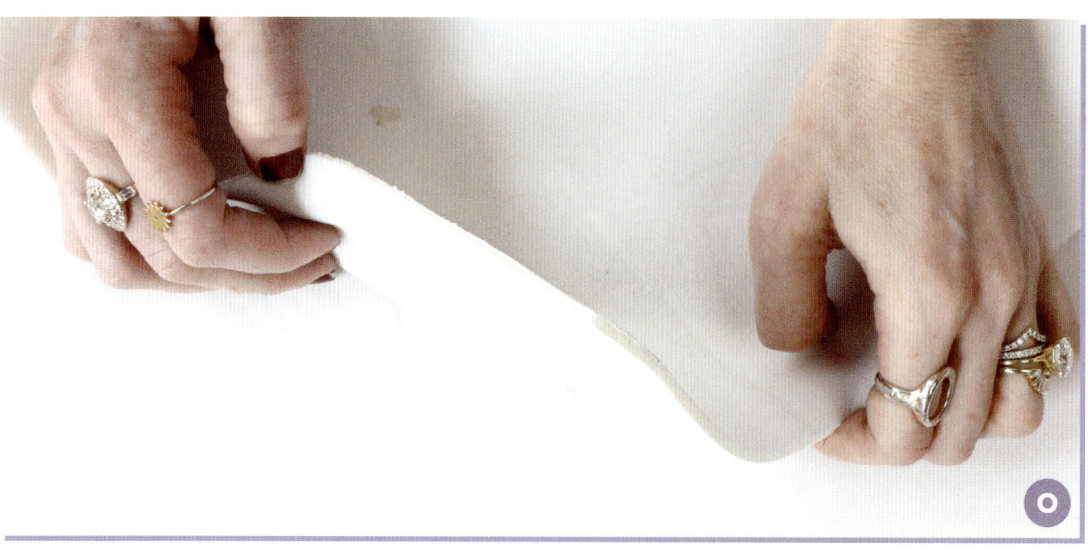

UNDERWIRES Underwires are rigid materials usually made from resin, metal, or plastic and available in different gauges. Gauge refers to the thickness of the wire, and the higher the number, the thicker it is. Plastic has a tendency to break and is usually used in mass produced lingerie or in swimwear because it doesn't rust. Wires also can have a coloured tip that indicates the size.

My favorite option are underwires made from carbonized steel with an exterior coating of nylon. Bonus if there is extra coating at the ends so the wire doesn't come through the wire casing.

When purchasing any new underwire, I recommend buying the size you measure and one size up and down. Always check to see what type of underwire a pattern is designed for.

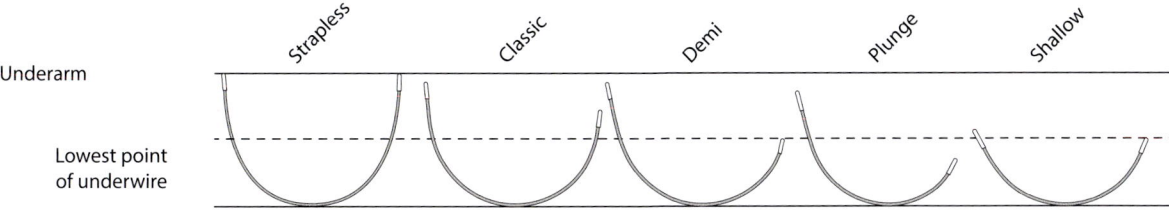

Classic/Regular: Traditional underwire that usually fits full coverage bras.

Demi: Underwires that end lower at the center front and are meant for demi style bras.

Plunge: Underwires that end ever lower than a demi at the center front and are meant for plunge styles.

Strapless: Underwires for strapless styles are usually shaped like the letter "U" with the underwire ending at the same point on the underarm and center front.

Shallow: A shallow underwire is arced slightly at the bottom and works best when used in vertical seam cupped bras and bralettes.

Monowire: A monowire is one continuous wire which looks like a soft 'w' shape. They offer lift and support, but not separation.

V-Wire/Separator: V-wires or separators are used in plunge style bras, bralettes, and corsets that dip below the breast. V-wires and separators can be used in combination with demi underwires or boning.

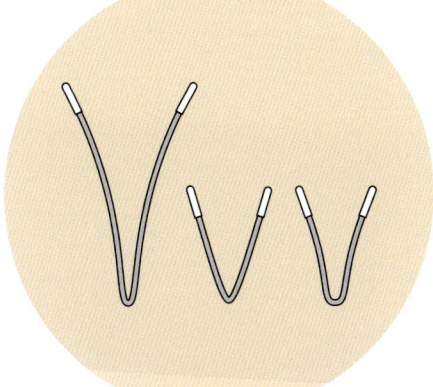

TOOLS AND MATERIALS 35

Tools

General Lingerie Sewing Tools

Duck billed scissors: Duck billed scissors have a flat, wide blade and a slightly angled handle. The blade, which resembles the bill of a duck, allows a sewist to cut close to stitches without cutting through them.

Rotary cutter: Rotary cutters have a handle on one end and a circular blade on the other end. Usually smaller blades (28mm) are used for small curves, and larger blades (45mm) are used for long, straight lines and wider curves.

Spray adhesive: Spray adhesive temporarily adheres two or more layers together. It also prevents fabric from shifting while cutting and sewing.

Pins: Regular pins are recommended for sewing most lingerie fabrics.

Dotted pattern paper: Dotted pattern paper is used for drafting and altering patterns. It has letters and symbols that are usually 1″ (2.5cm) apart.

Straight ruler: Straight rulers are also used in pattern making for drawing and measuring straight lines.

French curve ruler: French curved rules create smooth curved lines of varying radii.

Needle and Thread

Having the right needle and thread is another important element to achieving well sewn lingerie. Needles come in many shapes and sizes, and each package shows two numbers: the UK and US sizes. US sizes range from 8–20 and UK sizes range from 60–120. The lower the number, the finer the needle and vice versa. Below, you will find a table with recommended sizes for different lingerie fabrics.

FABRIC TYPE AND NEEDLE SIZE

Fabric	Examples	Needle Size
Sheer to lightweight	Sheer cup lining, stretch mesh, lace	60–80 or 8–11
Normal or Medium weight	Jersey, cotton, LYCRA	90 or 12
Heavyweight	Power net, stretch velvet	100 or 14

Ball point: Ballpoint needles have a medium rounded point designed to push through fibers rather than pierce them. A ballpoint needle is recommended when sewing most knits and jerseys. For highly elastic fabrics, choose a stretch or microtex needle instead.

Sharp or microtex: Sharp or microtex needles have a very sharp point and are designed to prevent skipped stitches when sewing highly elastic fabrics such as power net, stretch mesh, or stretch lace.

Stretch: Stretch needles have a slightly less rounded point than ballpoint needles and are also designed to prevent skipped stitches in highly elastic fabric.

Universal: Universal needles are used for fabric without spandex (example: sheer cup lining) as well as when sewing notions that are non stretch.

Thread: Polyester, polyester, polyester! Did I say polyester? Cotton and all purpose threads don't stretch. Polyester thread has a slight give, which is needed for lingerie fabrics. My preferred type is Gutermann Mara 120, which has a silk like sheen and is completely dust and lint free. The recommended needle size for this thread is 70–80/10–12.

Sewing Machines

Let me get straight to the point—you *do not* need the fanciest sewing machine to make beautiful lingerie. But, I do recommend a machine that is higher quality than the basic ones you may find at craft and hobby stores. I find that those machines often have recurring tension issues. Madalynne Studios uses high-end sewing machines now, but I used a basic PFAFF passport 2.0 and passport 3.0 for my first two years of sewing lingerie. If a new machine at the quality and price point of the passport 2.0 or passport 3.0 does not fit your budget, look for a used machine at your local sewing dealer, neighborhood for-sale group, or on Ebay.

Whether you have been sewing for a few months or for a few decades, I highly recommend visiting your local sewing machine dealer if you're in the market for a new machine. Buying a machine from a sewing dealer not only supports a local business but also provides you with support. A good dealer will guide you through getting familiar with your machine. When something goes wrong with your machine—believe me, it will—they offer technical support.

So, what should you look for in a sewing machine? Here are the features I suggest paying attention to when planning to sew lingerie:

Dual Feed: Essentially, dual feed is when the top and the bottom layer fabrics are fed into the sewing machine at the same rate. Have you ever sewn a long seam, and when you reached the end, one layer was shorter than the other? This happens a lot when using a regular presser foot because the feed dogs on a sewing machine push the bottom fabric through faster than the top.

Dual feed presser feet such as a walking foot and other accessories pull on the top layer at the same rate as the bottom layer. Even though seams on bras and panties are not long, using fine fabrics increases the chance that the seams won't match up.

Don't want to spend money on another sewing accessory like a new foot? I highly recommend the PFAFF range of sewing machines and their IDT technology. IDT stands for Integrated Dual Feed System. Basically, it's a built in walking foot that gives controlled, no slip sewing.

Adjustable Presser Foot: Adjustable presser foot pressure is beneficial for lingerie, but also any kind of sewing. Loosening the foot pressure helps the presser foot glide over fabric instead of pushing over it, which can cause mismatched or wavy seams.

Adjustable Zigzag Stitches: The only thing that is essential for sewing lingerie is a straight stitch and a zigzag stitch!

How and Where To Shop For Lingerie Materials

Local craft and hobby stores haven't hopped on the bra making bandwagon for the most part (at least not yet). Fortunately, online bra making supply stores have popped up around the world, so you will be buying from a web-based retailer for the majority of your supplies. Etsy is also a great resource. When working with small businesses, if you can't find something, I recommend emailing the owner. As a small business who sells bra making supplies, I love hearing from customers!

As you sit down to purchase supplies for a project, make sure to check the following things:

Fiber Content

What is the fabric made of? How does it behave? Some businesses use keywords in their titles for SEO purposes, so it's best to double check the product description to make sure that the item is what it says it is.

Width

This comes especially important when dealing with bra cups for larger sizes. Make sure you're purchasing the correct width of lace or elastic. If you're looking at a stretch galloon lace, I recommend buying lace that is at least 6" (15cm) wide.

Bulk

Because you'll be buying mostly online, you'll also be paying for shipping (if the vendor doesn't offer free shipping). Instead of paying for shipping multiple times, stock up and buy for multiple projects at a time. For notions like elastic, you can also ask the vendor if they will offer a discount if you buy more than 10 yards.

Kits

I cannot recommend DIY kits more! Not only do they offer all the fabric, trims and notions packaged together (and usually for a discount!), but for new makers, DIY kits help you get familiar with the types of materials without getting overwhelmed by the need to find and purchase all the little different doodads.

> **HASHTAGS**
>
> Turn to social media and get creative searching for hashtags relevant to bra making. Some that I recommend are #bramaking, #bramakingsupplies, #diylingerie, #handmadelingerie. Most of the time, the maker will include where they source their materials.

TECHNIQUES

No matter the style of lingerie, the fabrics being used, or what size is being sewn, there are fundamental techniques that are beneficial for you to know. This chapter goes over tips, tricks, and basic knowledge that will make your bra making experience more enjoyable.

Measurements and Sizing

The search for the right size in lingerie can feel like an impossible mission with uncomfortable pinching, poking underwires, too narrow straps, too wide straps, bands riding up, unsightly bulging, and more! You may have come to the point where you want to throw in the towel, admit defeat and buy white, cream, and black sports bras from a big box retailer for the rest of your existence. Or you may want to just go braless. **Don't give up!**

The first step to good fitting lingerie is taking measurements! There is no standardization in sizing from company to company and country to country, which can be hard and frustrating. So, when you take your measurements and one brand calls you a 38C and another brand calls you a 40D, you're like, *"What the heck?"* Each brand will determine their own sizing, and that sizing might even vary from bra style to bra style. So, it's important to focus on measurements, not on an arbitrary size that a brand determines. Your measurements do not define you. They are a tool for achieving the best fit for looking and feeling good.

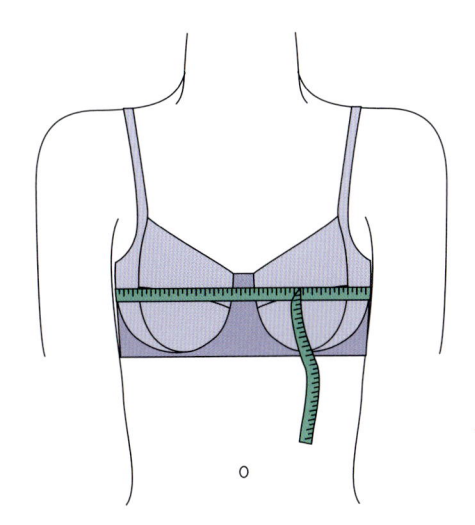

Measure Your Full Bust

Wearing a lightly lined or a non push up bra, wrap a measuring tape around the fullest part of your breasts. Breathe in and breathe out. Make sure the measuring tape is level and parallel to the floor. The tape measure should be tight enough so that it stays in place (level) on its own, but it should not be digging into your skin, cause indentations, or be painful. Write down the measurement.

Measure Your Underbust

Wearing a lightly lined or non push up bra, wrap the measuring tape directly under your breasts (on the ribcage). Breathe in and breathe out. Again, make sure the measuring tape is level, parallel to the floor, and not too tight. Write down the measurement.

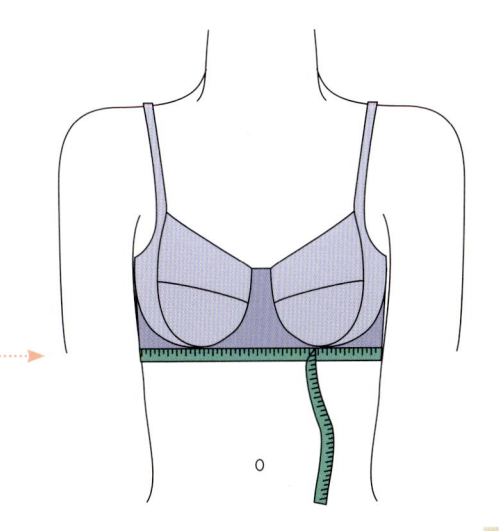

Calculate Your Cup Size

Subtract your underbust measurement from your full bust measurement. The difference between the two measurements determines your cup size. Every inch increase equals one cup size up. Refer to the chart below:

CUP SIZES

Difference Between Full Bust and Underbust	Cup Size (US)
0" (0cm)	AA
1" (2.5cm)	A
2" (5cm)	B
3" (7.5cm)	C
4" (10cm)	D
5" (13cm)	DD/E
6" (15cm)	DDD/F
7" (18cm)	G
8" (20cm)	H
9" (23cm)	I
10" (25.5cm)	J
11" (28cm)	K
12" (30.5cm)	L
13" (33cm)	M
14" (35.6cm)	N

Measure Your Waist

Wrap the measuring tape around the smallest part of your torso. Your waist is not necessarily where your belly button is. Write down the measurement.

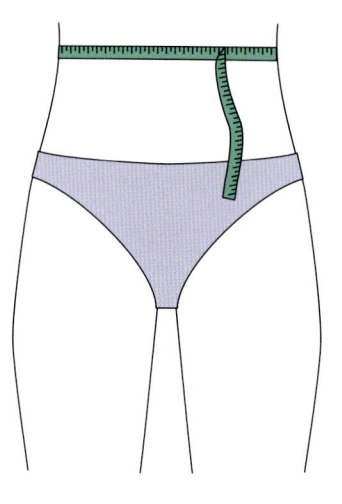

Measure Your Hips

Wrap the measuring tape around the widest part of your butt. Some people carry the weight of their hips higher or lower than others—it will depend on your shape. What's important is that you measure the widest part. Write down the measurement.

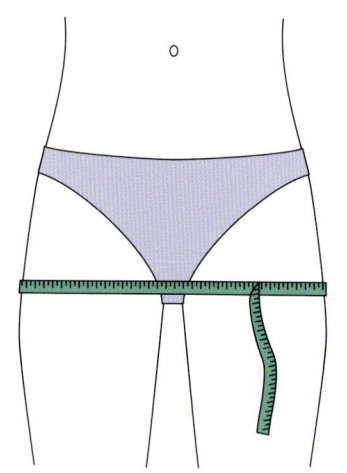

Full Bust vs. Plus Size

The terms "plus size lingerie" and "full bust lingerie" are often used interchangeably, but they mean two very different things. A person who is plus size can wear an A cup, and a petite person can be full busted.

Full busted means a cup size of D or larger (a difference of 4" (10cm) or greater between full bust and underbust). Don't get this confused with the term "full coverage", which is a type of bra style and is available in many sizes.

Plus size means a band size of 40 or greater. Some brands define 38 as plus size, so double check the brand's size chart.

So, a 34DD is full busted, a 40C is plus size, and a 42D is full busted AND plus size.

Sister Sizing

One of my favorite bra making aphorisms relates to sister sizing. It goes: "*A B cup is not a B cup is not a B cup.*" Basically, it means that the cup size of a bra is relative to the band size. Confused? Defining sister sizing will help it make more sense.

Bras that are sister sizes are bras that have the same cup volume even though the band size and cup letter are different. An example is a size 34A and a 32B—they have the same cup volume, but a different band size. As the band size gets larger, the cups will have the same volume if the letter gets smaller. An easy way to think of it is that they're reciprocals. As one moves up, the other moves down and vice versa.

Sister Size Down: This means one size smaller for the band and one letter bigger for the cups. Example: If you wear a 34C, your sister size down would be 32D.

Sister Size Up: This means one size larger for the band and one letter smaller for the cups. Using the same example as above, if you wear a 34C, your sister size up would be 36B.

How to Use Sister Sizing: If you sew a 34B and the cups fit but the band is loose, sister size down to a 32C. You *would not* go down to a 32B, which would reduce the cup volume. Sister sizing can be super helpful, both in DIY lingerie as well as ready made shopping, but use it with caution. I only recommend sister sizing down one, or maybe two sizes. This is because the construction and/or the grading changes across sizes. Yes, the cup volume of a 32D and a 38A are the same, but the 32 is most likely lined with a standard lining whereas the 38 is lined with a firm, supportive lining. Also, the shape of the pattern pieces may have been altered to maintain a proportionate grade from a 32D to a 38A.

Sizing In Different Countries

So you've measured yourself numerous times and have a number that you are confident is correct. Then you check the size chart on a pattern and discover that you're a GG. Now you're thinking: *"I've never heard of a GG cup!?"* To make bra sizing even more confusing, different countries and brands have different numbering systems based on their customer base or population. Oi vey! Don't get your panties in a knot. Keep the following chart handy and refer to it if you're trying to find your equivalent size in other countries sizing systems. Please note that cup sizes can go beyond what is listed in the chart.

CUP SIZE CONVERSION

US	UK	EUR	AUSTRALIA
A	A	A	A
B	B	B	B
C	C	C	C
D	D	D	D
DD/E	DD	E	DD
DDD/F	E	F	E
G	F	G	F
H	FF	H	FF
I	G	I	G
J	GG	J	GG
K	H	K	H
L	HH	L	HH
M	J	M	J
N	JJ	N	JJ
O	K	O	K

BAND SIZE CONVERSION

UK + USA	EURO	FRANCE
28	60	75
30	65	80
32	70	85
34	75	90
36	80	95
38	85	100
40	90	105
42	95	110
44	100	115
47	105	120
48	110	125
50	115	130

Working with Delicate Fabrics

Lace and other delicate fabrics are fun to look at, touch, and buy, but let's face it: They aren't the easiest fabrics to sew. They can get sucked into the feed dogs, burn easily, and shift during cutting or sewing. The following tips, tricks and tools will help you handle fine fabrics like a pro!

Backstitching

Backstitching is necessary to secure each line of stitches, but this can get complicated with fine fabrics. So, whether you're sewing lingerie or normal garments, I recommend you start sewing with the fabric aligned with the **back** of the presser foot. Why? Well, underneath the presser foot are feed dogs that move fabric through the sewing machine. If you place the fabric in front of the presser foot, then the feed dogs have nothing to grab onto and the fabric won't move. Similarly, if you start sewing with the fabric directly underneath the needle, there is a good chance it will get sucked into the bobbin, especially when the fabric is delicate.

Now, you may be thinking, if I start sewing with the fabric aligned with the back of the presser foot, then the backstitching won't go all the way to the edge. In most cases, seams are sewn into another seam or finished with elastic. So there is about ¼″ (6mm)–½″ (12mm) from the edge of the fabric that can be left unstitched without causing an issue.

Another tip for backstitching: If you're sewing a short seam, you don't have to start sewing at one end and sew to the other. Start in the middle! Begin stitching in the center and sew to one side. Then go back to the center and start stitching again to the other side, making sure your stitches overlap one or two stitches, which will lock the seam.

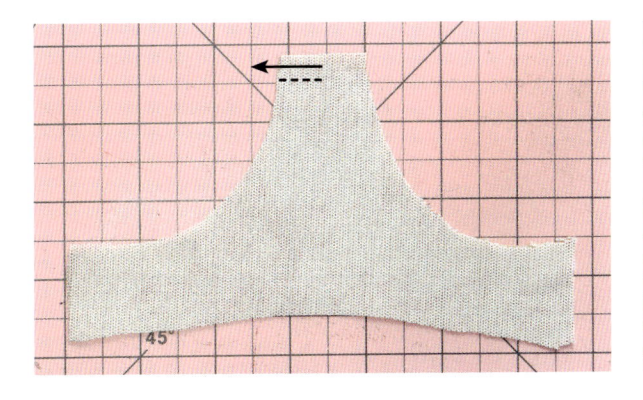

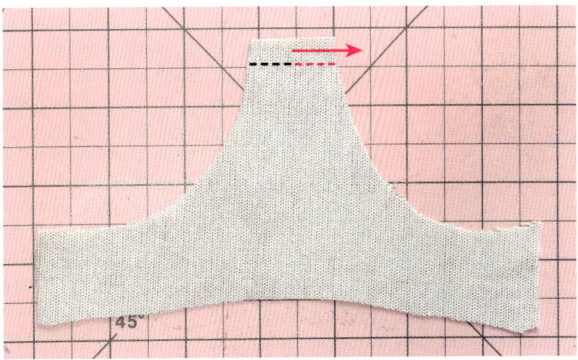

Stabilizers

If your machine is eating your fabric while you're sewing or serging, regardless of the thread, needle, or backstitching technique you're using, stabilizers can come to your rescue! They are available in many forms, but my preferred is Solvy Water Soluble Stabilizer, which is a clear film that can be dissolved by water. It comes on a roll, so I cut it into ¼″ (6mm)–½″ (12mm) strips. I place it on top of and/or below my fabric while I sew. When I'm finished, I run the piece under water, and voila! Another option is to wait to finish the project and then wash the garment as a whole.

In a pinch and can't wait to order a stabilizer online or make a mad dash to your nearest craft store? You can use pattern paper or newspaper! Cut it into the same width strips and place it on top of and/or below the fabric while sewing. When you're finished, slowly and carefully tear it away.

Directional vs. Non-Directional Patterns

Laces can have patterns that are directional or non-directional. Directional patterns must be oriented a certain way so that when looking at a piece of lingerie, the patterns go in the same direction from left to right. Non-directional patterns look the same no matter how they are oriented.

The easiest way to cut lace that has a directional pattern is to cut one pattern piece, then flip it over, line up the directional pattern, and then cut the other pattern piece.

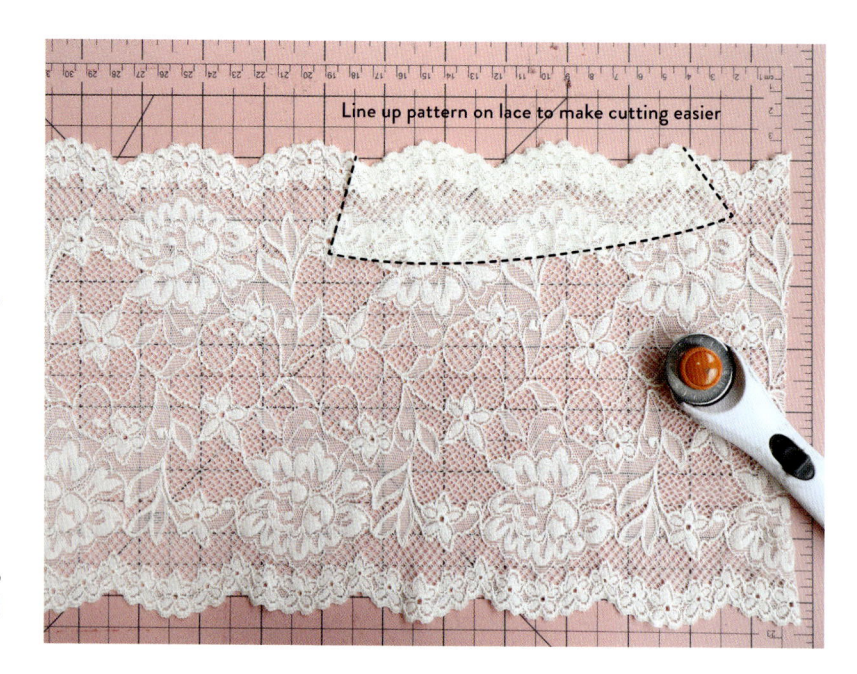

Straight Stitch or Zigzag Stitch

In bra making, you will use a straight stitch and a zigzag stitch most of the time. Zigzag stitches stretch, making them perfect for lingerie. But, straight stitches are necessary too, even though they don't stretch.

Generally speaking, our bodies move more widthwise, and less lengthwise. We twist and turn around horizontally, stretching our bodies more than when we reach up or down. So zigzag stitches are used most often on horizontal seams in lingerie, and straight stitches are preferred for vertical seams. Straight stitches can also be used to add a tiny bit of stability. The vertical seam on a bra cup is a perfect example of a place where straight stitches work great. A straight stitch also allows seams to be pressed open or to one side without the stitches being seen. Zigzag stitches are visible on the exterior after pressing seams. Backstitching is optional when using a zigzag stitch.

Ironing

Never ever, ever, ever use an iron on the highest heat to press a delicate or spandex fabric. The higher heat does not equate to a better pressed seam. More is not more here. Most of the time, your fabric will have spandex or a synthetic fiber in it. If it does, when you press it on the highest setting, it will melt. Ask me how I know. If you're using 100% cotton for your project, then yes, you can disregard the first sentence. The point is—always match the setting on your iron to the fabric you are using.

Making a Toile

The most accurate way to test the fit of a bra is to make a test fit, called a toile. It's an extra step, but if you bought really nice fabric that was super expensive, you might not want to run the risk of it not fitting comfortably. The great thing about toiles in bra making is that they are super quick to sew. Test cups take a few minutes, a fitting band takes approximately an hour, and a full toile takes shape quickly after that.

It may take a few toiles to get the fit right. In my experience with making custom lingerie, it takes an average of three. For a plus size or full bust, it can take four or more. For small or petite sizes, it's usually one to two. Only make one to three fit changes per toile. Fixing one fit issue may also affect another one!

Use a toile fabric that has a similar stretch percentage to your final fabric. If you use a fabric that has 30% stretch when the pattern calls for using fabric that only has 10% stretch, you won't be able to accurately assess the fit.

A **Test cups:** Sew the bra cups only. This is usually done when you know the band size but want to double check the cup size.

B **Fitting band:** This is done with underwire bras only. Sew the entire frame and back band, including the channeling and underwire, but leave the cups out. This is mostly done to determine if the underwire size and shape are correct.

C **Full toile:** Sew the bra in its entirety. The construction doesn't have to be haute couture. It can be quick, with uneven stitching and threads hanging everywhere. The point is to assess the fit. Wash away thread is a great tool for a full toile. After sewing and making fit adjustments, you can then dissolve the thread. Then, adjust the pieces to draft a revised pattern.

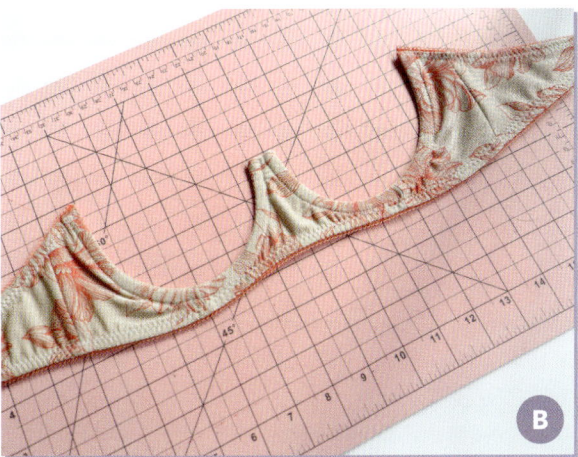

Evaluating Fit

With so many elements coming together to make a well fitting bra, it's important to evaluate the fit piece by piece. To make adjustments based on the fit recommendations in this chapter, see Adjusting Patterns (page 56).

Band Fit

Always fit the band first; many other fit issues could potentially be resolved with a band that fits correctly.

The band should be tight enough to fit approximately two fingers underneath the hook and eye. It should feel like a tight hug from your best friend after not seeing them for a year. The band should be level all the way around the body and not riding up in the back or sliding down in the front.

Many people comment that their bra causes indentations in their skin after wearing it for a day. This is okay. The bra, especially the band, must be tight in order to support the weight of the breasts. Even people with A cups have indentations in their skin after wearing a bra for a day. But, your bra should not be painful. If it hurts, the band is too tight.

When evaluating band fit, how do you know how many sizes to go up or down on the band? If the bra is too tight, use a bra extender, which is a small piece of fabric with hook and eye closures that attaches to your current bra to extend it. The amount you extend the bra in order for it to fit correctly determines how much to increase the length of the band (how many sizes to go up). If the bra is too loose, fasten the hook and eye on a tighter setting or pin out the excess band fabric to determine how much to decrease the length of the band (how many sizes to go down).

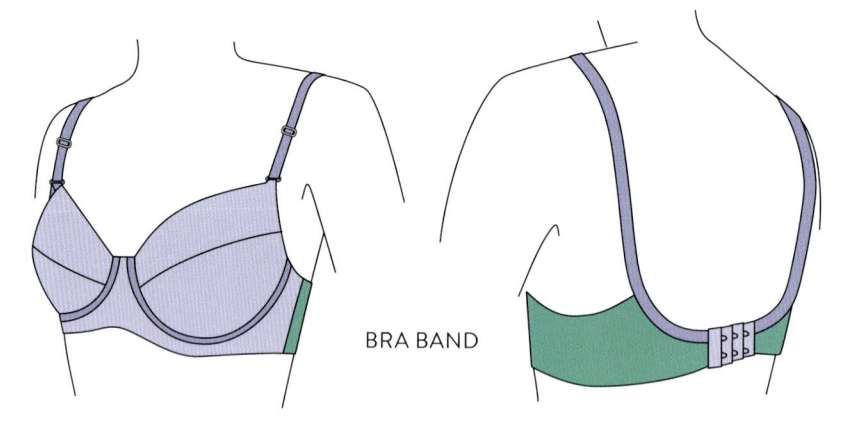

BRA BAND

REMINDER
A bra should always be fastened on the loosest hook when you first wear it. Over time, as it stretches, it should be fastened tighter and tighter.

SEW LINGERIE

Frame Fit

Next up is the frame. If the bra has an underwire, it should fully encapsulate the breast tissue and the wire should be sitting right next to the breast tissue with no gaps or spaces in between. If the wire is laying on top of the breast tissue, it is not the right size. The gore should be tacking down at the center front, meaning it should be lying against the chest wall and not standing away from it. If it isn't, this is a key indicator that the bra cups are too small. See Gore (page 21).

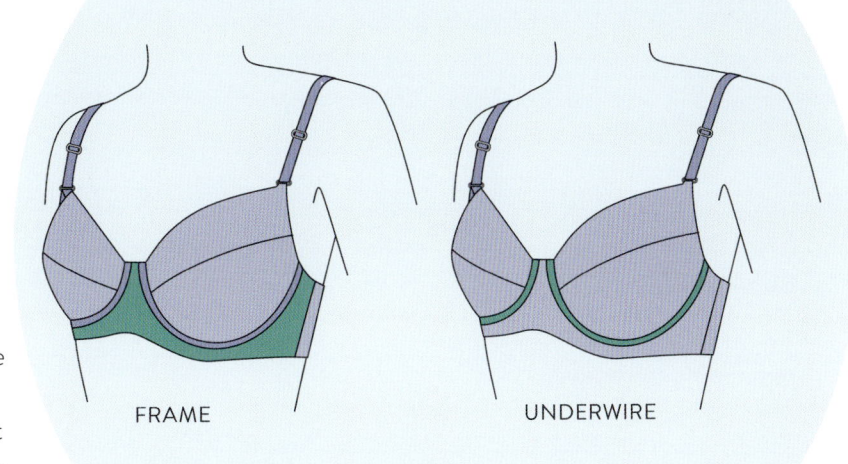

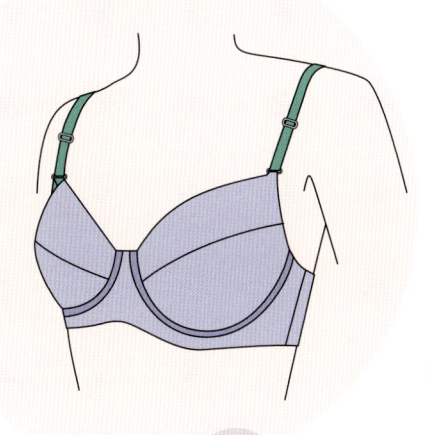

FRAME

UNDERWIRE

Strap Fit

The straps should be located midway between the neck and the shoulder, unless the bra is designed so that the straps are located closer or farther way (example: racer back bra). There should be tension on the straps, but it shouldn't be digging into the skin or causing pain. The straps only account for a small percentage of the support in a bra—if the shoulder straps are knocked off the shoulders, the bra should stay in place.

Cup Fit

Cups are the last thing to fit. If you need to make changes, you will either increase volume or decrease volume of the cups. The need to increase volume is usually indicated by the gore not tacking against the chest wall. The need to decrease volume is indicated by gaping at the neckline or overall excess fabric in the cups, meaning the breasts are not filling the cups.

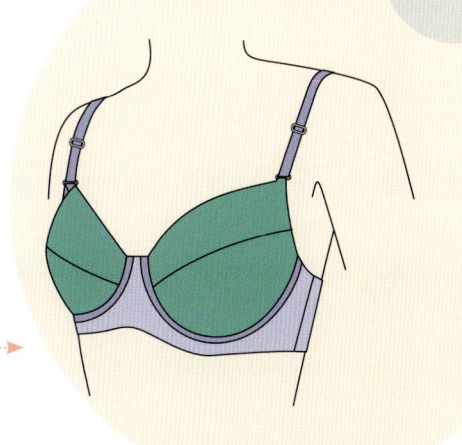

Cutting Fabric

Use the following tools and techniques to make cutting a smooth process, pun intended!

Pattern Weights

Pattern weights hold the fabric in place while cutting, preventing it from shifting. You don't have to have a fancy or expensive pattern weight. Soup cans will work!

Temporary Spray Adhesive

This has become my secret weapon. I use it mostly to spray baste the main fabric to the lining fabric prior to cutting. Doing so reduces the time it takes me to cut a pattern. There's no drying time, so you can spray, adhere, and cut immediately. It's also odorless and does not gum up on needles. My preferred brand is Odif's 505.

Spray one side of one fabric, and then lay the other layer of fabric on top. Firmly press down, starting from the center of the fabric and moving outwards towards the edge. Sometimes, the adhesive doesn't stick when only one fabric is sprayed. In that case, spray both sides and then lay one on top of the other and press. **A**

Be cognizant of the time between when you spray and cut to when you sew. I make sure to sew within a couple days after adhering. If I don't, the glue wears off and the lining and main fabric become independent. It's a real hassle to spray baste back together again! I also use spray adhesive during sewing, like when I attach hooks and eyes. I open the tape at the end of the hook and eye, spray a little inside, fit it over the back opening, press in place, and then sew it. Having it firmly secured before sewing helps with getting the topstitching straight and even. **B**

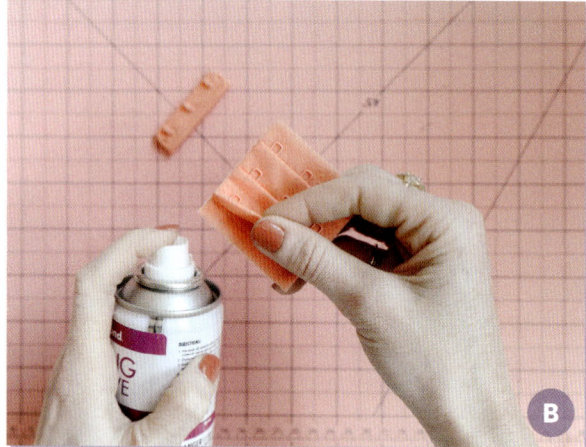

Rotary Cutter vs. Scissors

Scissors and rotary cutters can both get the job done, however, rotary cutters don't cause hand fatigue like scissors and are best for long, straight cuts. When it comes to lingerie, rotary cutters also produce the cleanest edge. When using scissors, the bottom blade slightly picks up the fabric when it is cut. Since lingerie fabrics are fine and delicate, this can cause it to shift.

I usually use a 28mm cutter, which refers to the size of the blade. I will use a size 18mm if cutting sharp corners, and 45mm if cutting a long seam, such as on a slip.

Sewing Elastic

Should you stretch elastic when sewing? Is there math you can use or marks you can put on your sewing machine? Yes and yes! Calculating and marking stretch is very helpful if you're a new lingerie sewist. But, the goal is to eventually develop an intuitive sense of how much to stretch elastic. Why? Because the amount of stretch applied will depend on many things and vary from project to project. The type of elastic, the type of fabric, and where the elastic is being sewn can all affect the amount of stretch, and it can be difficult to calculate considering all of these factors.

In general, elastic is generally stretched between 3–8%, with 8% being used only in parts where you want the garment to "hug" the body (i.e. at the underarm on a bra). So if the circumference of the waistline on a panty is 26" (66cm) and you want to apply 5% stretch, multiply 26" (66cm) by 0.05. The result is 1.3" (3.3cm). Subtract 1.3" (3.3cm) from 26" (66cm) to equal 24.7" (62.7cm), and cut that length of elastic. Then, as you sew, stretch the elastic to reach the entire 26" (66cm) waistband. If you are overlapping the elastic ½" (1.2cm) to finish it, add ½" (1.2cm) to the length.

> 26" (66cm) waistline × 0.05 stretch percentage = 1.3" (3.3cm) stretch amount
>
> 26" (66cm) waistline − 1.3" (3.3cm) stretch amount = 24.7" (62.7cm) elastic length
>
> 24.7" (62.7cm) elastic length + ½" (1.2cm) elastic overlap = 25.2" (64cm) total elastic length

If you don't want to use math, but want a guide to help with how much to stretch the elastic, you can also put marks or tape in front of the presser foot. First, test stretching the elastic with your intended fabric to see how much stretch is the right amount. Make a note of where you stretch the elastic to on your sewing machine. Then put a piece of tape there and use it as a guideline for where to pull your elastic to while sewing for your project.

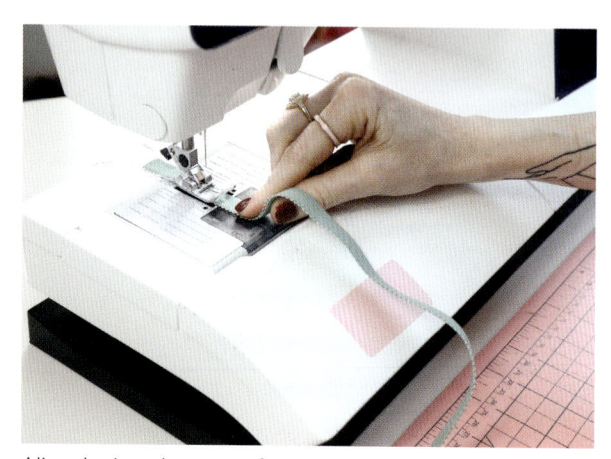

Align elastic under presser foot

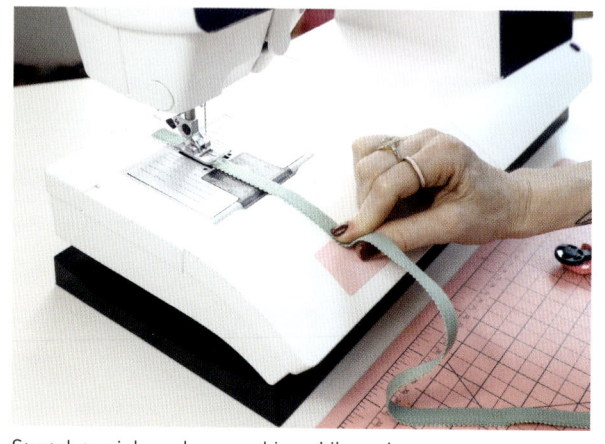

Stretch to pink mark on machine while sewing

Regardless of which method you use, you will eventually develop a "feel" for how much to stretch elastic through muscle memory.

SEW LINGERIE

Stitch Length

Stitch length, especially for zigzag stitches, will vary from machine to machine. My recommendation for getting zigzag stitches the correct width and spacing for lingerie is to compare it to your ready made bras. It doesn't have to be exact—just adjust your machine settings so that it looks similar. The more spacing apart between the zigzag stitches, the more similar it is to a straight stitch and the less stretch it has. The closer the spacing between the zigzag stitches, the more holes are going into the elastic, which damages it. Too many holes can also cause wavy elastic, a common headache for new lingerie sewists. Try to find that sweet spot!

Finishing Seams

Don't get discouraged if you don't have a serger and want to sew lingerie. The projects in this book say to finish seam allowances with a serger, but there are alternative options if you don't have one.

First, most lingerie fabrics do not fray. The point of a serger's overlock stitch is to finish seam allowances so they won't fray; so technically, overlocking is not needed. So why is it done? For the sake of finishing seam allowances. Traditionally, raw edges on the inside of a garment are considered messy and unprofessional. But, this isn't always the case. In certain cases, adding an overlock stitch on a delicate fabric adds bulk and can cause the seam to pucker. It's preferable to have a smooth, even appearance on the exterior than having the interior seam allowances finished just for the sake of it. So, if you don't have a serger, leave the edges raw or fold them to one side and sew them down with a zigzag stitch the width of the seam allowances.

Another alternative to the serger is to "clean finish" the seam allowances. This means enclosing the seam allowance within a seam. There is another example of using this technique on the Rey Underwire Bra (page 124).

Seam finished with zigzag stitch

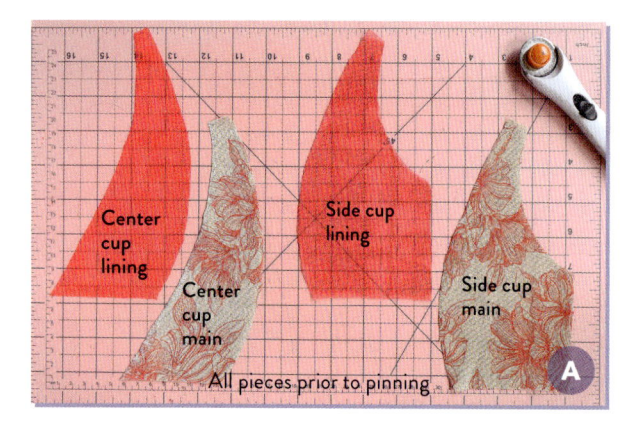

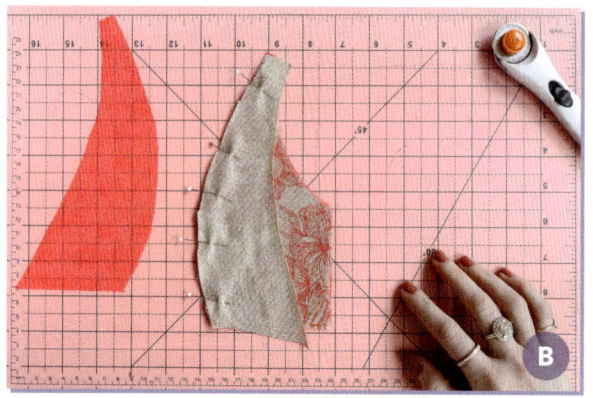

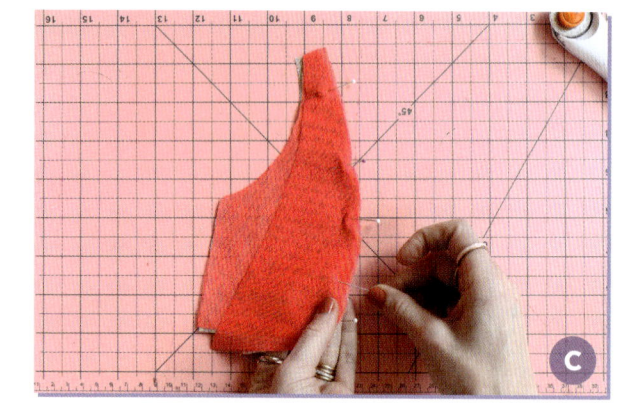

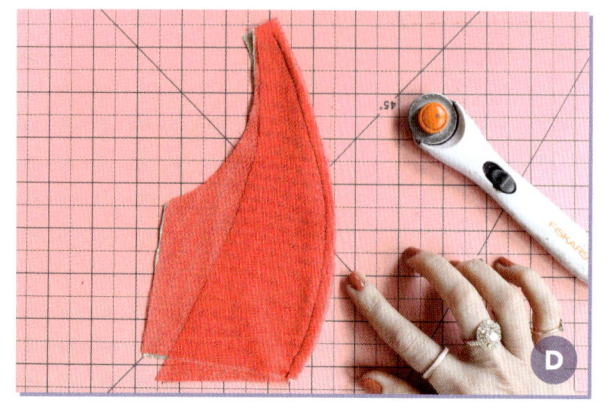

Clean Finishing

This technique demonstrates how to clean finish on a bra or bralette that has a vertical seam with a side cup and center cup.

1. Place side cup **main fabric** on top of center cup **main and lining fabric**. Right sides of the main fabrics should be facing. Pin along the vertical seam. **A B**

2. Flip over. Place the lining of the side cup on top of the center cup **lining fabric**. lining fabrics should be next to each other and main fabrics should be next to each other. Repin along the vertical seam through all layers. **C**

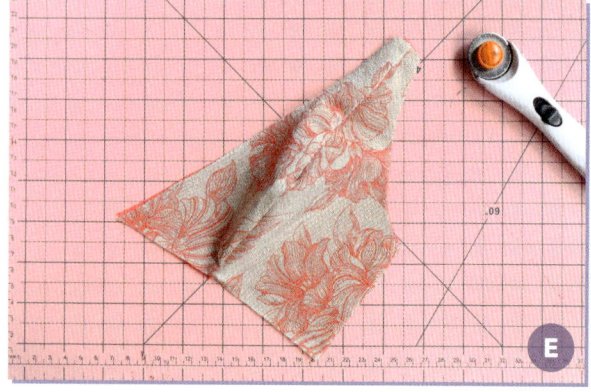

3. Sew the vertical seam with a straight stitch. Backstitch at the beginning and end. After, flip the bra cups right side out. **D E**

54 SEW LINGERIE

Piecing Lace Together

If you run into an instance where the lace you're using does not fit onto the pattern piece, it doesn't mean that you can't use it. "Piecing" lace together is a common technique where strips of galloon lace fabrics are sewn together until the piece is wide enough.

1. Decide where you want the lace pieces to be connected. The goal is that you won't be able to tell that the lace is pieced, but depending on the design, this might not be possible. I try to piece lace together in the most inconspicuous spot. The example shown is the Ryan Center Front Bralette pattern piece. **Ⓐ**

2. Cut strips of lace to be larger than the size of the pattern piece. You can piece them together with the lining or without the lining. In this example, there is no lining.

3. Overlap the lace pieces so that the scallop edges are aligned. Pin together along the scallop edge, or for more security, use a washable glue stick to adhere the layers together. **Ⓑ**

4. Sew a zigzag stitch along the scallop edge. The width and length of the zigzag stitch will vary depending on the design of the scallop lace, but usually about ¼" (6mm) wide will work. **Ⓒ**

5. Cut out the pattern piece. **Ⓓ**

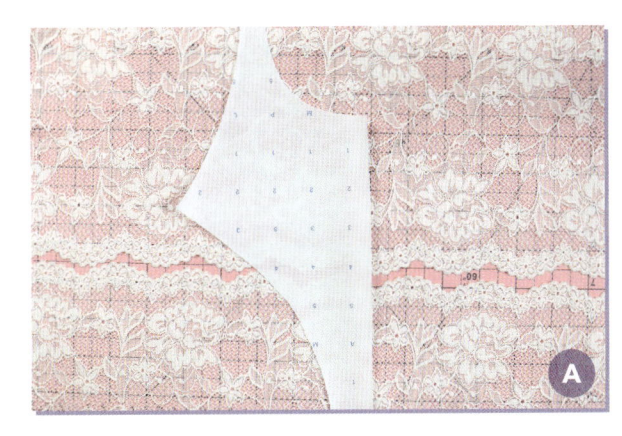

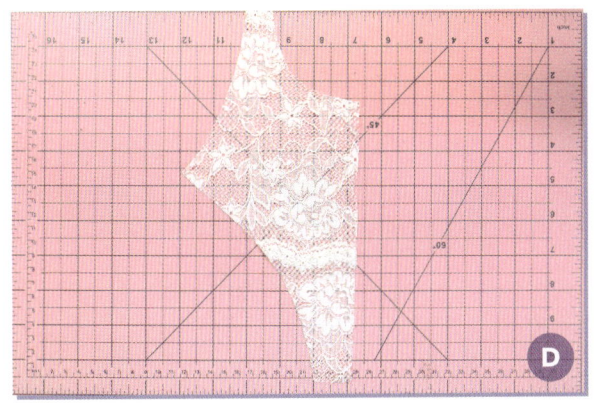

TECHNIQUES 55

ADJUSTING PATTERNS

56 SEW LINGERIE

I once bought the most beautiful French lace to make a self drafted underwire bra and panty. The fabric was gorgeous—a blend of black and beige with lurex detailing, making it sparkle whenever the light hit it. Every time I thought about sewing it, I was filled with self doubt. What if I messed up and ruined the fabric? For a year—a whole year!—I waited until I was 100% confident and had the courage to cut into it.

Many sewists fear pattern making like I feared sewing that beautiful lace. But, pattern making generally follows the same fundamental methods, which means that once you learn them, you use them over and over and can alter almost any pattern. Sounds easy, right? I encourage you to conquer any pattern making fears you may have and remind you that pattern making is a fun exercise that truly puts you in control.

Pattern Making Terms

First, let's go over pattern making terms that you will be using in this chapter. Gather a pencil or pen, dotted pattern paper, a straight ruler, and a French curve ruler (See Tools, page 36).

Slash and open: A pattern making technique that is used to add fullness, width, or length by cutting the pattern apart and spreading it open.

Slash and close: The opposite of slash and open, this technique removes fullness, width, or length by cutting the pattern apart and overlapping the pieces.

Trueing: The process of checking that the seams on a pattern are blended and that adjoining seams are the same length.

Blending: A process of creating smooth lines and transitions from one point or area to another.

Seam allowance: The area between the stitch line and the edge of the fabric. For pattern alterations shown in this chapter, seam allowances have been removed from the patterns.

Wire splay: Wire splay is the difference between the underwire when it is flat (not on body) and when it is being worn (on body). When the underwire is worn, there is tension on the band, causing it to pull open so that the underwire is slightly wider. This is called splay. How much splay depends on the type of underwire and the bra style. Generally, wire splay varies from ⅛" (0.45cm) to ⅝" (1.58cm) with shallower (less "U" shaped) underwires having less wire splay.

Play room: Play room is the extra length that is added to the wire seam line that prevents the underwire from bursting through the bra. It allows the underwire to move back and forth inside the channeling while the bra is being worn. If play room isn't added to the pattern, then the underwire will poke through the channeling and the fabric, which can be quite painful. Generally, ¼" (0.63cm) is added to either side.

ADJUSTING PATTERNS

Common Bra Pattern Alterations

Pattern alterations should be done in the same order in which the bra or bralette was fit. See Evaluating Fit (page 48). For the following pattern alterations, I'm using pattern pieces that are very similar to the Rey Bra (page 124).

Back Band Alterations

Increase Length

You'll know you need to increase a back band if it feels so tight that it is constricting normal movement and sometimes is painful. There also may be horizontal stress lines, which are a key indicator that the fabric is being stretched too much. To increase the length of the back band, use a slash and open method.

1. With a pen or pencil, draw a vertical line on the back band pattern piece that is parallel to the side seam and midway between the side seam and center back.

2. Cut along the vertical line. **A**

3. Place the left and right back band pieces on the pattern paper so that they are separated by the desired amount you want to increase. See Evaluating Fit (page 48) for help determining how much to increase.

4. Blend the increase by drawing a continuous, smooth line (A) from the side seam to the center back on both the top and the bottom. **B**

Decrease Length

You'll know you need to decrease a back band if it rides up in the back. Another key indicator is if you're able to fit more than two fingers between the bra and the body at the center back. To decrease the length of the back band, use the slash and close method, overlapping the pattern pieces instead of spreading them open.

1. With a pen or pencil, draw a vertical line on the back band pattern piece that is parallel to the side seam and midway between the side seam and center back.

2. Cut along the vertical line. **C**

3. Place the left and right back band pieces on the pattern paper so that they are overlapping by the desired amount you want to decrease. See Evaluating Fit (page 48), for help determining how much to decrease.

4. Blend the decrease by drawing a continuous, smooth line (B) from the side seam to the center back on both the top and the bottom. **D**

Frame Alterations

Increase Width of the Gore

You'll know you need to increase a gore if the channeling is not sitting on the breast root. It is important to determine where the gore needs to be increased: at the top only, at the bottom only, or through the entire length. In this example, width is being added through the entire length of the gore. Use a slash and open method.

Knowing how much to increase the gore is difficult because getting the most accurate adjustment requires cutting through the length of the gore and letting it spread open until the channeling sits on the breast root. You may not want to cut into your bra to figure this out. So, I recommend increasing in $\frac{1}{8}''$ (0.3cm) increments.

1. With a pen or pencil, draw a vertical line down the center of the gore pattern piece.

2. Cut along the vertical line. **E**

3. Place the left and right gore pieces on the pattern paper so that they are separated by the desired amount you want to increase.

4. Blend the two pattern pieces by drawing horizontal lines (C) at the top and the bottom of the gore. **F**

SEW LINGERIE

ADJUSTING PATTERNS 59

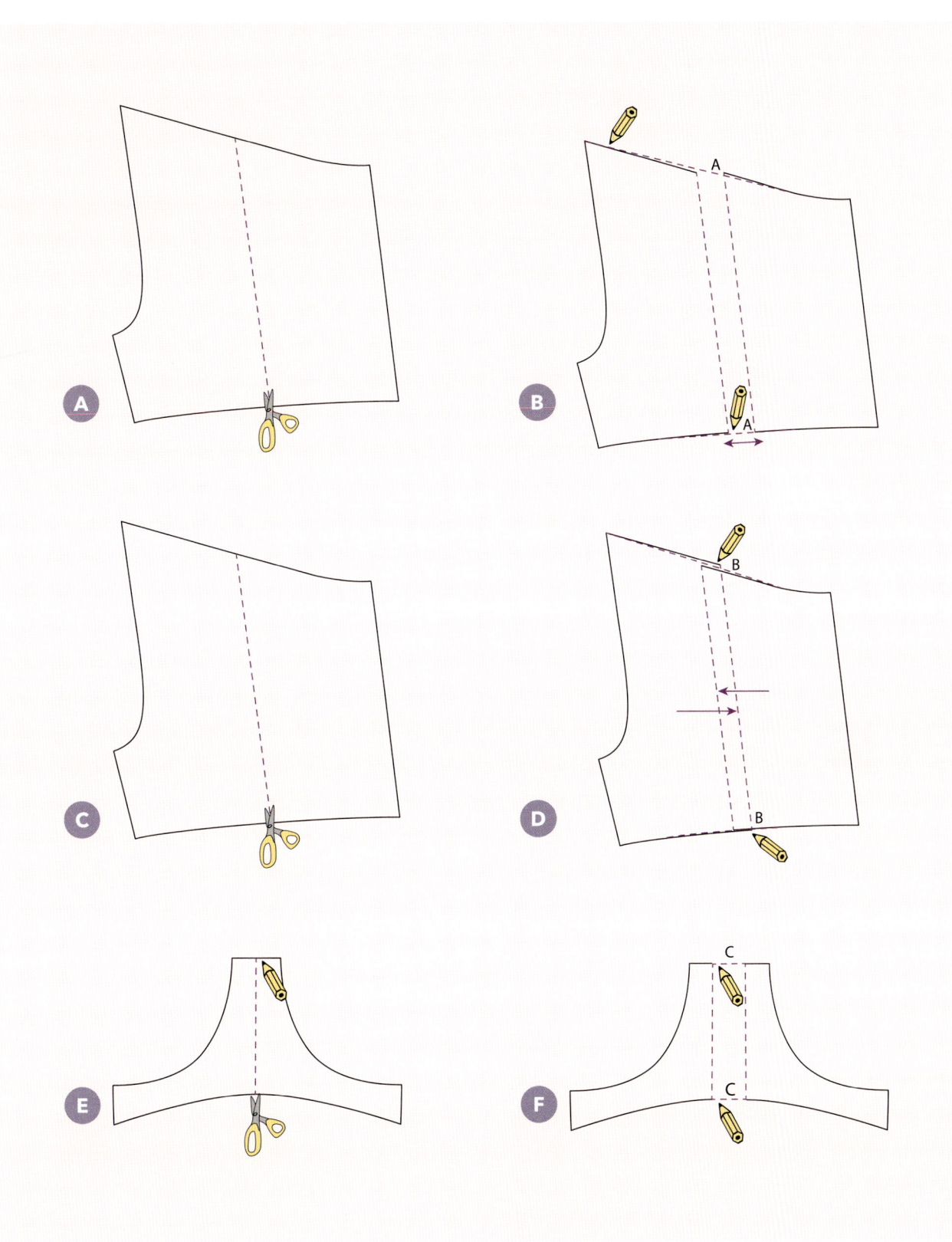

Decrease the Width of the Gore

You'll know you need to decrease the gore if the channeling is sitting on top of the breast tissue, is not tacking, or there is excess fabric in between the cups. It is important to determine where the gore needs to be decreased: at the top only, at the bottom only, or through the entire length of the gore. In this example, width is being removed through the entire gore. Use the slash and close method.

To determine how much to decrease, pin out the excess fabric until the channeling is sitting on the breast root and there is no excess.

It is also important to note that the channeling will meet at the center front top edge of the gore. So, if you do not want to overlap the channeling, the width at the top edge should be ¾" (1.9cm). Since each channeling is ⅜" (0.9cm), that width ensures there is enough fabric without the channeling overlapping.

1. With a pen or pencil, draw a vertical line down the center of the gore pattern piece.

2. Cut along the vertical line. **Ⓐ**

3. Place the left and right gore pieces on the pattern paper so that they are overlapping by the desired amount you want to decrease.

4. Blend the decrease by drawing a continuous, smooth line (D) at the top and the bottom of the gore. **Ⓑ**

Increase at Base of the Gore

If the base, or bottom, of the gore is too narrow, there will be horizontal drag or stress lines at or near the bottom only. To increase the width of the gore at the bottom, use the slash and open method. The width of the gore at the top will remain the same.

Just like when increasing the entire gore, knowing how much to increase is difficult. If you don't want to cut into the bra, I recommend increasing in ⅛" (0.3cm) increments.

1. With a pen or pencil, draw a vertical line down the center of the gore pattern piece.

CHANNELING OVERLAP

If you reduce the width of the gore using Steps 1–4 and the gore is still not tacking, there is still excess fabric, or the gore is still sitting on the breast tissue, then you will have to reduce the gore width to less than ¾" (1.9cm) and overlap the channeling.

When sewing the underwire channeling, sew the inner and outer lines of stitching just as you normally would to the point where they overlap. Then, insert the underwires. Once the underwires are situated inside the channeling, finish sewing the inner and outer lines of stitching to the top edge of the gore. Sewing channeling with the underwires inside requires meticulous attention, so I recommend going slow and if needed, manually turning the handwheel until you get to the top edge.

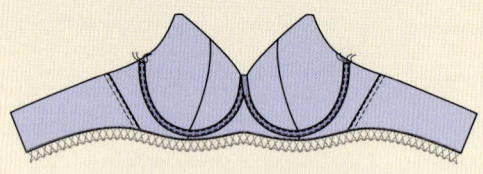

Sew until the point of overlap

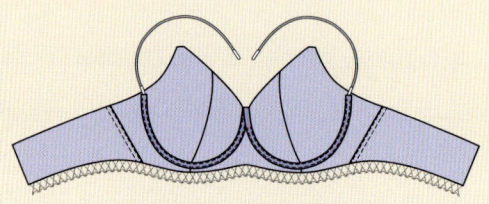

Insert the underwires

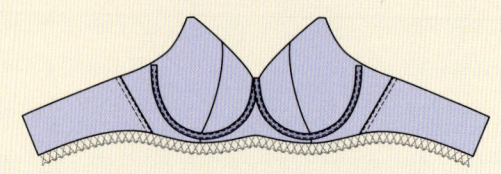

Finish sewing to the top of the gore

SEW LINGERIE

2. Cut along the vertical line from the bottom to the top. Cut all the way to, but not through, the top edge. This creates a hinge with a tiny portion of the paper intact at the top that allows you to spread the gore open at the bottom, leaving the top the same width. **C**

3. Spread open the gore at the bottom the desired amount.

4. Blend the decrease by drawing a continuous, smooth line (E) at the top and the bottom of the gore. **D**

Decrease at Base of the Gore

If the base, or bottom, of the gore is too wide, there will be excess fabric or gaping at or near the bottom only. To decrease the width of the gore at the bottom, use the slash and close method. The width of the gore at the top will remain the same.

To determine how much to decrease, pin out the excess fabric using pins until the channeling is sitting on the breast root.

1. With a pen or pencil, draw a vertical line down the center of the gore pattern piece.

2. Cut along the vertical line from the bottom to the top. Cut all the way to, but not through, the top edge. This creates a hinge with a tiny portion of the paper intact at the top that allows you to overlap the gore at the bottom, leaving the top the same width. **E**

3. Overlap the gore at the bottom the desired amount.

4. Blend the decrease by drawing a continuous, smooth line (F) at the top and the bottom of the gore. **F**

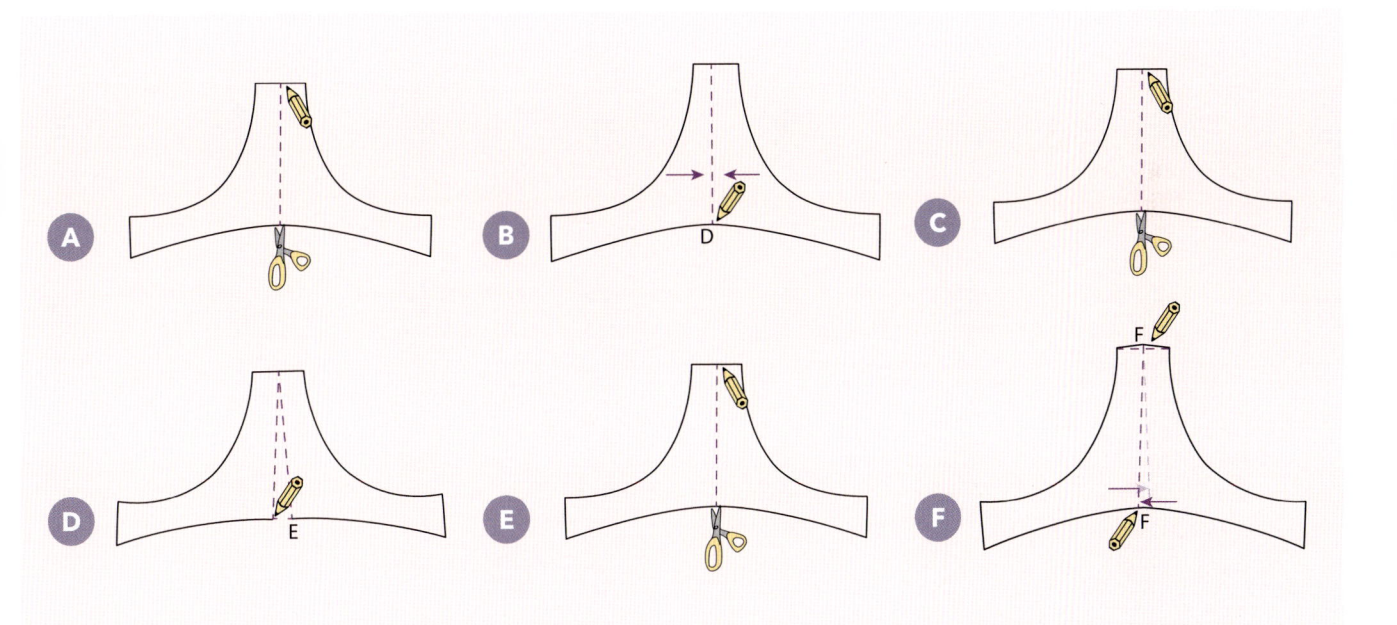

ADJUSTING PATTERNS   **61**

Increase at Top of the Gore

If the top of the gore is too narrow, the channeling will not sit on the breast root. To increase the width of the gore at the top, use the slash and open method. The width of the gore at the bottom will remain the same.

1. With a pen or pencil, draw a vertical line down the center of the gore pattern piece.

2. Cut along the vertical line from the top to the bottom. Cut all the way to, but not through, the bottom edge. This creates a hinge with a tiny portion of the paper intact at the bottom that allows you to spread the gore at the top, leaving the bottom the same width. **A**

3. Spread open the gore at the top the desired amount.

4. Blend the increase by drawing a continuous, smooth line (G) at the top and the bottom of the gore. **B**

Decrease at Top of the Gore

If the top of the gore is too wide, it will be indicated by the channeling sitting on top of the breast tissue at the top only. To decrease the width of the gore at the top, use the slash and close method. The width of the gore at the bottom will remain the same.

To determine how much to decrease, pin out the excess fabric using pins until the channeling is sitting on the breast root.

1. With a pen or pencil, draw a vertical line down the center of the gore pattern piece.

2. Cut along the vertical line from top to bottom. Cut all the way to, but not through, the bottom edge. This creates a hinge with a tiny portion of the paper intact at the bottom that allows you to overlap the gore at the top, leaving the bottom the same width. **C**

3. Overlap the gore at the top the desired amount.

4. Blend the decrease by drawing a continuous, smooth line (H) at the top and the bottom of the gore. **D**

Lower the Gore at Center Front (Decrease Coverage)

You may want to change the height of the gore at the center front because of a personal preference for comfort or coverage, or you may need to adjust it for a different underwire size or style. It is important to note that changing the height of the gore at the center front will also change the length of the wire seam line. So, depending on how much you increase or decrease it, and how much play room is built into the pattern, you may need to go up or down an underwire size.

1. With a pen or pencil, draw a horizontal line below the top of the gore pattern piece. The distance between the top of the gore and the line is equal to the desired amount you want to lower the gore.

2. On the upper cup pattern piece, measure down the same amount at the center front edge of the piece. Draw a new line (J) from the center front mark to the corner of the upper cup where it will attach to the side cup (no change made at that side). **E**

Raise the Gore at Center Front (Increase Coverage)

Just like lowering the gore at the center front, it is important to note that raising the height of the gore will also change the length of the wire seam line. So, depending on how much you increase or decrease it, and how much play room is built into the pattern, you may need to go up or down an underwire size.

1. With a pen or pencil, draw a horizontal line above the top of the gore pattern piece on pattern paper. The distance between the top of the gore and the line is equal to the desired amount you want to raise the gore.

2. On the upper cup, measure up the same amount above the center front edge. Draw a new line (K) from the center front mark to the corner of the upper cup where it will attach to the side cup (no change made at that side). **F**

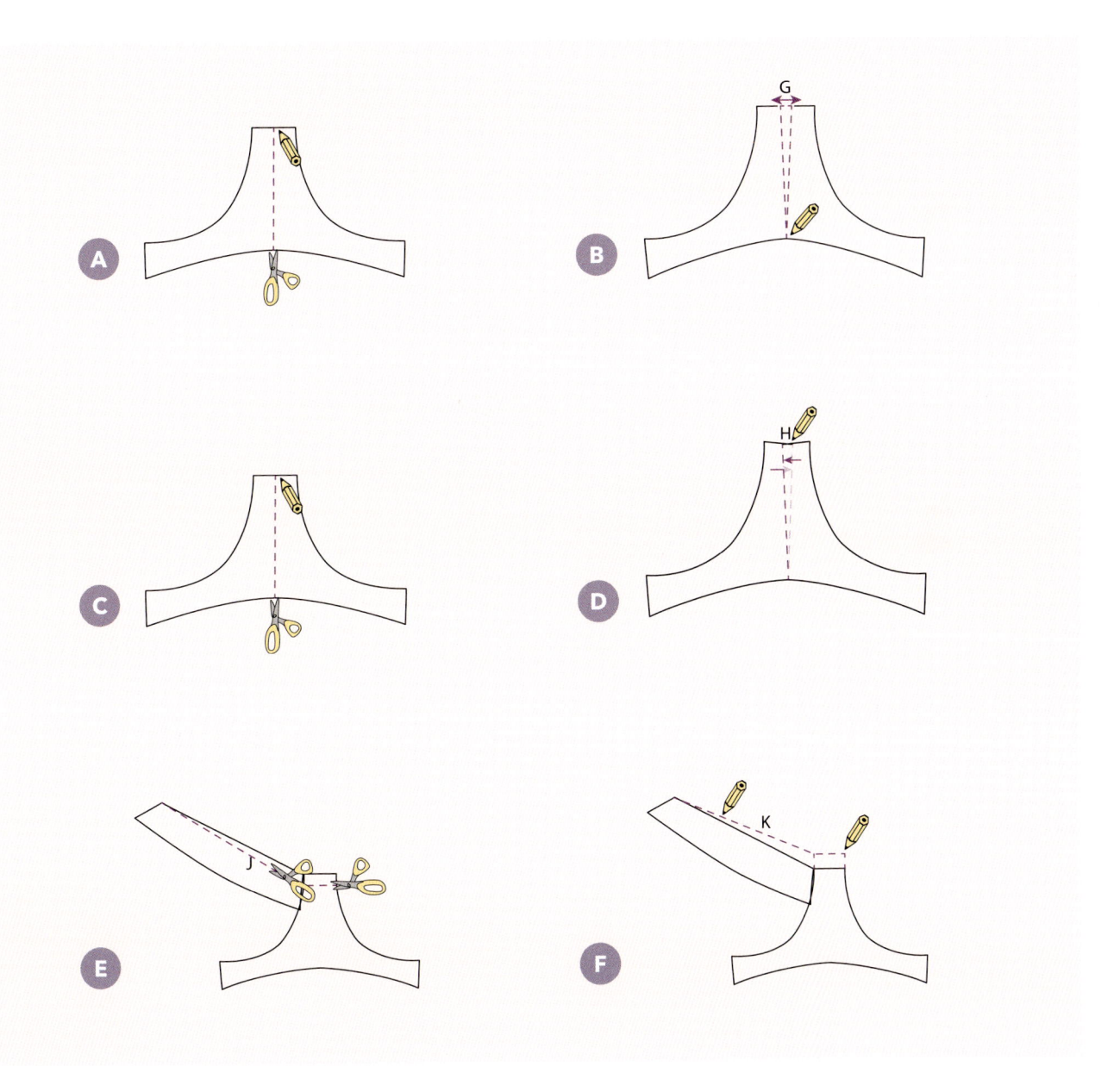

ADJUSTING PATTERNS **63**

Remove Gaping at the Underarm

To remove gaping at the underarm, use the slash and close method on the frame at the underarm.

1. With a pen or pencil, draw a diagonal line on the pattern piece from the frame at the underarm to the bottom edge, midway between the side seam and wire seam line.

2. Cut along the vertical line from the top of the frame to the bottom. Cut all the way to, but not through, the bottom edge. This creates a hinge with a tiny portion of the paper intact at the bottom that allows you to overlap at the top, leaving the bottom the same width. **A**

3. Overlap the frame at the underarm the desired amount. The most accurate way to figure out how much to overlap is to try the bra on and pin out the excess fabric where the bra is gaping.

4. Blend the decrease by drawing a continuous, smooth line (R) at the top edge of the frame. **B**

Lower the Underarm

Lowering the underarm reduces the amount of coverage.

1. Join the cup, frame and back band pattern pieces together at the underarm so that there is a continuous, smooth line from the strap point to the back band.

2. Using a pen or pencil, mark the desired amount you wish to lower at the underarm. The most accurate way to figure out how much to lower the underarm is to try the bra on and hold a ruler or a soft measuring tape up to the bra. Then draw a continuous smooth line (S) from the strap point to the back band with a French curve. It is important that the line starts and stops at the points from the original pattern pieces at the strap point and back band so that the strap placement and height of the hook and eye are not changed. It is also important that the amount reduced at the wire seam line is minimal or none so that you don't have to adjust the size of the underwire.

3. Cut the pattern pieces to reflect the decrease. **C**

Raise the Underarm

Raising the underarm provides more coverage.

1. Join the cup, frame and back band pattern pieces together at the underarm so that there is a continuous, smooth line from the strap point to the back band.

2. Using a pen or pencil, mark the desired amount you wish to raise at the underarm. Then, on pattern paper, draw a continuous smooth line (T) from the strap point to the back band with a French curve. It is important that the line starts and stops at the points from the original pattern pieces at the strap point and back band so that the strap placement and height of the hook and eye are not altered. It is also important that the amount reduced at the wire seam line is minimal or none so that you don't have to adjust the size of the underwire. **D**

Strap Alterations

Move Straps Towards Center Back on Back Band

Strap adjustments are very common and in my opinion, the easiest pattern adjustments to make on a bra. Even though people are built differently—some people have wide shoulders and some people have narrow shoulders—I have found that strap placement is often just a personal preference. But, if the straps are falling off your shoulders, they need to be adjusted. Demi and balconette bras tend to have straps that are wider.

1. Measure the desired amount you want to move the straps from the top of the back band curve. The most accurate way to figure out how much to move the straps towards the center back is to try the bra on and hold a ruler or a soft measuring tape up to the back band. Another option is to move the straps at ¼" (0.64cm) increments until the straps are in the correct position.

2. Using a pen or pencil, draw a smooth, curved line (L) that starts at the point you marked and ends at the existing center back edge. The height of the back band at the center back must remain the same so that the hook and eye can fit into it. **E**

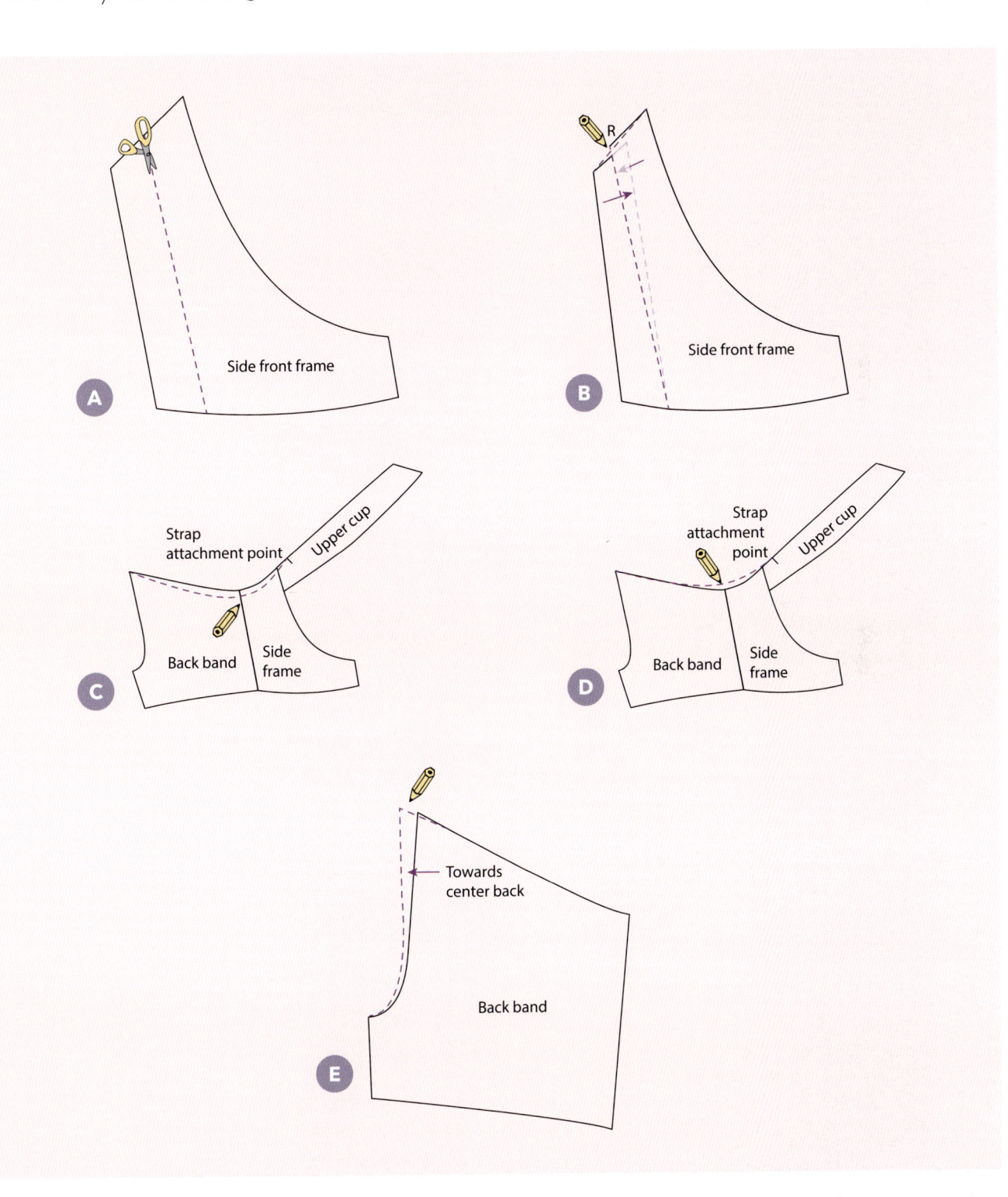

A — Side front frame

B — Side front frame

C — Strap attachment point / Upper cup / Back band / Side frame

D — Strap attachment point / Upper cup / Back band / Side frame

E — Towards center back / Back band

ADJUSTING PATTERNS 65

Move Straps Towards Shoulders on Back Band

1. Measure the desired amount you want to move the straps from the top of the back band. The most accurate way to figure out how much to move the straps towards the shoulders is to try on the bra and pin the straps where you want them to be. If the straps have already been sewn to the bra, unpick the stitches and repin the straps in the correct position.

2. Using a pen or pencil, draw a smooth, curved line (M) that starts at the point you marked and ends at the existing center back edge. The height of the back band at the center back must remain the same so that the hook and eye can fit into it. **Ⓐ**

Move Straps Towards Center Front on Cups

1. Measure the desired amount you wish to move the straps from the top cup at the underarm. The most accurate way to figure out how much to move the straps towards the center front is to try on the bra and pin the straps where you want them to be. If the straps have already been sewn to the bra, unpick the stitches and repin the straps in the correct position.

2. Using a pen or pencil, draw a smooth line (N) that starts at the point you marked and ends at the bottom of the top cup at the underarm (where the top cup meets the lower cup). **Ⓑ**

Move Straps Towards Shoulders on Cups

1. Measure the desired amount you wish to move the straps from the top cup at the underarm. The most accurate way to figure out how much to move the straps towards the shoulders is to try the bra on and hold a ruler or a soft measuring tape up to the strap points. Another option is to move the straps at ¼" (0.64cm) increments until the straps are in the correct position.

2. Using a pen or pencil, draw a smooth line (O) that starts at the point you marked and ends at the bottom of the top cup at the underarm (where the upper cup meets the lower cup). **Ⓒ**

Cup Alterations

Increase Volume

If the cups need more volume, the gore will not tack at the center front, and stress lines will appear on the cups. The pattern alteration shown is the simplest version when there is only a side cup and center front cup. If there were more bra cup pattern pieces, volume would need to be added to all parts.

1. Using a pen or pencil, mark the desired amount you want to increase the volume. The most accurate way to figure out how much to increase is to cut partially through each bra cup vertically using scissors, try them on, and measure how much the cups spread open. If you don't want to cut your bra, another option is to increase it at ¼" (0.64cm) increments until the volume is enough.

2. Using a French curved ruler, draw a smooth line (P) on pattern paper from the top of the cup pattern piece, to the marked point, and then to the bottom. It is important that the line starts and ends at the top and bottom points of the original cup pattern pieces. **Ⓓ**

3. Put the cup pattern pieces on top of each other so that the vertical seam is aligned. You want to make sure that the vertical seam lines are the same length and they have the same curve. **Ⓔ**

Decrease Volume

If the cups need less volume, it will be indicated by excess fabric and gaping.

1. Using a pen or pencil, mark the desired amount you want to decrease the volume. The most accurate way to figure out how much to decrease is to try the bra on and pin out the excess.

2. Using a French curved ruler, draw a smooth line (Q) from the top, to the marked point, and then to the bottom. It is important that the line starts and ends at the top and bottom points of the original cup pattern pieces. **Ⓕ**

3. Put the patterns on top of each other so that the vertical seam is aligned. You want to make sure that the vertical seam lines are the same length as well as the same curve. **G**

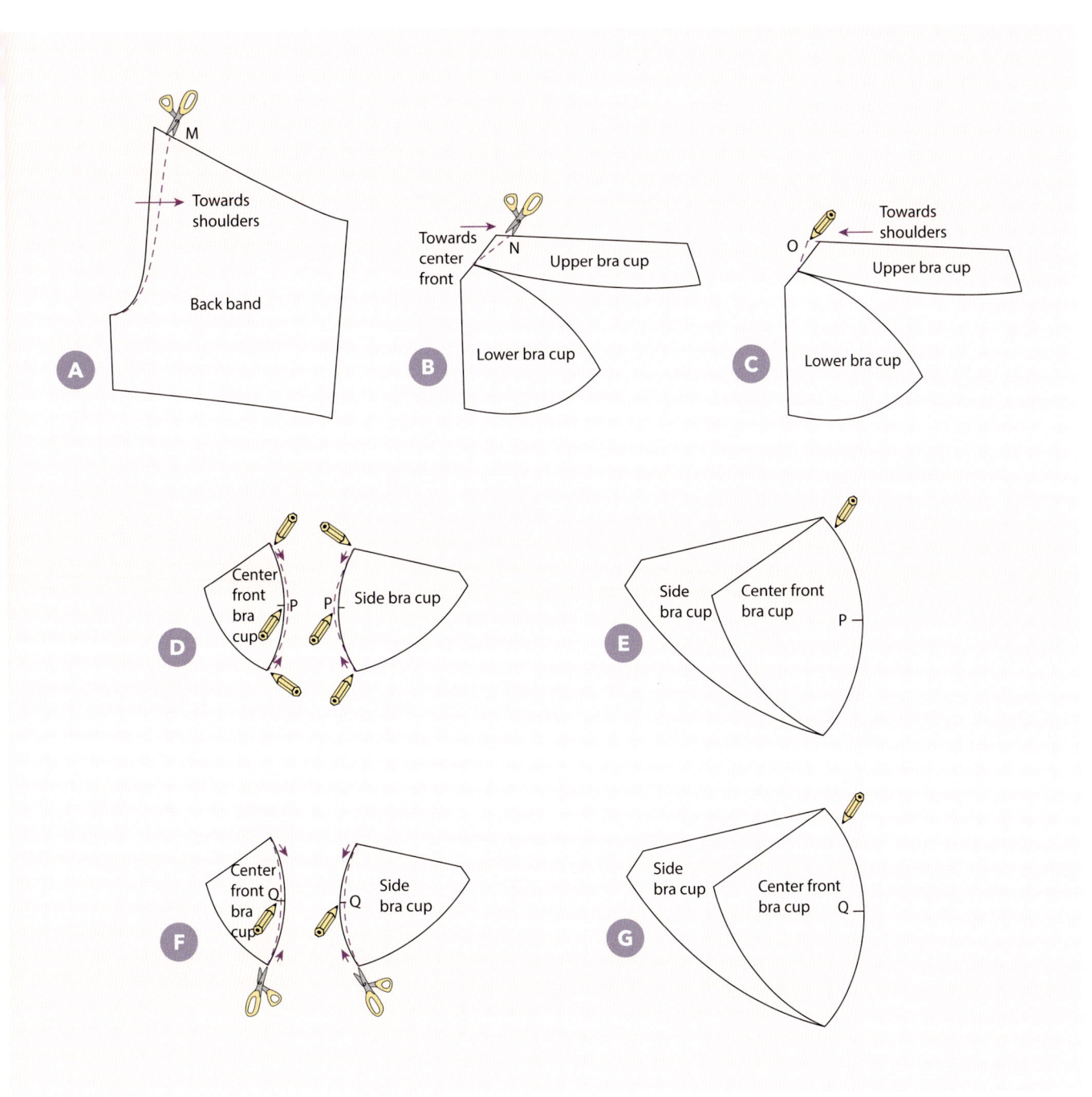

A — Back band, Towards shoulders, M

B — Upper bra cup, Lower bra cup, Towards center front, N

C — Upper bra cup, Lower bra cup, Towards shoulders, O

D — Center front bra cup, Side bra cup, P

E — Side bra cup, Center front bra cup, P

F — Center front bra cup, Side bra cup, Q

G — Side bra cup, Center front bra cup, Q

ADJUSTING PATTERNS **67**

Adjusting Patterns Without Cup Sizes

I love bralettes for their comfort and because they offer wireless support, but they have one major drawback. Most are based on a B cup, and many people are not a B cup. So, I've developed a method that I have been using for years to incorporate cup sizing if a bra or bralette pattern doesn't have cup sizes. If you measure any cup size other than A–C cup, you can use this method for cutting the bra or bralette patterns in this book.

Cut the pattern size you measure based on the full bust for the front bra or bralette pieces. Cut the size you measure based on the underbust for the back band pieces. This will give you enough coverage for the front, but also fit around your ribcage. So, if you are very full busted, you might cut a size 2X for the front bra or bralette and a small for the back band.

When you cut a smaller size back band, you need to make a very minor pattern alteration (there are no changes to the sewing). Even if you have no experience with pattern making, you can totally handle this!

Using the same example, let's say you cut a 2XL for the front bralette cups and a small for the back band. Now, the side seam will not match between the two pieces. So, you need to increase the height of the smaller piece or decrease the height of the larger piece at the side seam. Whether you increase or decrease is up to you. A wider back band will be more supportive. Align the two pieces and cut the side cup to match the height of the back band, or grab a sheet of paper and add a strip to the back band so it matches the height of the side cup. **Ⓐ**

Adjusting Bra Patterns for Different Underwires

You might need a different underwire style than the pattern calls for, like changing from a classic underwire to a demi. Or you may discover that the shape of the underwire doesn't match the shape of the wire seam on your pattern. Luckily, you can make adjustments!

First, it's important to note that adjusting a pattern for a different underwire has limitations. Just like fitting a toile, only a few alterations (1–3) should be made at a time and I don't recommend changing the seam line more than ½" (1.2cm). Since one alteration can affect another part of the bra, I also suggest making a toile after each change.

1. If it isn't already indicated on the pattern, mark the lowest point of the frame. It is usually easy to find—you can eyeball it. **Ⓑ**

2. Mark the lowest point on the new underwire. You can usually eyeball the lowest point. Or, if you have dotted pattern making paper, place the underwire on top of the grid and find the lowest point. You can also put the underwire up to your chest and mark the lowest point while the underwire is on your body, again eyeballing. **Ⓒ**

3. Place the underwire on top of the frame pattern piece and align the marks indicating the lowest points. **Ⓓ**

4. Redraw the wire seam line (W) to match the shape of the underwire. The new wire seam line should be drawn based on the inner edge of the underwire. **Ⓔ**

5. Add wire splay and play room (see Pattern Making Terms, page 57), indicated by line Y, at the underarm. Then adjust the frame at the center front. Double check that there is enough room for the channeling at the center front. There will be two strips of channeling, and if channeling measures ⅜" (0.95cm), then the center front needs to be at least ¾" (1.9cm) wide so that the channeling does not overlap. **Ⓕ**

SEW LINGERIE

6. Last, true the pattern by measuring the length of the wire seam line on the bra cups and the length on the underwire. The underwire should measure less than the wire seam line.

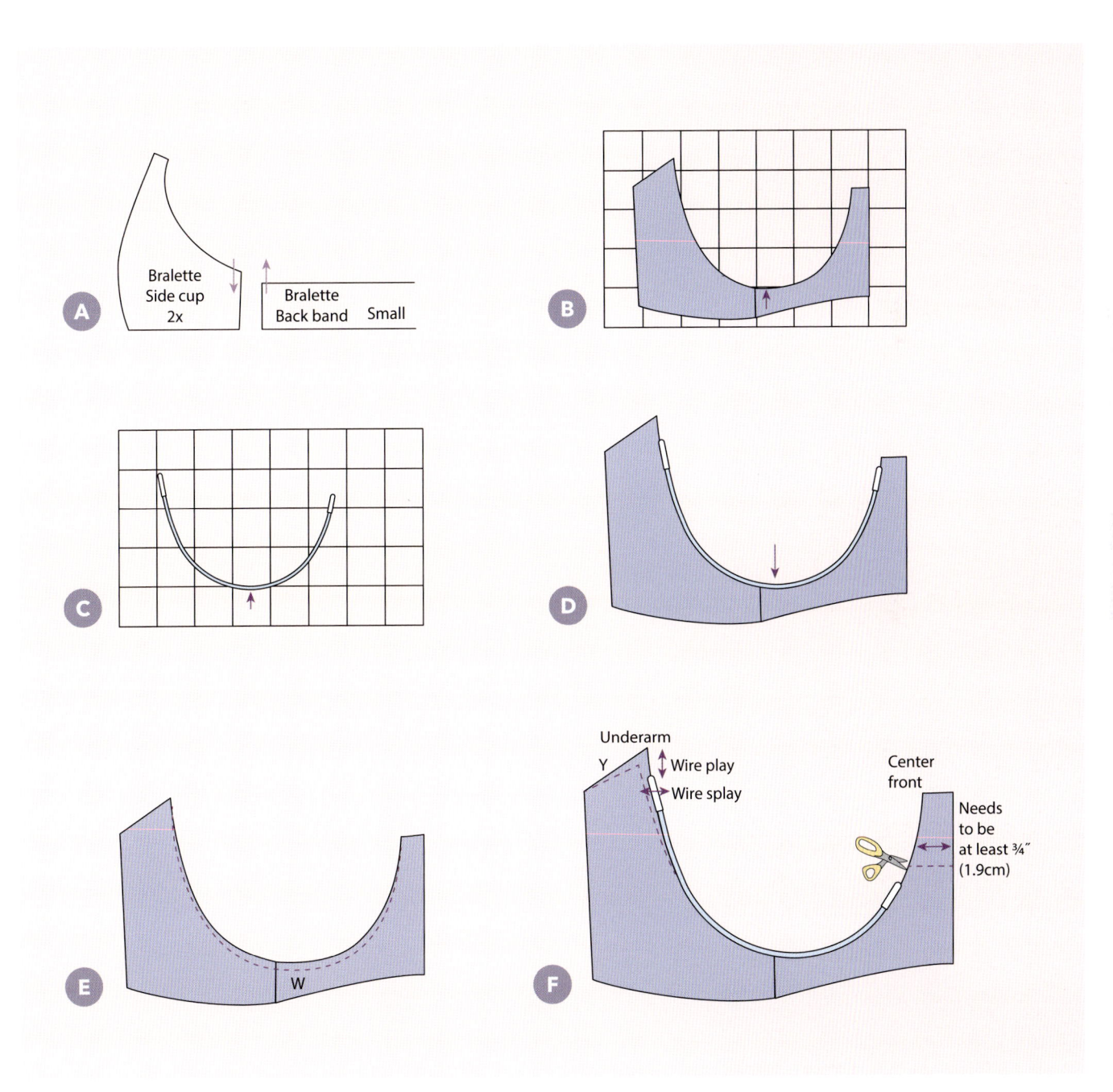

A. Bralette Side cup 2x / Bralette Back band Small

B.

C.

D.

E. W

F. Underarm Y / Wire play / Wire splay / Center front / Needs to be at least ¾" (1.9cm)

ADJUSTING PATTERNS 69

Common Panty Pattern Alterations

If you've worn ill-fitting panties, then you know that they are a pain in the you know what! Whether it's visible panty lines underneath a tight fitting pair of pants or a skirt, a waistband that is too tight, excess fabric that is bunching up, or not enough fabric that causes panties to ride up (AKA a wedgie), even small details can cause discomfort all day long. With just a few tweaks, it's possible to get the perfect pair for all day comfort.

Gusset Width

Generally, the width of the gusset is around 2" (5cm) no matter what size you are. So, the gusset width on a size X-small and a size 3XL are the same. If panties have vertical folds or excess fabric in the gusset area or the front and back of the panty, then the gusset width needs to be decreased. If panties don't have enough coverage and are exposing parts of your body, then the gusset width needs to be increased. Use the slash and open or slash and close method.

To increase the width:

1. With a pen or pencil, draw a vertical line down the middle of the gusset pattern piece.

2. Cut along the vertical line. **A**

3. Place the left and right gusset pieces on the pattern paper so that they are separated by the desired amount you want to increase. The most accurate way to determine how much to add is to try on the panty and measure with a measuring tape. An alternative method is to increase it to the standard 2" (5cm).

4. Blend the two pattern pieces by drawing a straight line at the top and bottom. **B**

5. True the front and back seams to match the gusset, and adjust the pattern pieces to have a smooth curve on both sides. **C**

ADJUSTING PATTERNS

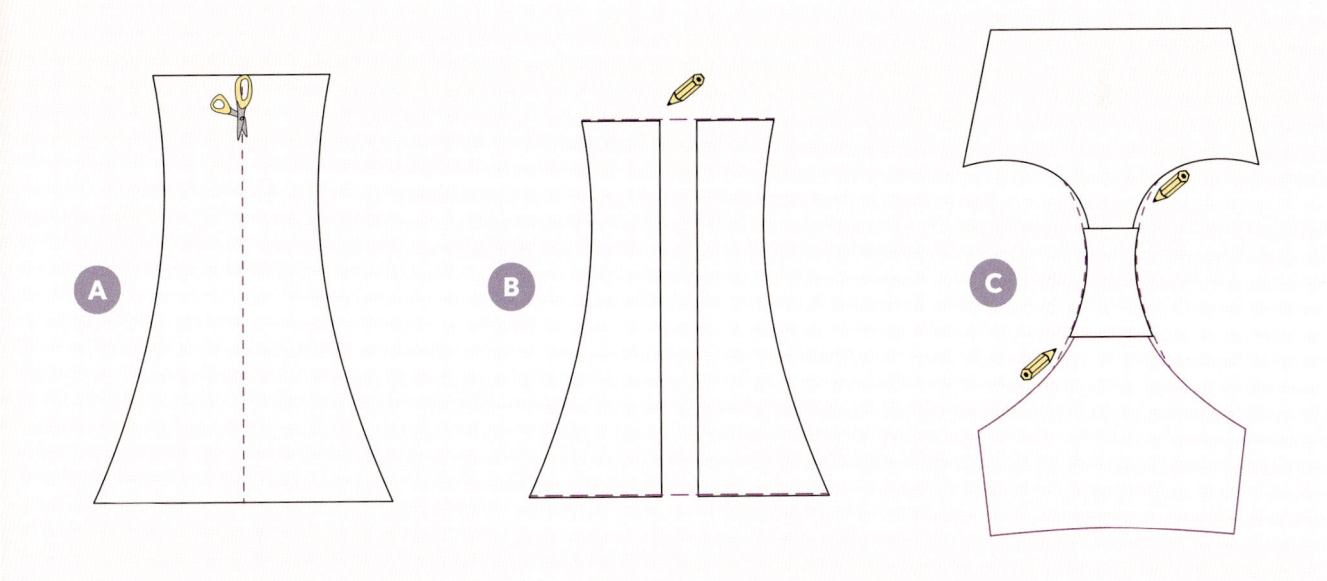

To decrease the width:

1. With a pen or pencil, draw a vertical line down the middle of the gusset pattern piece.

2. Cut along the vertical line. **A**

3. Place the left and right gusset pieces on the pattern paper so that they are overlapping by the desired amount you want to decrease. The most accurate way to determine how much to decrease is to try on the panty and pin out the excess. An alternative method is to decrease to the standard 2″ (5cm).

4. Blend the two pattern pieces by drawing a straight line at the top and bottom. **B**

5. True the front and back seams to match the gusset, and adjust the pattern pieces to have a smooth curve on both sides. **C**

Full Tummy Adjustment

Panties need a full tummy adjustment if the front of the panty dips lower than the back. This can be due to a full stomach or midsection, or an anterior rear tilt (when the spine is curved in a way that causes a person's rear to protrude). Either way, more fabric is needed on the front so that the panty is level all the way around.

1. Using a pen or pencil, draw a horizontal line approximately 2″ (5cm) below the top of the front panty panel pattern piece.

2. Cut along the horizontal line from center front to side seam. Cut all the way to, but not through, the side seam. This creates a hinge with a tiny portion of the paper intact at the side seam that allows you to spread the center front open without changing the length. **D**

3. Spread open at the center front the desired amount, making sure that the side seam does not increase in length.

4. Blend by drawing a continuous, smooth line across the top of the pattern pieces starting at the center front crossing the side seam, and ending at the center back. **E**

Adjusting Rise for Torso Length

You may want to change the rise on a panty for personal preference, or to better fit a certain body shape. For increasing and decreasing the rise, use the slash and open and slash and close method.

To increase the rise:

1. Using a pen or pencil, draw a horizontal line 2″ (5cm) below the top of the front panty panel pattern piece.

2. Cut along the horizontal line. **F**

3. Place the upper and lower panty pieces on the pattern paper so that they are separated by the desired amount you want to increase. The most accurate way to determine this is to try on the panty and hold a ruler or a soft measuring tape up to the top of the waistline and make a note how much you want to increase it.

4. Blend the two pattern pieces by drawing a continuous, smooth line at the center front and side seam. **G**

5. Repeat steps 1–4 for the back panty pattern, and then true the side seams to ensure that the front and back side seams are the same length and angle.

ADJUSTING PATTERNS

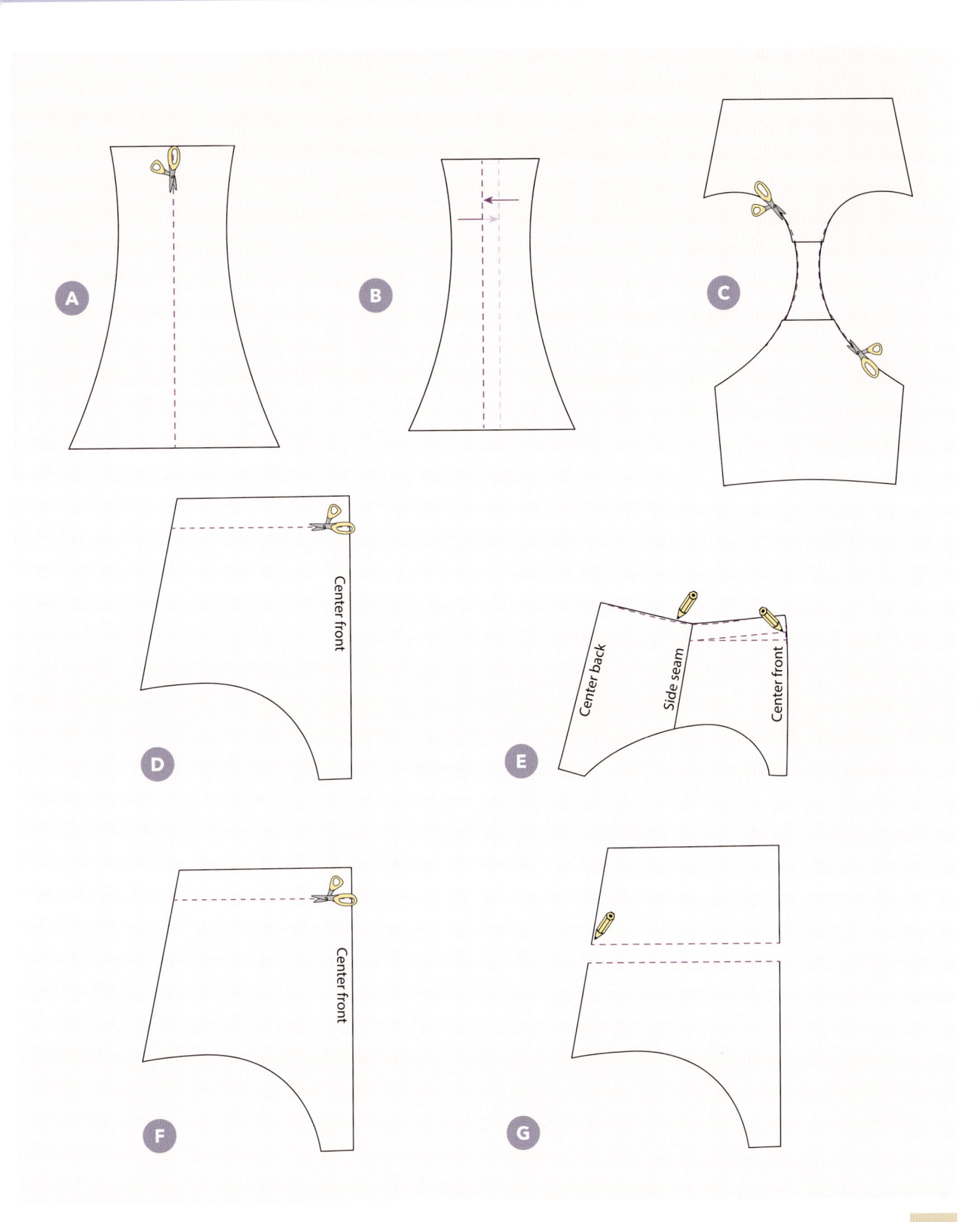

To decrease the rise:

1. Using a pen or pencil, draw a horizontal line 2″ (5cm) below the top of the front panty panel pattern piece.

2. Cut along the horizontal line. **A**

3. Place the upper and lower panty pieces on the pattern paper so that they are overlapping by the desired amount you want to decrease. The most accurate way to determine how much to decrease the rise is to try on the panty and pin out fabric until the waistline hits where you want it to be.

4. Blend the two pattern pieces by drawing a continuous, smooth line at the center front and side seam. **B**

5. Repeat steps 1–4 for the back panty pattern, and then true the side seams to ensure that the front and back side seams are the same length and angle.

Adjusting the Leg Line

You may want to adjust the leg line to achieve a different style (example: french cut versus boyshort).

1. Butt the front and back panty pieces together at the side seam.

2. Using a pen or pencil, mark the desired amount you want to raise or lower the side seam. The most accurate way to determine this is to try on the panty and hold a ruler or a soft measuring tape up to the leg line and make a note how much you want to adjust it.

3. Blend the two pattern pieces by drawing a continuous, smooth line from the front leg line to the back leg line. **C D**

Fix Wedgies

If you count yourself as one of many people who don't wear a thong because you don't like having a thin piece of fabric between your rear all day long, you're not alone. But, what's the point of wearing regular underwear if it *also* gives you a wedgie? Isn't that pretty much a thong?

There are several causes of wedgies. It could mean something is too small—when fitting pants, a clear indication that the rise needs to be increased is if the seam starts to creep into your rear. A wedgie can also mean something is too big—if there's too much fabric, the fabric is going to bunch up. Wedgies can also be caused by the type of fabric, sewing mechanics, or the shape of the pattern.

Sizes

It may sound silly, but make sure you're wearing the right size. Double check your measurements and compare them to the size chart of that particular brand and style. It's easy to assume that your measurements haven't changed since your last project or when you last measured, but they could have. I also suggest taking your measurements throughout the month to know when/if you fluctuate.

Fabric Choice

In contrast to cotton panties, panties made of synthetic fabrics tend to bunch less since they have more inherent stretch and better recovery. This allows the fabric to move and flex with the movement of your body. It's also important to note that the spandex and recovery in synthetic fabrics will fade over time. So if your underwear didn't used to give you a wedgie, but it does now, it could be that they're old and need to be replaced.

SEW LINGERIE

Elastic

The elastic could have stretched out when sewing, causing there to be excess fabric. If the fabric is too loose around the butt, the fabric will slide around and cause a wedgie. See Sewing Elastic (page 52) for more on stretching while sewing.

Pattern

If you choose the correct size, use the right fabric, and add the right amount of tension when sewing the elastic, there are two pattern changes that might help. The first is adding a slight curve to the back panty pattern piece (A). The other is to curve the crotch seam (B). **E**

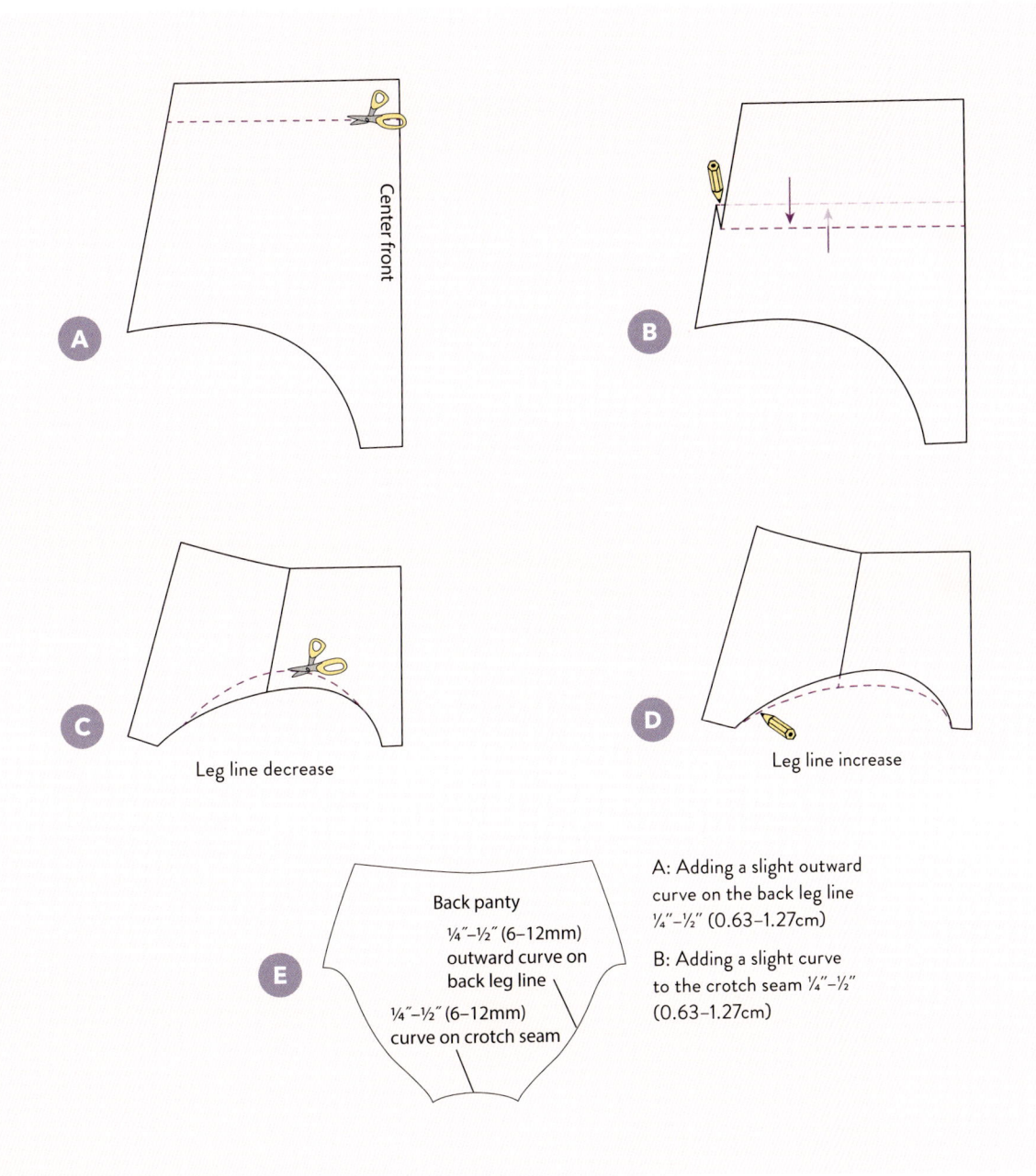

A

B

C — Leg line decrease

D — Leg line increase

E — Back panty
¼″–½″ (6–12mm) outward curve on back leg line
¼″–½″ (6–12mm) curve on crotch seam

A: Adding a slight outward curve on the back leg line ¼″–½″ (0.63–1.27cm)

B: Adding a slight curve to the crotch seam ¼″–½″ (0.63–1.27cm)

ADJUSTING PATTERNS 75

panty PROJECTS

To access each pattern, scan the QR code in each individual project. You can then download the pattern at full size, or in print-at-home format.

All seam allowances are included in patterns and are ¼" (0.6cm), unless otherwise noted. Whenever instructed to serge a seam allowance, if you do not have a serger, you can skip this step and leave the edges unfinished or push seam allowances to one side and sew them down with a zigzag stitch that is ¼" (0.6cm) wide.

Panty Size

Size	XS	S	M	L	XL
Waist	23"–25" (58.4–63.5cm)	25"–27" (63.5–68.6cm)	27"–29" (68.6–73.7cm)	29"–31" (73.7–78.4cm)	31"–34" (78.4–86.4cm)
Hip	33–35" (83.8–88.9cm)	35"–37" (88.9–94cm)	37"–39" (94–99.1cm)	39"–41" (99.1–104.1cm)	41"–44" (104.1–111.8cm)

Size	2X	3X	4X	5x
Waist	34"–37" (86.4–94cm)	37"–41" (94–104.1cm)	41"–45" (104.1–114.3cm)	45"–49" (114.3–124.5cm)
Hip	44"–47" (111.8–119.4cm)	47"–51" (119.4–129.5cm)	51"–55" (129.5–139.7cm)	55"–59" (139.7–149.7cm)

78

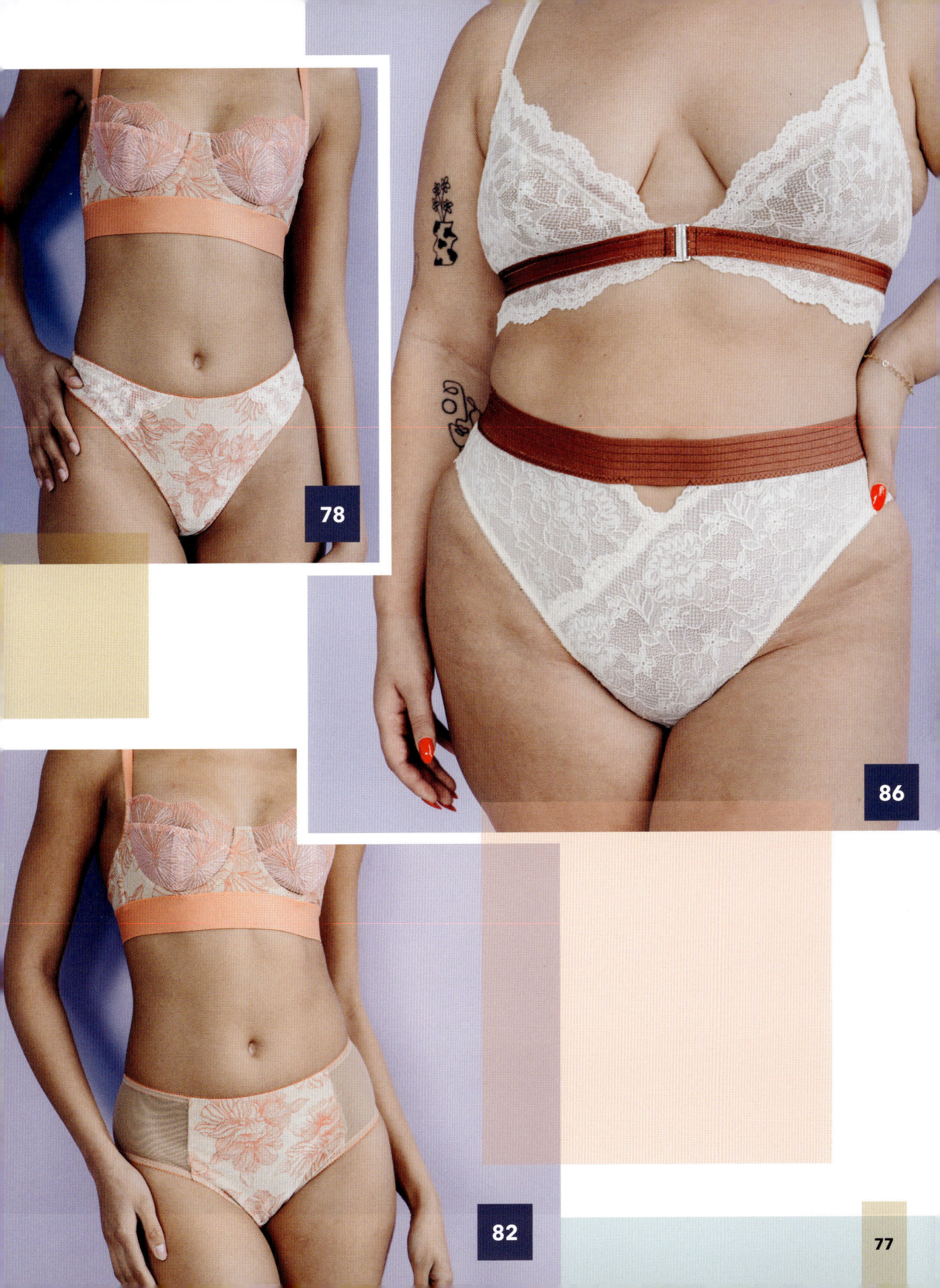

86

82

77

BEGINNER
BARKER *panty*

The Barker Panty is a basic, mid-rise brief that has side panels. The waistline and leg openings are finished with panty elastic. Use #barkerpanty to share your make!

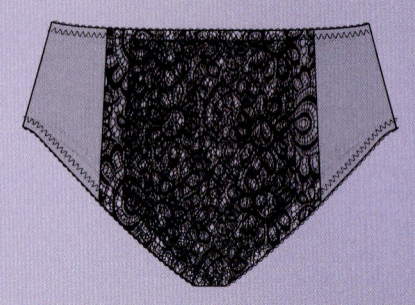

PANTY PROJECTS

Fabrics and Notions

MAIN FABRIC: Jersey, stretch mesh, LYCRA, or stretch all over lace

COMBO FABRIC: Jersey, stretch mesh, LYCRA, stretch all over lace, or stretch galloon lace at least 8″ (20cm) wide

LINING FABRIC: Stretch mesh

PANTY ELASTIC: 3½ yards (3.3m) ¼″ (6mm)–⅜″ (8mm) wide

COTTON JERSEY SWATCH/SCRAP FOR GUSSET

FABRIC CHART	XS–L	XL–5X
Main Fabric	½ yard (46cm)	¾ yard (69cm)
Combo Fabric	½ yard (46cm)	½ yard (46cm)
Lining Fabric	½ yard (46cm)	¾ yard (69cm)

Tools

SEWING MACHINE WITH STRAIGHT AND ZIGZAG STITCH

POLYESTER THREAD

PINS

ROTARY CUTTER

SPRAY ADHESIVE *(optional)*

SERGER *(optional)*

Scan this QR code or visit
tinyurl.com/11531-pattern1-downloads
to download and print the pattern pieces for this project.

Cutting List

MAIN FABRIC: Front Panty (A), Back Panty (B)

COMBO FABRIC: Side Panel (C)

LINING FABRIC: Front Panty (A), Back Panty (B)

COTTON JERSEY: Gusset (D)

Notes on Project

Pattern pieces A and B should be lined with stretch mesh. Spray baste the main fabric to the lining using a temporary adhesive before starting to construct the garment. In the instructions, the fabrics are treated as one layer. See Temporary Spray Adhesive (page 50). The cotton jersey gusset should stay separate. For additional finishing techniques without a serger, see Finishing Seams (page 53). Contrasting color threads are used to clearly show each step.

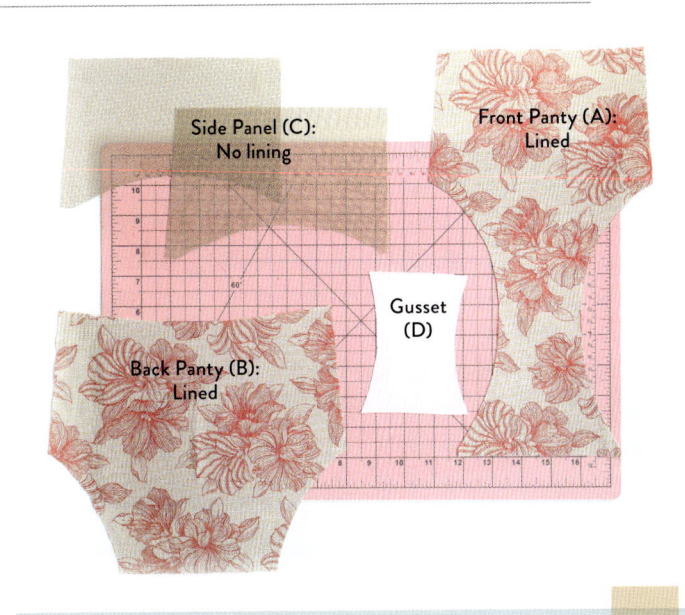

BARKER PANTY

Serge and Place Gusset

1. Serge front and back edges of the gusset. If you do not have a serger, you can skip this step and leave the edges unfinished.

2. With the wrong side of the gusset facing the wrong side of the front panty, pin in place. Refer to the pattern notches for correct placement. **A**

Sew Sides, Front, and Back Panty

1. With right sides facing, sew side panty panels to the front and back panty pieces with a straight stitch. Backstitch at beginning and end of each seam. Serge (overlock) seam allowances. **B**

2. With right sides facing, sew front and back panty panels together at gusset seam with a straight stitch. Backstitch at the beginning and end. Serge (overlock) seam allowances. **C** **D**

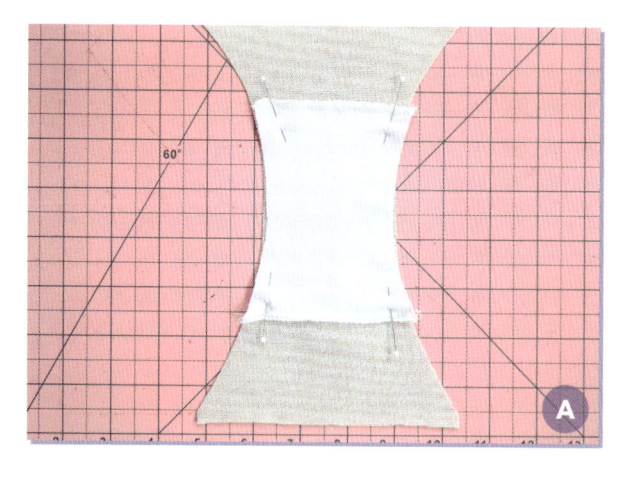

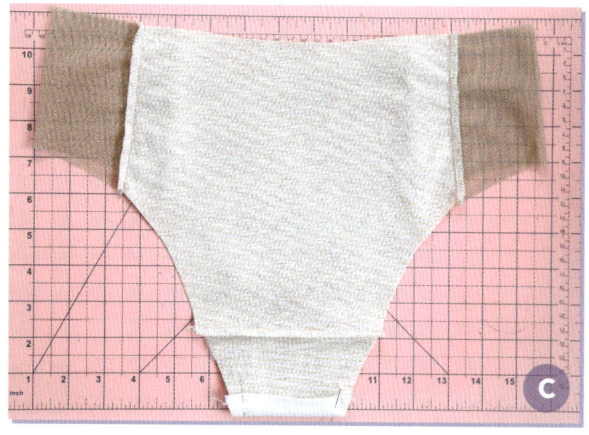

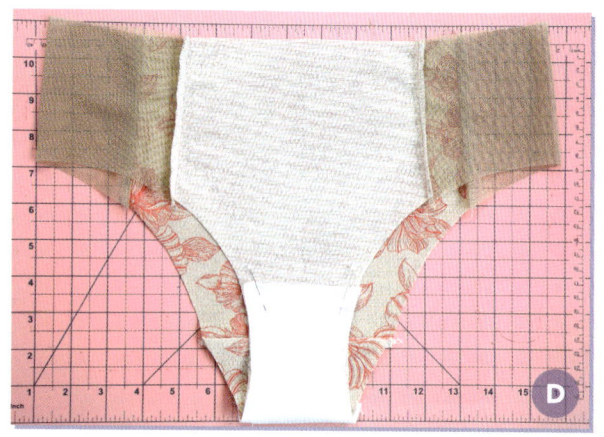

80 SEW LINGERIE

PANTY PROJECTS

Sew Panty Elastic at Waist and Leg Openings

1. With the right side of panty facing up, place panty elastic on top of the waistline. When sewing elastic on the waistline or the leg opening, I recommend starting approximately ½″ (1.2cm) behind a seam on the back portion of the panty so that when the garment is finished, the start/stop point is not visible when looking at the front of the garment.

If the panty elastic is ¼″ (0.6cm) wide, the flat edge of the elastic will align with the edge of the fabric (since the seam allowances are ¼″ or 0.6cm wide). If the panty elastic is wider, then it will extend past the edge of the fabric (example: If panty elastic is ½″ (1.2cm wide), then it will extend past the edge of the fabric ¼″ (0.6cm). Regardless of the width of the elastic, the picot edge should face inward towards the fabric and the plush side should face up.

2. Sew along the picot edge of the elastic with a zigzag stitch around the whole waistband. The zigzag stitch width should be adjusted for the width of the elastic. Stitch as close to the picot edge as possible all the way around the waistband of the panty. Overlap elastic at ends ½″ (1.2cm). Backstitching is optional. **E F**

3. Turn the elastic to the wrong side of the fabric and sew the opposite (flat) edge of the elastic with a zigzag stitch. Stitch as close to the edge as possible. **G H**

4. Repeat Steps 1–3 to attach the elastic to each leg opening. Remove the gusset pins. **I**

BARKER PANTY

BEGINNER
MILLIE *panty*

The Millie Panty is a basic, mid-rise thong with lace side panels. The back of the panty features a keyhole opening finished with fold over elastic. Use #milliepanty to share your make!

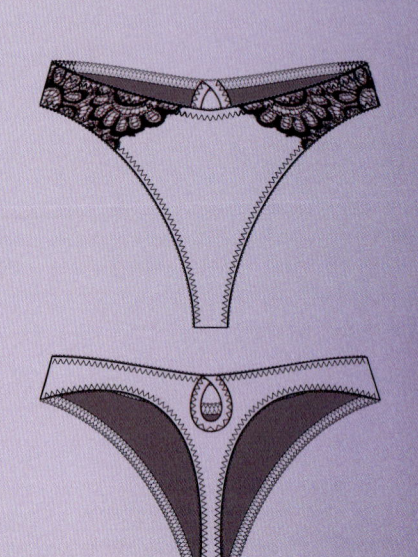

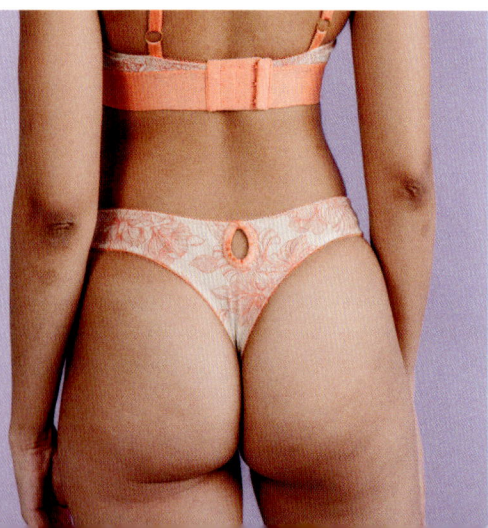

PANTY PROJECTS

Fabrics and Notions

MAIN FABRIC: Jersey, stretch mesh, LYCRA, or stretch all over lace

COMBO FABRIC: Stretch galloon lace at least 5″ (12.7cm) wide

LINING FABRIC: Stretch mesh

PANTY ELASTIC: 3½ yards (3.3m) ¼″ (6mm)–⅜″ (8mm) wide

FOLD OVER ELASTIC: ½ yard (46cm) ⅝″ (16mm) wide (⅜″ or 8mm when folded)

COTTON JERSEY SWATCH FOR GUSSET

FABRIC CHART	XS–L	XL–5X
Main Fabric	⅓ yard (31cm)	½ yard (46cm)
Combo Fabric	½ yard (46cm)	½ yard (46cm)
Lining Fabric	⅓ yard (31cm)	½ yard (46cm)

Tools

SEWING MACHINE WITH STRAIGHT AND ZIGZAG STITCH

POLYESTER THREAD

PINS

ROTARY CUTTER

DUCK BILLED SCISSORS

SPRAY ADHESIVE *(optional)*

SERGER *(optional)*

Scan this QR code or visit
tinyurl.com/11531-pattern2-downloads
to download and print the pattern pieces for this project.

Cutting List

MAIN FABRIC: Front Panty (A), Back Panty (B)

COMBO FABRIC: Lace Side Panel (C)

LINING FABRIC: Front Panty (A), Back Panty (B)

COTTON JERSEY: Gusset (D)

Notes on Project

All pattern pieces should be lined with stretch mesh. Spray baste the main fabric to the lining using a temporary adhesive before starting to construct the garment. In the instructions, the fabrics are treated as one layer. See Temporary Spray Adhesive (page 50). The cotton jersey gusset should stay separate. For additional finishing techniques without a serger, see Finishing Seams (page 53). Contrasting color threads are used to clearly show each step.

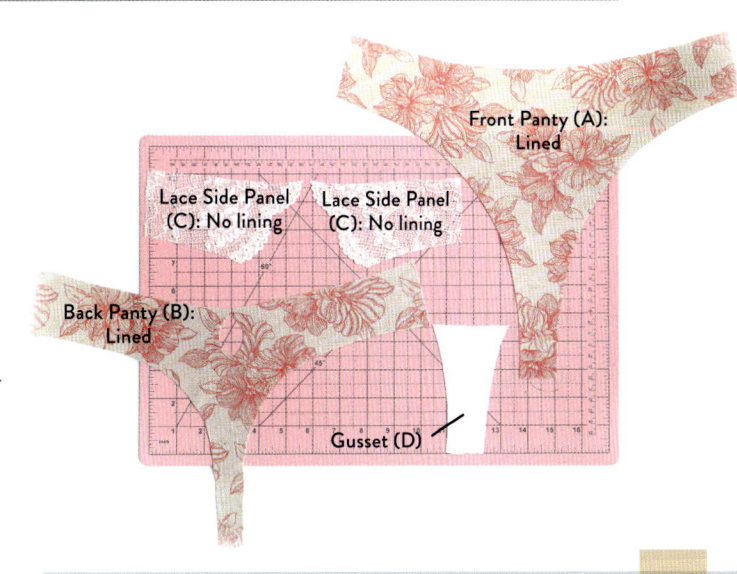

MILLIE PANTY

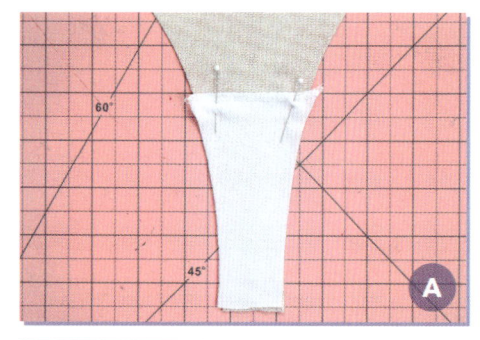

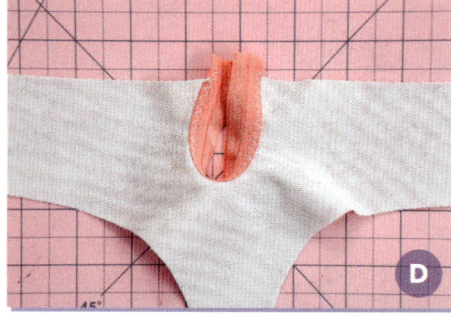

Serge and Place Gusset

1. Serge front edge of gusset. If you do not have a serger, you can skip this step and leave the edges unfinished.

2. With the wrong side of the gusset facing the wrong side of the front panty, pin in place. Refer to pattern notches for correct placement. **A**

Place Lace Side Panel

1. With the wrong side of the lace side panel facing the right side of the front panty, pin in place. Repeat for the second panel. **B**

2. Sew along the edges of the scallop lace using a zigzag stitch approximately ⅛" (0.3cm) wide. **C**

Sew Fold Over Elastic at Keyhole Opening

1. With the wrong side of the back panty panel face up, lay fold over elastic (FOE) on top of the keyhole so that the center of the FOE is aligned with the edge of the fabric. Sew fold over elastic to panty with a zigzag stitch that is approximately ¼" (0.6cm) wide. Zigzag stitches should be as close to the edge of the FOE as possible. **D**

2. Trim the seam allowances as close to the stitches as possible using duck billed scissors. After, turn the FOE to the right side of the fabric and sew a second pass that is approximately ¼" (0.6cm) wide. Zigzag stitches should be as close to the edge of the FOE as possible. Because a straight trim (FOE) is being sewn to a curved edge (keyhole opening), the fold over elastic may not lay in a circular shape. Use an iron set to a synthetic setting with steam to press it into shape. Let the fabric cool before removing it from the ironing or pressing board. It is the act of cooling that sets the elastic into the correct shape. **E**

3. Overlap fold over elastics at waistline and sew a straight stitch back and forth 2–3 times to secure in place. **F**

84 SEW LINGERIE

PANTY PROJECTS

Sew Front Panty to Back Panty

1. With right sides facing, sew front panty to back panty at side seams and crotch seam with a straight stitch. Backstitch at the beginning and end. Serge (overlock) seam allowances. If you do not have a serger, you can skip this step and leave the edges unfinished or push seam allowances to one side and sew down with a zigzag stitch that is ¼″ (0.6mm) wide. **G**

Sew Panty Elastic at Waist and Leg Openings

1. With the right side of panty facing up, place panty elastic on top of the waistline. When sewing elastic on the waistline or the leg opening of a panty, I recommend starting approximately ½″ (1.2cm) behind the side seam so that when the garment is finished, the start/stop point is not visible when looking at the front of the garment.

If the panty elastic is ¼″ (0.6cm) wide, the flat edge of the elastic will align with the edge of the fabric (since the seam allowances are ¼″ or 0.6cm wide). If the panty elastic is wider, then it will extend past the edge of the fabric (example: If panty elastic is ½″ or 1.2cm wide, then it will extend past the edge of the fabric ¼″ or 0.6cm). Regardless of the width of the elastic, the picot edge should face inward towards the fabric and the plush side should face up.

2. Sew along the picot edge of the elastic with a zigzag stitch. The zigzag stitch width should be adjusted for the width of the elastic. Stitch as close to the picot edge as possible all the way around the waistband of the panty. Overlap elastic at ends ½″ (1.2cm). Backstitching is optional. **H**

3. Turn the elastic to the wrong side of the fabric and sew the opposite (flat) edge of the elastic with a zigzag stitch. Stitch as close to the edge as possible. **I**

4. Repeat Steps 1–3 to attach the elastic to each leg opening. Remove the gusset pins. **J**

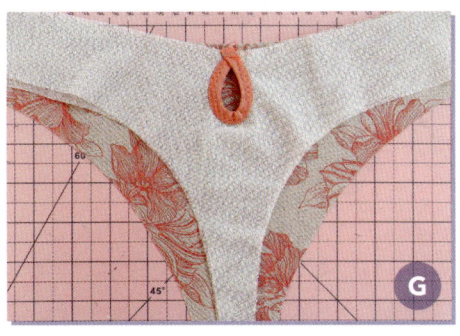

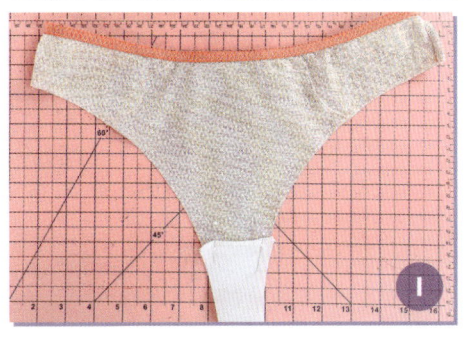

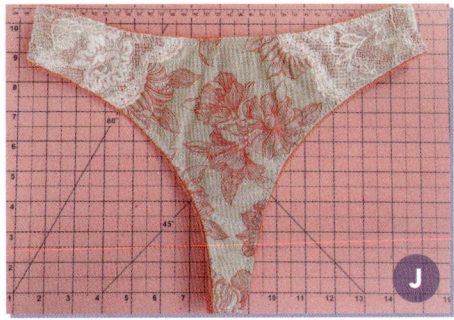

MILLIE PANTY 85

BEGINNER
ROSS *panty*

The Ross Panty is a high-rise, French cut style that has a cut out in the front and a triangular insert in the back. The waistline is finished with a wide band elastic and the front leg openings are finished with panty elastic. Use #rosspanty to share your make!

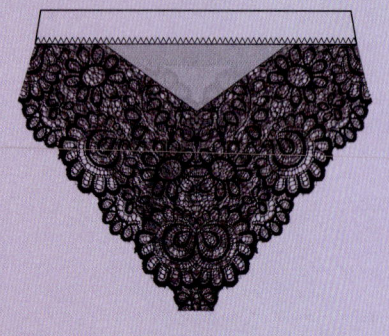

SEW LINGERIE

PANTY PROJECTS

Fabrics and Notions

MAIN FABRIC: Stretch galloon lace at least 9″ wide

COMBO FABRIC: Jersey, stretch mesh, LYCRA, or stretch all over lace

LINING FABRIC: Stretch mesh

PANTY ELASTIC: 2 yards (1.9m) ¼″ (6mm)–⅜″ (8mm) wide

WIDE BAND ELASTIC: 1½ yards (1.4m) 1½″ (38mm) wide

COTTON JERSEY SWATCH FOR GUSSET

FABRIC CHART	XS–L	XL–5X
Main Fabric	2¼ yards (2.1m)	2½ yards (2.3m)
Combo Fabric	⅓ yard (31cm)	⅓ yard (31cm)
Lining Fabric	⅓ yard (31cm)	½ yard (31cm)

Tools

SEWING MACHINE WITH STRAIGHT AND ZIGZAG STITCH

POLYESTER THREAD

PINS

ROTARY CUTTER

SPRAY ADHESIVE (optional)

SERGER (optional)

Scan this QR code or visit

tinyurl.com/11531-pattern3-downloads

to download and print the pattern pieces for this project.

ROSS PANTY 87

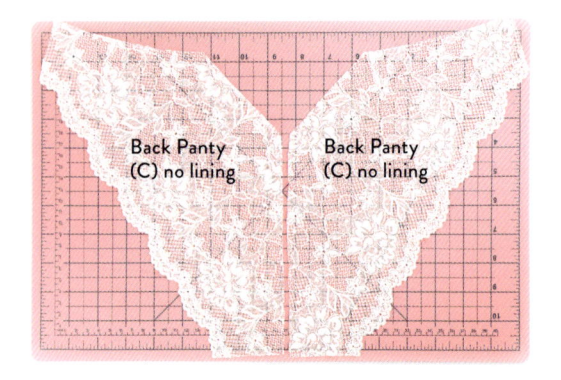

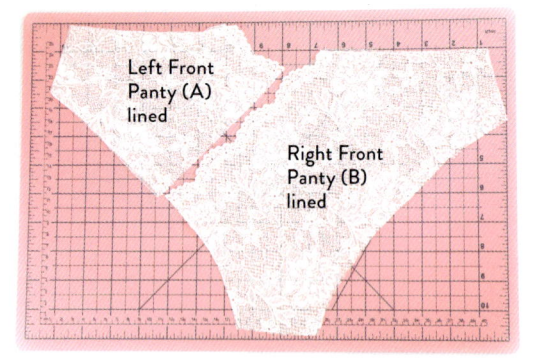

Cutting List

MAIN FABRIC: Left Front Panty (A), Right Front Panty (B), Back Panty (C), Gusset (E)

LINING FABRIC: Left Front Panty (A), Right Front Panty (B), Gusset (E)

COMBO FABRIC: Back Insert (D)

COTTON JERSEY: Gusset (E)

WIDE BAND ELASTIC (F)

Notes on Project

All pattern pieces except C should be lined with stretch mesh. Spray baste the main fabric to the lining using a temporary adhesive before starting to construct the garment. In the instructions, the fabrics are treated as one layer. See Temporary Spray Adhesive (page 50). The cotton jersey gusset should stay separate. For additional finishing techniques without a serger, see Finishing Seams (page 53). When cutting Back Panty (C), Left Front Panty (A), and Right Front Panty (B), align the edge of the pattern with the highpoint of the scallop on the galloon lace. Contrasting color threads are used to clearly show each step.

PANTY PROJECTS

Sew Back Panty

1. With right sides facing, sew back panty panels together at center back seam using a straight stitch. Start sewing ¼" (6mm) down from the top all the way down to the bottom edge. Backstitch at beginning and end. Serge (overlock) seam allowances. **A**

Attach Back Insert

1. With right sides facing, pin back insert to one side of back panty. Sew together with a straight stitch. Start sewing at the top edge of panty (waistline) and stitch down to where the center back seam is. **B**

2. With right sides facing, pin back insert to the other side of the back panty. Sew together with a straight stitch, making a sharp V shape. Start sewing at the top edge of panty (waistline) and stitch down to where the center back seam is. Serge (overlock) seam allowances. If you do not have a serger, you can skip this step and leave the edges unfinished. Whether you serged the seam allowances or left the seam allowances unfinished, push the seam allowances towards the back panty and sew down with a zigzag stitch that is ¼" (0.6cm) wide. **C D**

> ### SEWING A V SHAPE
> Sewing a V Shape can be difficult. Carefully pin prior to sewing the seam and continuing to check that the fabric isn't bunching underneath the presser foot while sewing. Sew slow and steady!

3. Use a steam iron set to a synthetic setting to press the back insert. Use your fingers to shape the V into a sharp point. Let the fabric cool before removing it from the ironing or pressing board. It is the act of cooling that sets the fabric into the correct shape.

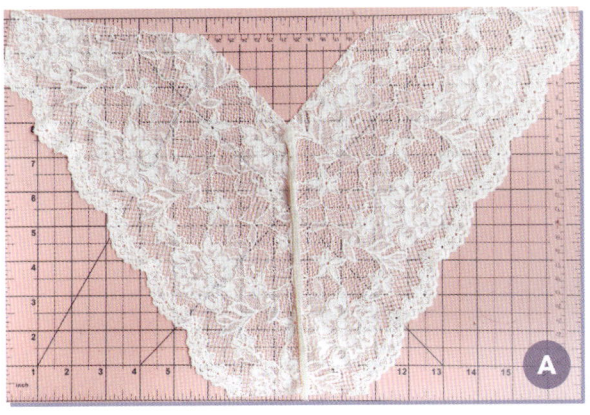

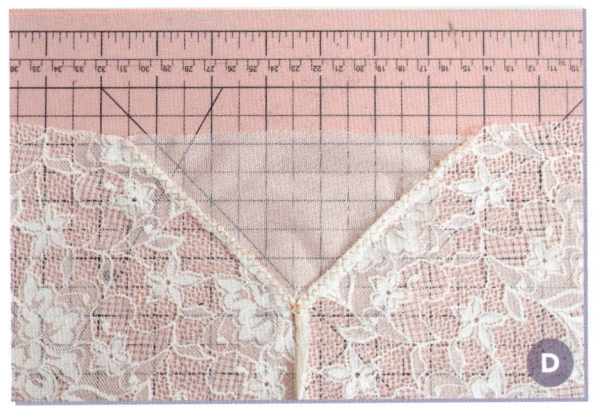

ROSS PANTY **89**

Sew Gusset to Front and Back Panty

1. Align the right side of the gusset main and lining fabric, which should be spray basted together, with the right side of the right panty front. Pin together. Align the right side of the cotton jersey gusset with the wrong side of the right panty front. Pin together. Sew through all the layers with a straight stitch. Backstitch at beginning and end. Press seam allowances open with an iron set to a synthetic setting. **E F**

2. Fold the gusset to the right side. **G**

Finish Cut Out Edge on Left Panty Front

1. With the wrong side of the left panty front face up, lay panty elastic on top along the cut out edge. The flat edge of the panty elastic should be aligned with the low point of the scallop edge. Sew down with a zigzag stitch that is approximately ¼" (0.6cm) wide. **H**

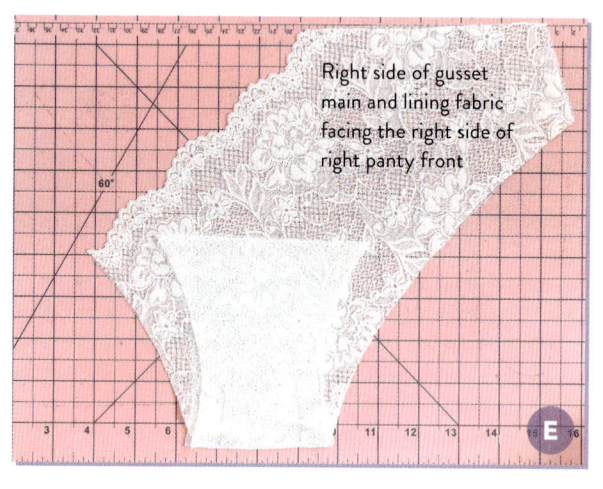

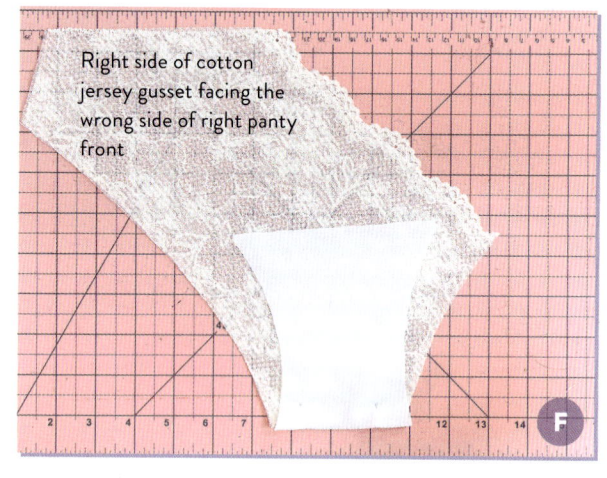

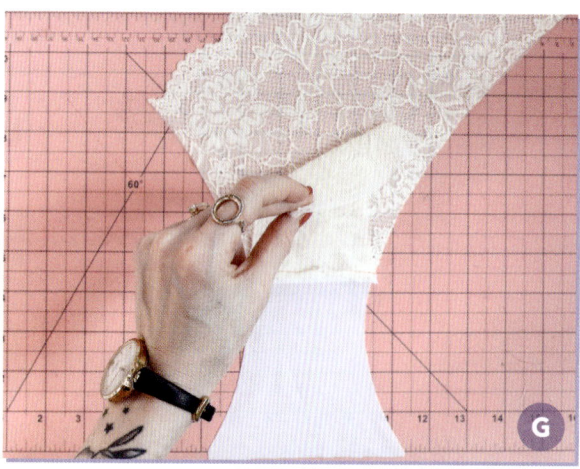

Right side of gusset main and lining fabric facing the right side of right panty front **E**

Right side of cotton jersey gusset facing the wrong side of right panty front **F**

G

H

SEW LINGERIE

PANTY PROJECTS

Sew Right Panty Front to Left Panty Front

1. Lay the left panty front underneath the right panty front so that it overlaps ¼" (0.6cm). Pin in place. **I**

2. With the wrong side of the front panty face up, lay panty elastic on top along the diagonal edge that connects left panty front to right panty front. The flat edge of the panty elastic should be aligned with the low point of the scallop edge. Sew down with a zigzag stitch that is approximately ¼" (0.6cm) wide. If the scallop edge of lace is standing away from the fabric, then sew along the scallop edges with a zigzag stitch that is approximately ⅛" (0.3cm) wide. **J**

Sew Panty Elastic to Front Leg Openings

1. With the right side of panty facing up, place panty elastic on top of the leg opening. If the panty elastic is ¼" (0.6cm) wide, the flat edge of the elastic will align with the edge of the fabric (since the seam allowances are ¼" (0.6cm) wide). If the panty elastic is wider, then it will extend past the edge of the fabric (example: If panty elastic is ½" (1.2cm) wide, then it will extend past the edge of the fabric ¼" (0.6cm). Regardless of the width of the elastic, the picot edge should face inward towards the fabric and the plush side should face up.

2. Sew along the picot edge of the elastic with a zigzag stitch. The zigzag stitch width should be adjusted for the width of the elastic. Stitch as close to the picot edge as possible. **K L**

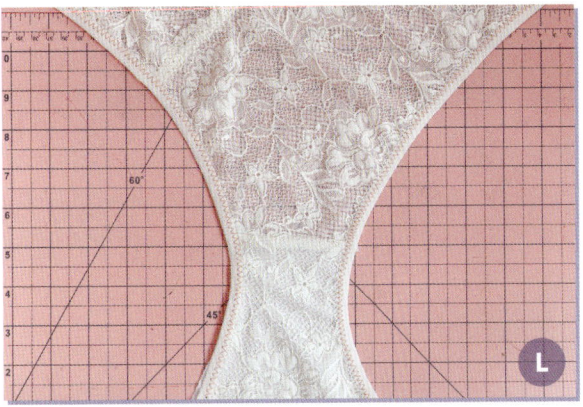

ROSS PANTY 91

3. Turn the elastic to the wrong side of the fabric and sew the opposite edge of the elastic with a zigzag stitch. Stitch as close to the flat edge as possible. **M N**

Sew Front Panty to Back Panty

1. With right sides facing, sew front panty to back panty at the side seams and gusset seam with a straight stitch. Backstitch at the beginning and end. Serge (overlock) seam allowances. If you do not have a serger, you can skip this step and leave the edges unfinished. Whether you serged the seam allowances or left the seam allowances unfinished, push the seam allowances to the side where they naturally fall and sew down with a zigzag stitch that is ¼" (0.6cm) wide. **O P**

92 SEW LINGERIE

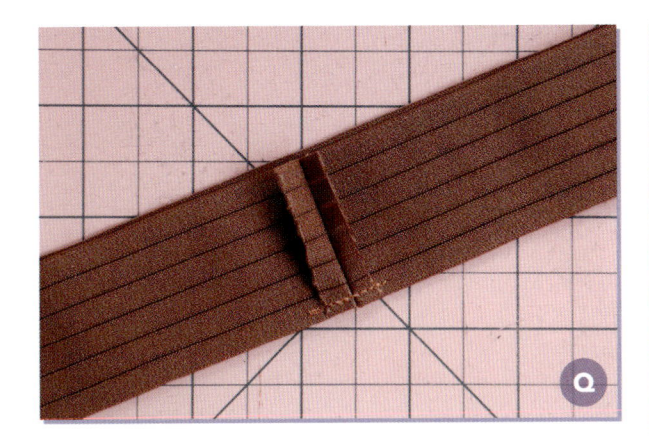

Sew Wide Band Elastic To Waist

1. With right sides facing, sew the short ends of wide band elastic together with a straight stitch. Backstitch at the beginning and end. The wide band elastic should now be a circle.

2. Finger press seams open and on one edge, and sew a straight stitch back and forth 3–4 times. This side will not be sewn to the panty, so its purpose is to keep seam allowance secure and in place. **Q**

3. With the seam on the wide band elastic aligned with one side seam, overlap the wide band elastic and waistline of the panty ¼" (0.6cm). The wide band elastic should be on top. Pin together all the way around. **R**

4. Sew wide band elastic to waistline with a zigzag stitch that is approximately ¼" (0.6cm) wide. Start at one cut out edge and sew all the way around to the other cut out edge. Even though backstitching zigzag stitches is optional, it is recommended to do it at this step to secure it in place. **S**

bra PROJECTS

To access each pattern, scan the QR code in each individual project. You can then download the pattern at full size, or in print-at-home format.

All seam allowances are included in the patterns and are ¼" (0.6cm), unless otherwise noted. Whenever instructed to serge a seam allowance, if you do not have a serger, you can skip this step and leave the edges unfinished or push seam allowances to one side and sew them down with a zigzag stitch that is ¼" (0.6cm) wide.

Bra Band Size (Numerical)

Size	28	30	32	34	36
Underbust (Ribcage)	28"–30" (71.1–76.2cm)	30"–32" (76.2–81.3cm)	32"–34" (81.3–86.4cm)	34"–36" (86.4–91.4cm)	36"–38" (91.4–96.5cm)

Size	38	40	42	44
Underbust (Ribcage)	38"–40" (96.5–101.6cm)	40"–42" (101.6–106.7cm)	42"–44" (106.7–111.8cm)	44"–46" (111.8–116.8cm)

Bra Size (Alpha)

Size	XS	S	M	L	XL
Full Bust	28″–30″ (71.1–76.2cm)	30″–32″ (76.2–81.3cm)	32″–34″ (81.3–86.4cm)	34″–36″ (86.4–91.4cm)	36″–38″ (91.4–96.5cm)

Size	2X	3X	4X	5x
Full Bust	38″–41″ (96.5–104.1cm)	41″–44″ (104.1–111.8cm)	44″–47″ (111.8–119.4cm)	47″–50″ (119.4–127cm)

Cup Size

Size	A	B	C	D	E	F	G	H	I	J
Difference between full bust and underbust/ribcage	1″ (2.5CM)	2″ (5cm)	3″ (7.5cm)	4″ (10cm)	5″ (13cm)	6″ (15cm)	7″ (18cm)	8″ (20cm)	9″ (23cm)	10″ (25.5cm)

124

114

136

104

96

95

INTERMEDIATE
BROOKLYN *bralette*

The Brooklyn Bralette is a basic, pull-on style bralette with side panels, adjustable shoulder straps, and a wide bottom band that adds support. The front neckline, armhole, and top back band are finished with fold over elastic. Use #brooklynbralette to share your make!

BRA PROJECTS

Fabrics and Notions

MAIN FABRIC: Jersey, stretch mesh, LYCRA, or stretch all over lace

COMBO FABRIC: Jersey, stretch mesh, LYCRA, stretch all over lace, or stretch galloon lace at least 9 (22.9cm) wide

LINING FABRIC:

   Stretch mesh for sizes XS–M

   Power net for sizes L–4X

FOLD OVER ELASTIC: 2½ yards (2.3m) ⅝″ (16mm) wide (⅜″ or 8mm when folded)

WIDE BAND ELASTIC: 1½ yards (1.4m) 1¼″ (32mm) wide or wider

SHOULDER STRAP ELASTIC:

   1½ yards (1.4m) ½″ (12mm) for sizes XS–M

   1½ yards (1.4m) ¾″ (18mm) wide or wider for sizes L–4X

RINGS AND SLIDERS: 1 pair, width should match the width of shoulder strap elastic

Tools

SEWING MACHINE WITH STRAIGHT AND ZIGZAG STITCH

BALLPOINT, STRETCH, OR MICROTEX NEEDLE
(size depends on the thickness of the fabric; see Needle and Thread, page 36)

POLYESTER THREAD

PINS

ROTARY CUTTER

DUCK BILLED SCISSORS

SPRAY ADHESIVE *(optional)*

SERGER *(optional)*

Scan this QR code or visit
tinyurl.com/11531-pattern4-downloads
to download and print the pattern pieces for this project.

FABRIC CHART	XS–L	XL–5X
Main Fabric	¼ yard (23cm)	⅓ yard (31cm)
Combo Fabric	¼ yard (23cm)	⅓ yard (31cm)
Lining Fabric	¼ yard (23cm)	⅓ yard (31cm)

BROOKLYN BRALETTE

Cutting List

MAIN FABRIC: Center Front Bralette (A), Side Front Bralette (B), Center Back Bralette (D)

COMBO FABRIC: Side Panel Bralette (C)

LINING FABRIC: Center Front Bralette (A), Side Front Bralette (B), Center Back Bralette (D)

WIDE BAND ELASTIC (E)

SHOULDER STRAP ELASTIC (F)

Notes on Project

Pattern pieces A, B, and D should be lined with a stretch mesh or power net. Spray baste the main fabric to the lining using a temporary adhesive before starting to construct the garment. In the instructions, the fabrics are treated as one layer. See Temporary Spray Adhesive (page 50). For additional finishing techniques without a serger, see Finishing Seams (page 53). Contrasting color threads are used to clearly show each step.

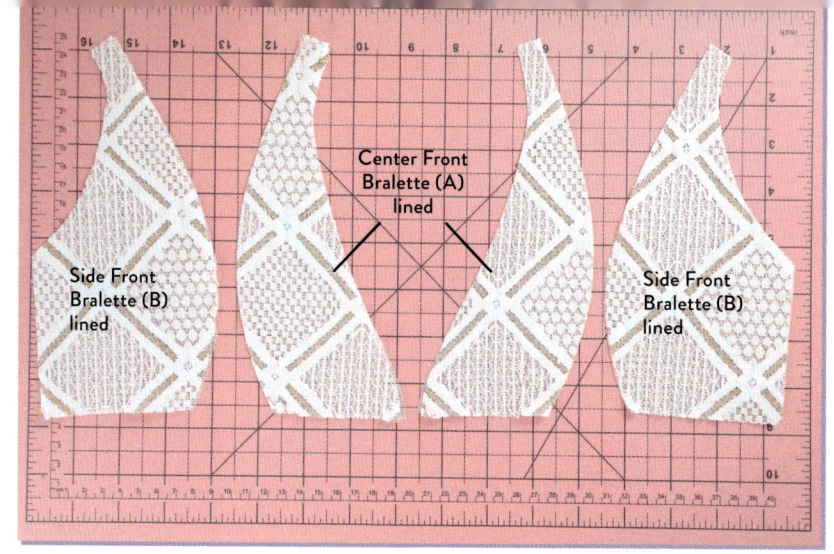

Right side of fabric

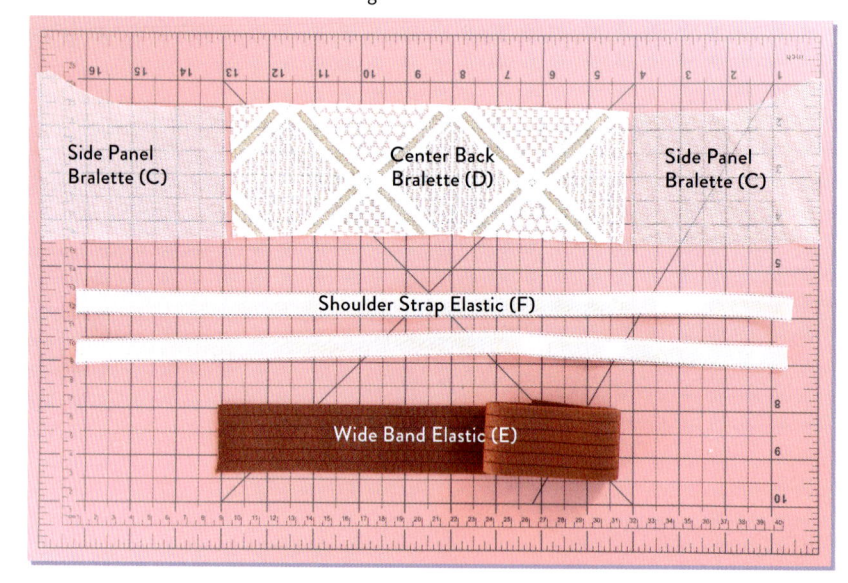

Attach Pattern Pieces

1. With right sides facing, sew center front bralette to side front bralette with a straight stitch. Backstitch at beginning and end. Serge (overlock) seam allowances. Repeat to make the second front bralette. **A**

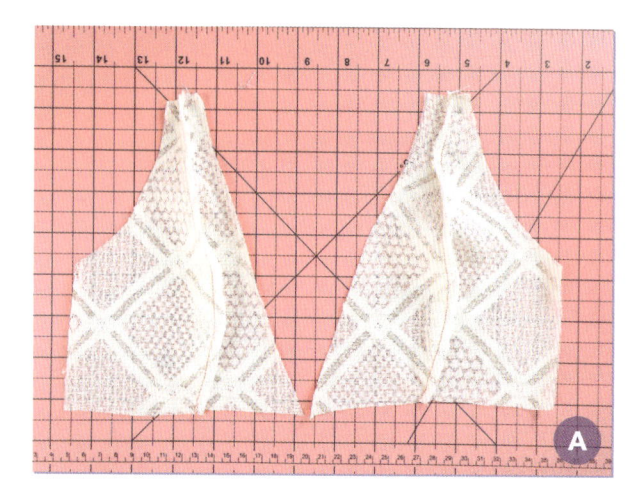

98 SEW LINGERIE

BRA PROJECTS

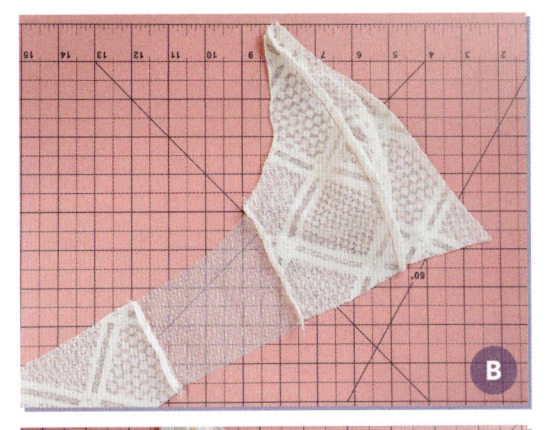

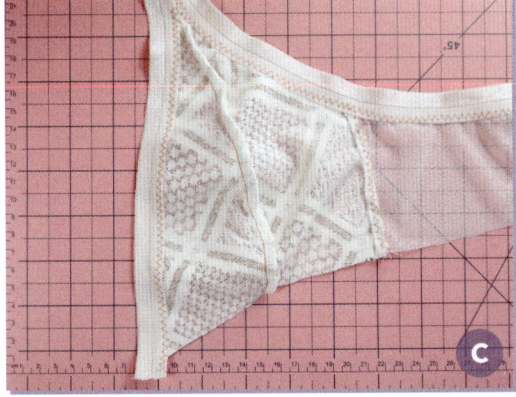

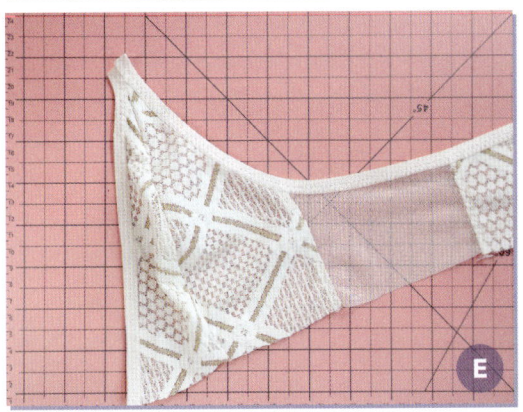

2. Using the same stitches and finishes as Step 1, sew the front bralette to the side panel and the center back. Then, sew the second side panel and front bralette to the other side of the center back. **B**

Sew Fold Over Elastic (FOE)

1. With the wrong side of the bralette facing up, lay the fold over elastic (FOE) on top of the fabric along the neckline, armhole, and top of the back band so that the center of the FOE is aligned with the edge of the fabric. Sew the FOE to the bralette with a zigzag stitch that is approximately ¼" (0.6cm) wide. The stitches should be as close to the edge of the FOE as possible. At the strap points, the FOE pieces should be parallel to each other, not crossing. **C D**

2. After sewing the first "pass," or line of zigzag stitches, trim seam allowances as close to stitches as possible using duck billed scissors. After, turn the FOE to the right side of the fabric and sew a second pass that is approximately ¼" (0.6cm) wide. Just like the first pass, the zigzag stitches should be as close to the edge of the FOE as possible. **E**

BROOKLYN BRALETTE 99

MORE ON FOLD OVER ELASTIC

What is fold over elastic and why is it used?

Fold over elastic is an alternative to the picot elastic that is often used as a binding to finish an edge. Also referred to as FOE, it gives a clean look to edges as well as a pop of contrast color. It can also be encased with clear elastic or twill tape and made into shoulder straps. It normally has a shiny side and a matte side with an indentation down the middle.

What is the best width to use?

The most common width is ⅝" (16mm), which is about ⅜" (8mm) when folded. Narrower FOE is hard to handle when sewing and FOE that is wider than ⅝" (16mm) doesn't curve nicely; it buckles.

Can FOE be sewn in one step?

If you use pins or spray adhesive to secure the FOE in place prior to sewing, it can be sewn in one pass of sewing. However, I find that no matter how carefully it is pinned, FOE always ends up wavy when I sew it in one step. Since FOE is visible on the exterior of a garment, it's noticeable if it isn't straight. So, even though sewing it in two passes is double the work, it results in a more accurate finish.

Bottom of Bralette

1. Serge (overlock) the bottom edge of the bralette. If you do not have a serger, you can skip this step.

2. With right sides facing, sew the short ends of the wide band elastic with a straight stitch. Backstitch at the beginning and end. The wide band elastic is now a circle.

3. Finger press the seam open, and on one edge, sew a straight stitch back and forth 3–4 times. This side will not be sewn to the bralette, so its purpose is to keep seam allowance secure and in place. **F**

> ### DO YOU HAVE A SMALL WAIST?
> Do you have a small waist compared to your ribcage? If so, angle the seam inwards ¼″–½″ (0.6cm–1.2cm) when sewing the wide band elastic into a circle. This will help the wide band elastic to be snug against your body and not stand away from it.

4. With the seam on the wide band elastic aligned with one side seam on the bralette, overlap the wide band elastic and the bottom of the bralette ¼″ (0.6cm). The right side of the bralette should be facing the wrong side of the band. The wide band elastic should be on top. Pin together all the way around. At the center front, the bralette cups should be "kissing", or side by side. **G**

5. Starting in the center front, sew the wide band elastic to the bottom of the bralette with a zigzag stitch that is approximately ¼″ (0.6cm) wide. Overlap the zigzag ¼″ (0.6mm)–½″ (1.2cm) at beginning/end. **H**

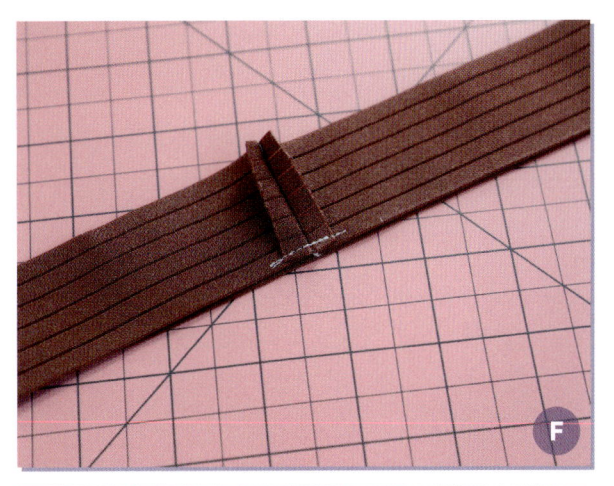

BROOKLYN BRALETTE

Make and Attach Shoulder Straps

1. Put each ring through the strap points and turn them back ½″ (1.2cm). Sew a straight stitch back and forth 3–4 times as close to the ring as securely as possible. Trim the seam allowance close to the stitching. **I**

> **TIP!**
> After trimming the elastic close to the stitching, you can apply clear nail polish or fray check to the cut ends of elastic to prevent it from fraying/wearing over time.

2. Feed one end of the shoulder strap elastic through the bottom of one slider, over the center bar, and then down through the other side. It should look like a belt buckle with one short end and one long end. Fold back ¾″ (1.9cm). Repeat for the other strap. **J**

3. Sew a straight stitch back and forth 3–4 times as close to the slider as possible, attaching the short end of the elastic to the long side. It is difficult to sew this step with the slider underneath the presser foot, so if your machine has this setting, move the needle position all the way to the right. This will allow you to butt the edge of the slider against the edge of the presser foot and stitch really close to it. **K**

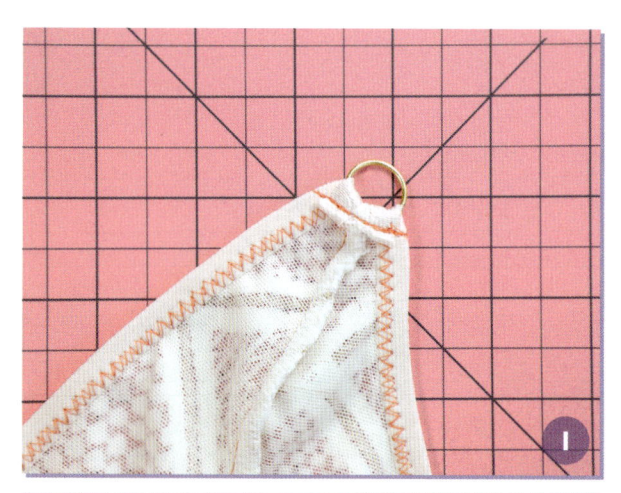

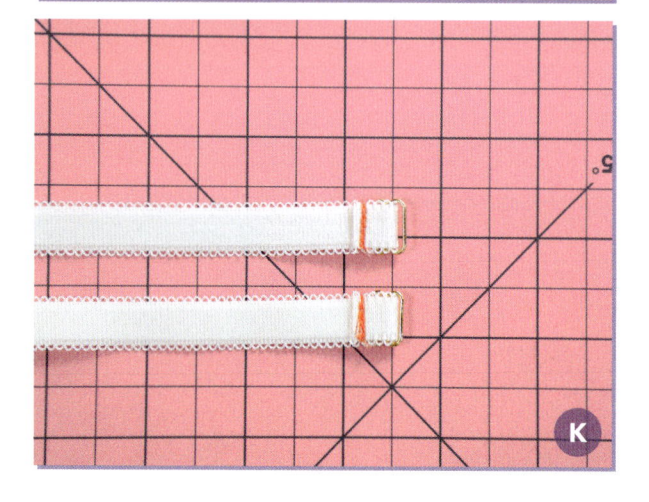

SEW LINGERIE

BRA PROJECTS

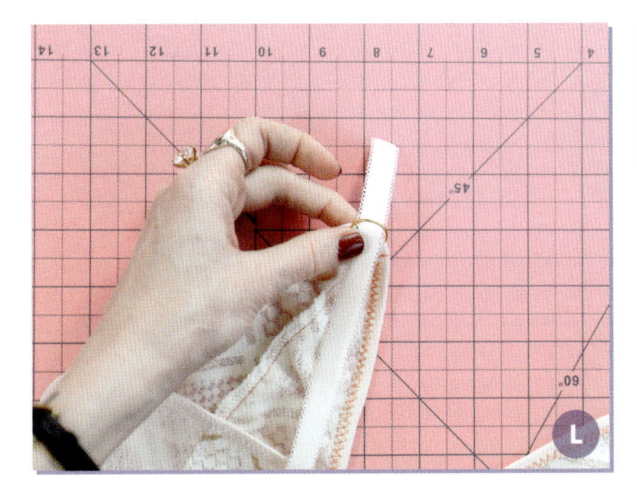

4. Weave the unstitched side of the strap elastics through rings from back to front. Then weave the same end up and over the center bar of the slider again just like in Step 3. The "standard" length from slider to ring is approximately 2″ (5cm). **L M N**

5. With the back of the bra right side facing up, lay the loose end of the shoulder strap elastic underneath the back band. Refer to the pattern notches for placement. Sew the shoulder straps to the top and the bottom of the back band. Use a straight stitch and stitch back and forth 3–4 times. If there is any elastic hanging below the stitch, trim it close to the stitching. **O**

BOUTIQUE SHOULDER STRAPS

Most bras have sliders located on the back of a bra or bralette. Boutique straps, like on the Brooklyn Bralette, have the sliders located on the front, allowing the wearer to adjust the length of the straps more easily.

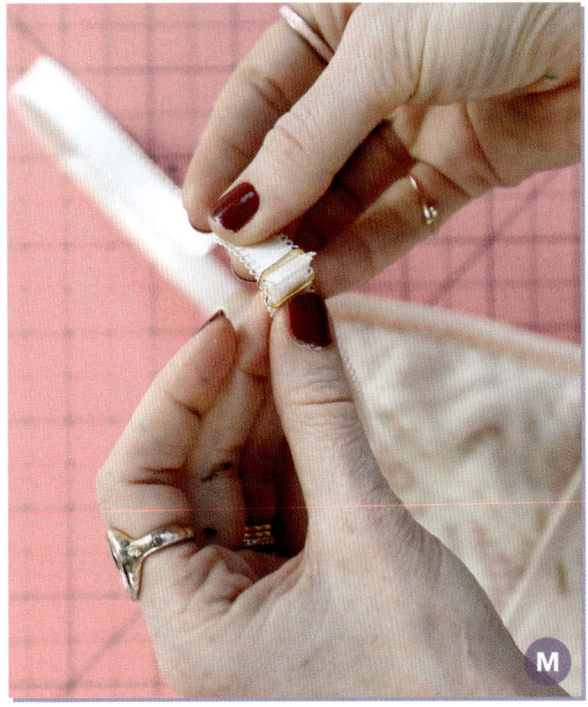

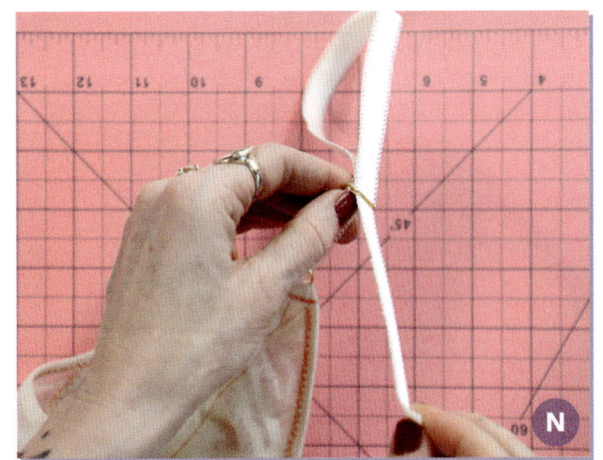

BROOKLYN BRALETTE

INTERMEDIATE
MARGO *bralette*

The Margo Bralette is a front closure style bralette that has scallop lace edging along the neckline and at the bottom. It also has adjustable shoulder straps and band elastic where the bralette meets the lace edging at the bottom. Use #margobralette to share your make!

SEW LINGERIE

BRA PROJECTS

Fabrics and Notions

MAIN FABRIC: Jersey, stretch mesh, LYCRA, stretch all over lace, or stretch galloon lace at least 8″ (20cm) wide

COMBO FABRIC: Stretch galloon lace at least 8″ (20cm) wide

LINING FABRIC:
- Stretch mesh for sizes XS–M
- Power net for sizes L–4X

PICOT ELASTIC:
- 2 yards (1.9m) 3/8″ (8mm) wide for sizes XS–M
- 2½ yards (2.3m) ½″ (12mm) wide or wider for sizes L–4X

BAND ELASTIC: 1½ yards (1.4m) 1¼″ (32mm) wide

1 FRONT CLOSURE: 1¼″ (32mm)

SHOULDER STRAP ELASTIC:
- 1½ yards (1.4m) ½″ (12mm) wide for sizes XS–M
- 1½ yards (1.4m) ¾″ (18mm) wide or wider for sizes L–4X

RINGS AND SLIDERS: 1 pair, width should match the width of shoulder strap elastic

Tools

SEWING MACHINE WITH STRAIGHT AND ZIGZAG STITCH

BALLPOINT, STRETCH OR MICROTEX NEEDLE (size depends on the thickness of the fabric; see Needle and Thread, page 36)

POLYESTER THREAD

PINS

ROTARY CUTTER

DUCK BILLED SCISSORS

SPRAY ADHESIVE *(optional)*

SERGER *(optional)*

Scan this QR code or visit
tinyurl.com/11531-pattern5-downloads
to download and print the pattern pieces for this project.

FABRIC CHART	XS–L	XL–5X
Main Fabric	¼ yard (23cm)	⅓ yard (31cm)
Combo Fabric	¼ yard (23cm)	⅓ yard (31cm)
Lining Fabric	¼ yard (23cm)	⅓ yard (31cm)

MARGO BRALETTE 105

Cutting List

MAIN FABRIC: Center Front Bralette (A), Side Front Bralette (B), Back Band (D)

COMBO FABRIC: Bralette Cup Lace Edging (C), Lower Lace Edging (E)

LINING FABRIC: Center Front Bralette Cup (A), Side Front Bralette Cup (B), Back Band (D)

SHOULDER STRAP ELASTIC (F)

BAND ELASTIC (G)

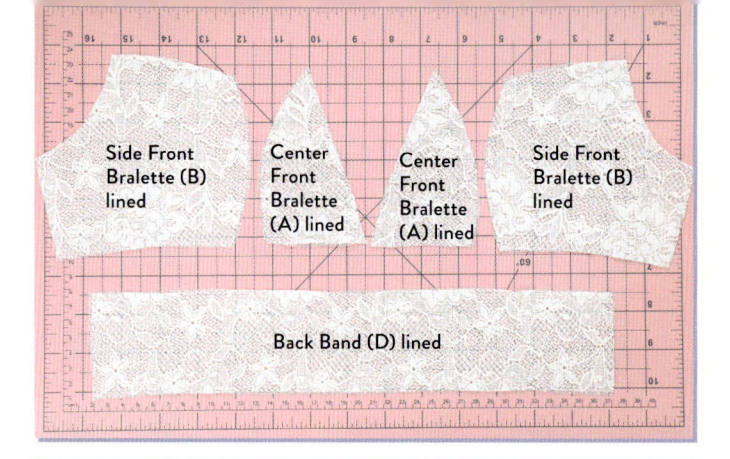

Notes on Project

Pattern pieces A, B, and D should be lined with a stretch mesh or power net. Spray baste the main fabric to the lining using a temporary adhesive before starting to construct the garment. In the instructions, the fabrics are treated as one layer. See Temporary Spray Adhesive (page 50). For additional finishing techniques without a serger, see Finishing Seams (page 53). Contrasting color threads are used to clearly show each step.

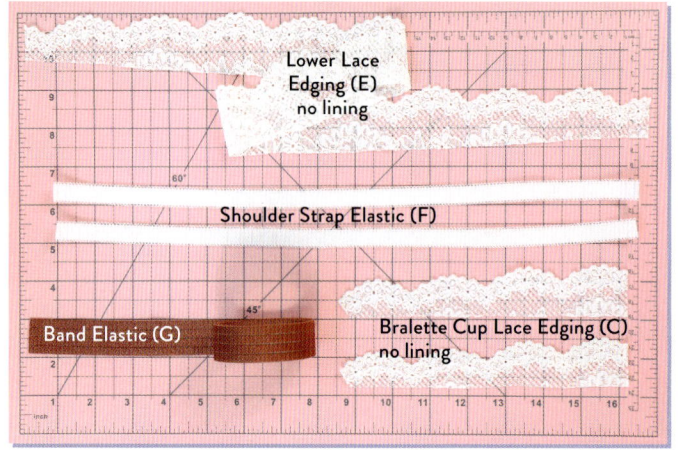

Sew Center Front Bralette Cups Together

1. With right sides facing, sew the center front bralette to side front bralette with a straight stitch. Backstitch at beginning and end. Serge (overlock) seam allowances. Repeat to make the second cup. **A**

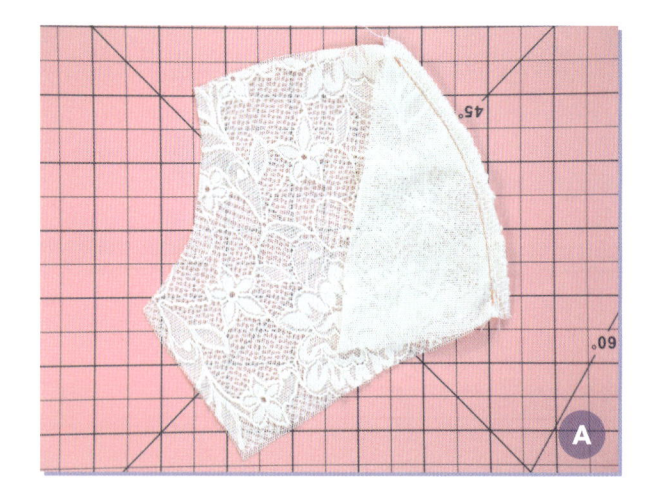

106　SEW LINGERIE

BRA PROJECTS

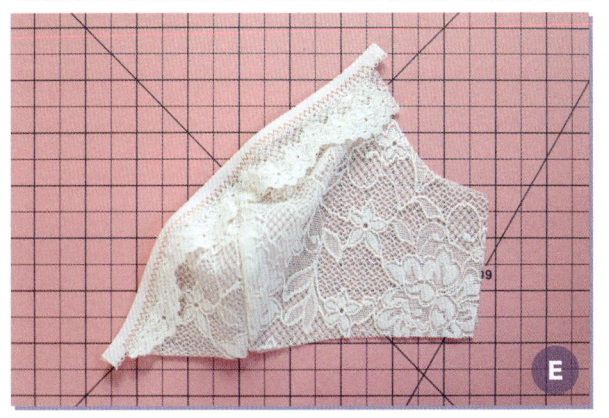

Sew Bralette Cups to Bralette Cup Lace Edging

1. With right sides facing, pin bralette cups to the bralette cup lace edging. Sew together with a zigzag stitch that is ¼" (6mm) wide. **B C**

Sew Picot Elastic Along Horizontal Bra Cup Seam

1. With seam allowances facing one direction and bra cups and lace edging facing the other direction, place the picot elastic on top. The picot edge of the elastic should be right on top of, or aligned with the zigzag stitches. The plush side of the elastic should be face up. **D**

2. Sew through the seam allowance and elastic using a zigzag stitch that is approximately ¼" (0.6cm) wide. The stitches should essentially be on top of the stitches sewn to attach the lace edging, and the stitches should be as close to the picot edge as possible. **E**

3. Fold the picot elastic down towards the bralette and sew another line of zigzag stitches that are approximately ¼" (0.6cm) wide. This time, sew through the seam allowance and bralette. Stitches should be as close to the flat edge of the elastic as possible. **F**

MARGO BRALETTE

Side Seam

1. With right sides facing, sew one cup to the back band at the side seam with a straight stitch. Backstitch at beginning and end. Serge (overlock) seam allowances. Repeat to attach the other cup to the other side of the back band. **G**

Sew Picot Elastic

1. With the right side of the bralette facing up, place the picot elastic on top of the back band and cup from strap point to strap point. If the picot elastic is ⅜″ (1cm) wide, the edge of the elastic will extend ⅛″ (0.4cm) past the edge of the fabric. If the picot elastic is wider, then it will extend past the edge of the fabric more (i.e. if the picot elastic is ½″ or 12mm wide, then it will extend past the edge of the fabric ¼″ or 6mm). Regardless of the width of the picot elastic, the picot edge should face inward towards the fabric and the plush side should face up.

2. Sew along the picot edge of the elastic from strap point to strap point with a zigzag stitch approximately ¼″ (0.6cm) wide. Zigzag stitches should be as close to the picot edge as possible. **H**

3. Flip the picot elastic to the inside of the bra and sew along the flat edge of the elastic with a zigzag stitch approximately ¼″ (0.6cm) wide. Zigzag stitches should be as close to the flat edge as possible, and the picot edge should now face the outer edge of the garment. **I**

Serge Bottom of Bralette

1. Serge (overlock) the bottom edge of the bralette. If you do not have a serger, you can skip this step.

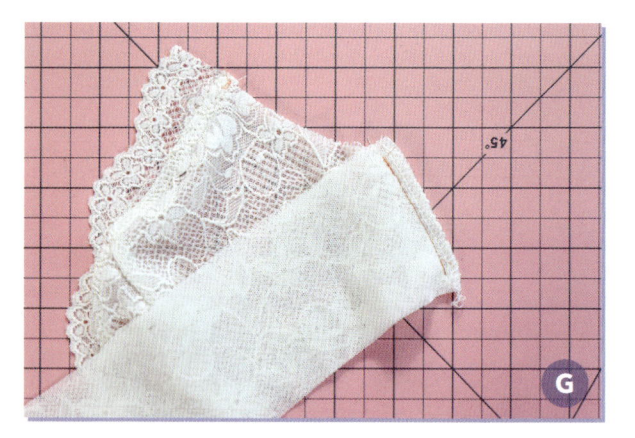

SEW LINGERIE

BRA PROJECTS

Sew Band Elastic

1. Overlap the band elastic and the bottom of the bralette ¼" (0.6cm). The band elastic should be on top. Pin together all the way around with approximately 1" (2.5cm) extending past the beginning and the end of the bralette.

2. Sew the band elastic to the bottom of the bralette with a zigzag stitch that is approximately ¼" (0.6cm) wide. The zigzag stitch should be sewn along the edge of the elastic band. **J**

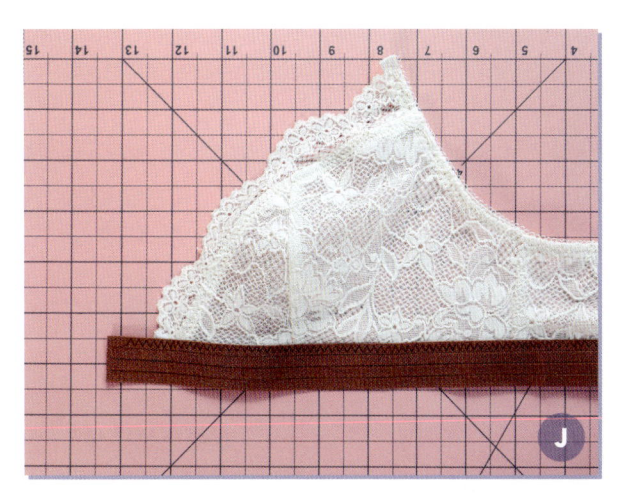

Sew Bottom Lace Edging

1. Overlap the band elastic and the bottom lace edging ¼" (0.6cm). Ensure that the pattern notches on the bottom lace edging and the wide band elastic match, and that the band elastic is on top. Pin together all the way around. The lace edging should be angled so that it disappears behind the band at the center front. **K**

2. Sew the band elastic to the bottom lace edging with a zigzag stitch that is approximately ¼" (0.6cm) wide. The zigzag stitch should be sewn along the edge of the elastic band. **L**

MARGO BRALETTE

Attach Front Closure

1. Wrap the band elastic around one side of the front closure and fold back. When folding back, try your best to position the front closure so that it is slightly underneath the bralette cups. This will help the bra cups stay closer together (not spread open when it is worn) and provide a better fit. Refer to More About Front Closures (right). **M N**

2. Sew as close to the front closure as possible with a straight stitch. If needed, adjust your needle position so that you can stitch as close to the front closure as possible. Backstitch at beginning and end. Trim excess as close to stitch as possible with duck billed scissors. **O P**

MARGO BRALETTE WITHOUT A FRONT CLOSURE

The Margo can be sewn without a front closure. It's actually easy! Use the Brooklyn Bralette (see Bottom of Bralette, page 101) method when attaching the band elastic. When pinning the band elastic to the bottom of the bralette prior to sewing, ensure that the front bralette cups are next to each other, or "kissing". You could also have the front bralette cups overlap ½" (1.2cm) to create a cross over style.

SEW LINGERIE

BRA PROJECTS

MORE ABOUT FRONT CLOSURES

Front closure bralettes offer an easy way to get a bralette on and off for people who have limited mobility or trouble securing a hook and eye that is normally sewn at the back. For many people, having to reach behind their back to fasten a bra or bralette is difficult and in some cases, painful. The great thing about front closures is that if you do not like it, you can eliminate it!

Pros: Front closure bralettes fasten between breasts. This is a great style for people who have difficulty reaching a hook and eye closure due to limited mobility. Also, a traditional hook and eye can be visible through form fitting or clingy clothes. So, a front closure bra or bralette creates a smoother look from behind. Because a front closure bralette has a lower center panel, it's a great choice for a V-neck top or a dress.

Cons: People with wide-set breasts can easily wear front closure styles since there is more space to fit the front closure, however, people with large cup sizes or close set breasts may find that front closures don't correctly sit in between their breasts. Since there is only one clasp in the front, there is no adjustability with front closure bras. This means that the band must fit since you won't be able to tighten or loosen it.

Adding Stability: If you like a front closure, but need to add stability, you can add a strip of stabilizer (a super lightweight yet very strong fabric), when sewing it. Add this when feeding the wide band elastic through the front closure and folding it back. This will help stop the front from spreading open.

MARGO BRALETTE   111

Make and Attach Shoulder Straps

1. Feed one end of the shoulder strap elastic through the bottom of one slider, over the center bar, and then down through the other side. It should look like a belt buckle with one short end and one long end. Fold back ¾" (1.9cm). Repeat for the other strap. **Q R**

2. Sew a straight stitch back and forth 3–4 times as close to the slider as possible. It is difficult to sew this step with the slider underneath the presser foot, so if your machine has this setting, move the needle position all the way to the right. This will allow you to butt the edge of the slider against the edge of the presser foot and stitch really close to it. **S**

3. Cut a strip of shoulder strap elastic that is 4" (10.2cm) long, and feed it through the ring. With the wrong side of the back band face up, lay strap elastic on top. Refer to the pattern notches for placement. The shoulder strap elastic and ring should extend ½" (1.2cm) above the edge of the back band. Stitch back and forth 3–4 times approximately ¼" (0.6cm) from top edge. Trim near the stitches. **T**

112 SEW LINGERIE

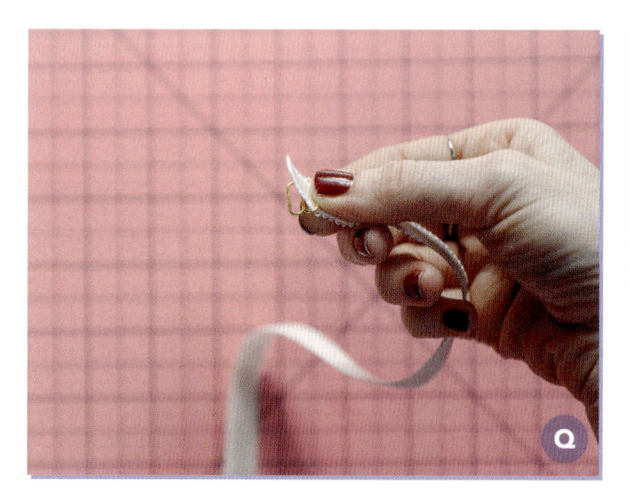

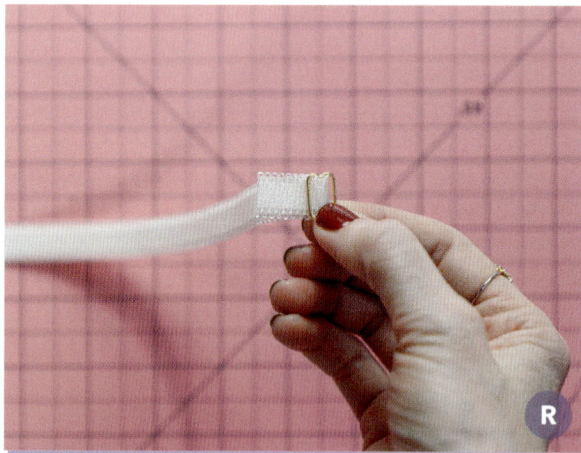

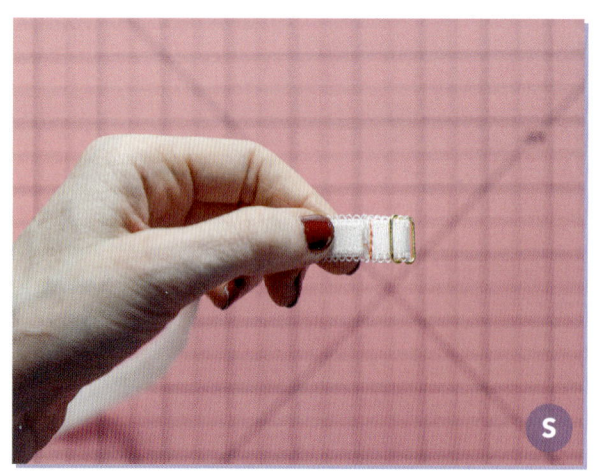

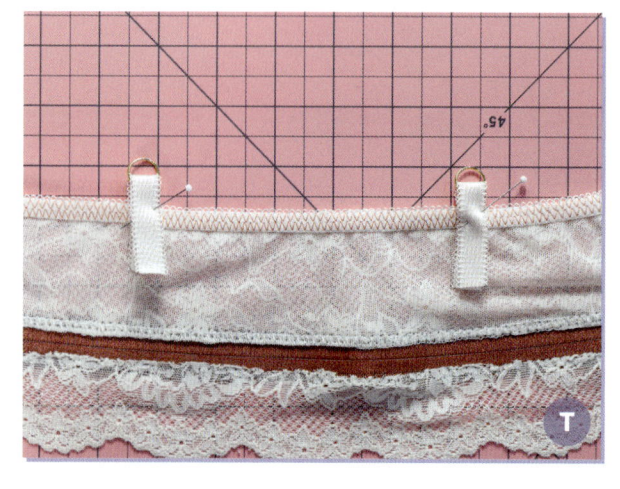

BRA PROJECTS

4. Weave the unstitched edge of the strap elastics through the rings from back to front. Then weave up and over the center bar of the slider again just like in Step 1. The "standard" length from slider to ring is approximately 2″ (5cm). **U V**

5. With the wrong side of the bralette cups face up, lay strap elastic on top so that it is overlapping ½″ (1.2cm) and laying right on top of the picot elastic that is along the underarm. The right side of the shoulder strap elastic should face the wrong side of the bralette cup. Stitch back and forth 3–4 times with a straight stitch approximately ¼″ (0.6cm) from the top edge of the bra cup. For extra security, stitch back and forth 3–4 times with straight stitch times approximately ¼″ (0.6mm) below the previous stitch. If there is any elastic hanging below the stitch, trim it close to the stitching. **W**

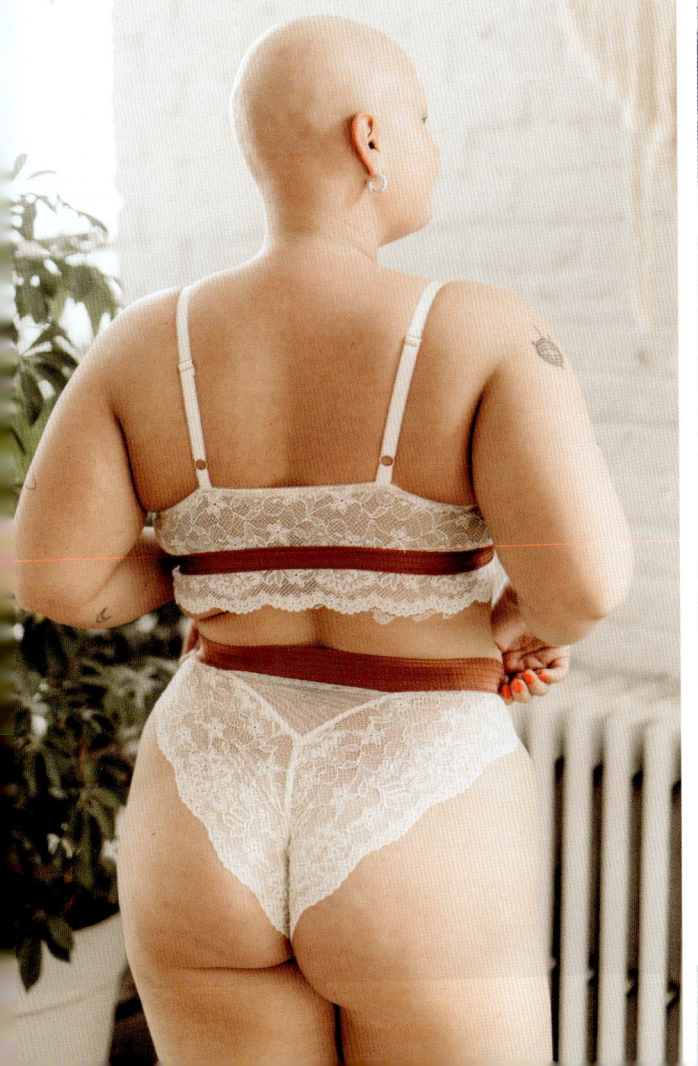

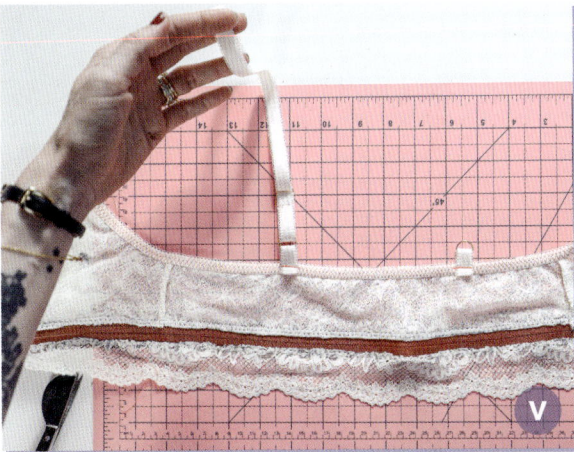

MARGO BRALETTE

INTERMEDIATE
RYANN *bralette*

The Ryann is a high neck, racerback style bralette. Instead of having a wide elastic band, Ryann has a bottom band made of fabric. Both the front and the back feature curved seaming which allows for creative uses of fabrics. A decorative trims runs from the neckline down to the bottom band at the center front. Wear the Ryann as lingerie, a layering piece, or a crop top! Use #ryannbralette to share your make!

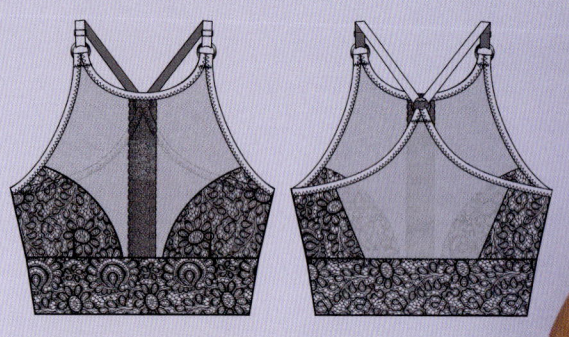

BRA PROJECTS

Fabrics and Notions

MAIN FABRIC: Stretch mesh, LYCRA, or stretch all over lace

COMBO FABRIC: Stretch mesh, jersey, LYCRA, stretch all over lace, or stretch galloon lace at least 9″ (22.9cm) wide

LINING FABRIC:
- Stretch mesh for sizes XS–M
- Power net for size sizes L–4X

PICOT ELASTIC: 2½ yards (2.3m) ⅜″ (8mm) wide

FOLD OVER ELASTIC: 2½ yards (2.3m) ⅜″ (8mm) wide

CENTER FRONT TRIM: 1 yard (1m) 1½″ (38mm) wide

SHOULDER STRAP ELASTIC:
- 1½ yards (1.4m) ½″ (12mm) wide for sizes XS–M
- 1½ yards (1.4m) ¾″ (18mm) wide for sizes L–4X

3 RINGS, 2 SLIDERS: Width should match the width of the shoulder strap elastic

Tools

SEWING MACHINE WITH STRAIGHT AND ZIGZAG STITCH

BALLPOINT, STRETCH, OR MICROTEX NEEDLE (size depends on the thickness of the fabric; see Needle and Thread, page 36)

POLYESTER THREAD

PINS

ROTARY CUTTER

DUCK BILLED SCISSORS

SPRAY ADHESIVE (optional)

SERGER (optional)

Scan this QR code or visit
tinyurl.com/11531-pattern6-downloads
to download and print the pattern pieces for this project.

FABRIC CHART	XS–L	XL–5X
Main Fabric	⅓ yard (31cm)	½ yard (46cm)
Combo Fabric	¼ yard (23cm)	⅓ yard (31cm)
Lining Fabric	⅓ yard (31cm)	½ yard (46cm)

RYANN BRALETTE

Cutting List

MAIN FABRIC: Side Front Bralette (B), Side Back Bralette (D), Back Bottom Band (E), Front Bottom Band (F)

COMBO FABRIC: Center Front Bralette (A), Center Back Bralette (C)

LINING FABRIC: Side Front Bralette (B), Side Back Bralette (D), Back Bottom Band (E), Front Bottom Band (F)

CENTER FRONT TRIM (G)

SHOULDER STRAP ELASTIC (H)

Notes on Project

Pattern pieces B, D, E, and F should be lined with a stretch mesh or power net. Spray baste the main fabric to the lining using a temporary adhesive before starting to construct the garment. In the instructions, the fabrics are treated as one layer. See Temporary Spray Adhesive (page 50). For additional finishing techniques without a serger, see Finishing Seams (page 53). Contrasting color threads are used to clearly show each step.

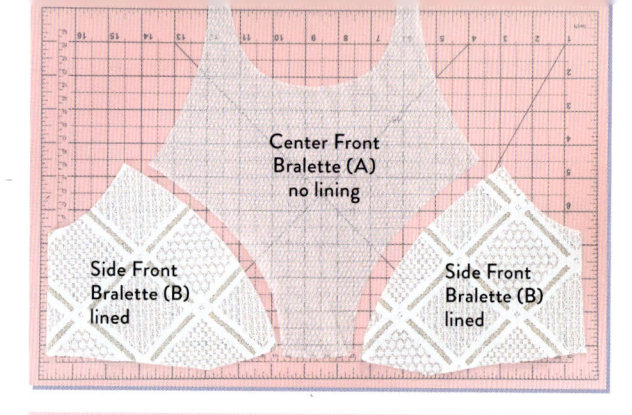

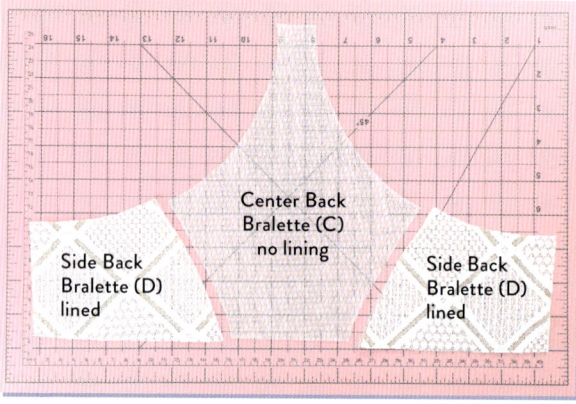

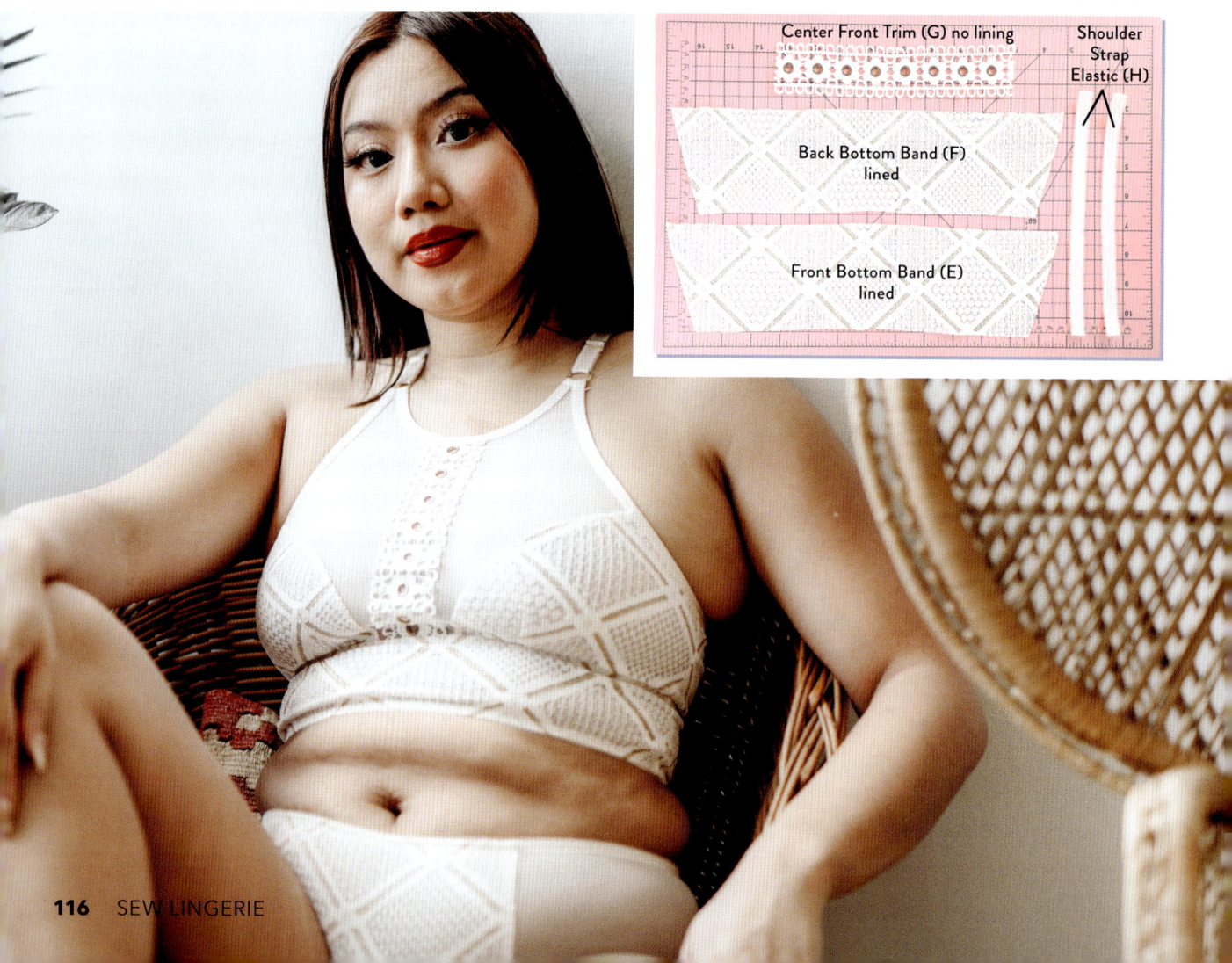

Sew Bust Darts

1. With right sides together, sew bust darts on the side front bralette pieces by folding darts in half and pinning in place along dart legs. Sew from bottom edge to dart point. At dart point, sew off fabric and leave a long thread tail (do not backstitch). Tie in a knot to secure. Be sure not to pull the knot tight against the fabric as it will cause puckering. **A**

Sew Center Front Trim

1. Lay the center front trim down the middle of the center front bralette. Right side of the center front should face the wrong side of the trim. Sew along both edges of the center front trim with a zigzag stitch approximately ¼″ (0.6cm). **B**

Sew Center Front Bralette to Side Front Bralette

1. With right sides facing, sew the center front bralette to the side front bralette with a straight stitch. Backstitch at the beginning and end. Serge (overlock) seam allowances. Repeat to attach the other side. **C**

Sew Side Back Bralette to Center Back Bralette

1. With right sides facing, sew center back bralette to side back bralette with a straight stitch. Backstitch at beginning and end. Serge (overlock) seam allowances. If you do not have a serger, you can skip this step and leave the edges unfinished or push seam allowances to one side and sew down with a zigzag stitch that is ¼″ (6mm) wide. Repeat to attach the other side. **D**

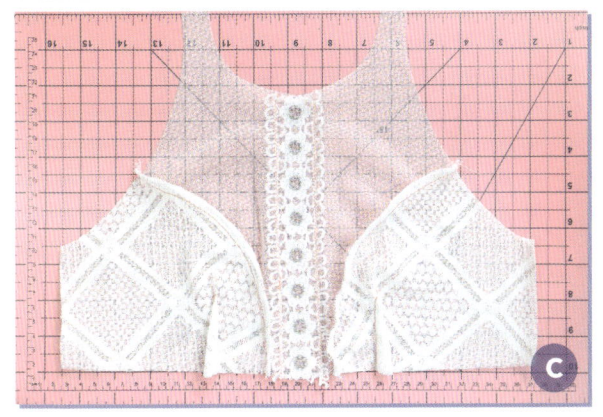

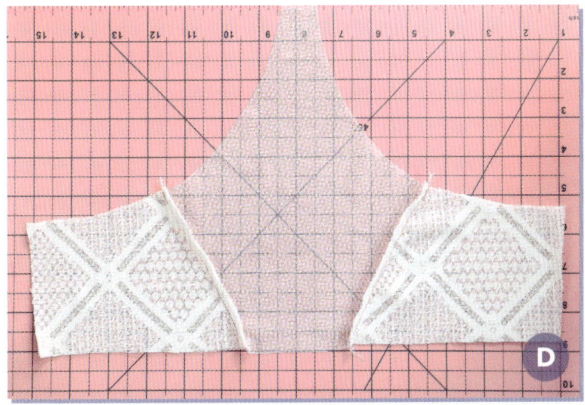

Sew Front Bralette, Back Bralette and Bottom Bands Together

1. With right sides facing, sew the front bralette to the back bralette at the side seams with a straight stitch. With right sides facing, sew the front bottom band to the back bottom band at the side seams with a straight stitch. Backstitch all seams at the beginning and end. Serge (overlock) all seam allowances. If you do not have a serger, you can skip this step and leave the edges unfinished or push seam allowances to one side and sew down with a zigzag stitch that is ¼" (0.6mm) wide. **E**

Sew Bralette to Bottom Band

1. With right sides facing and side seams aligned, sew bralette to bottom band with a zigzag stitch that is approximately ¼" (0.6mm) wide, or a lightning stitch. **F G**

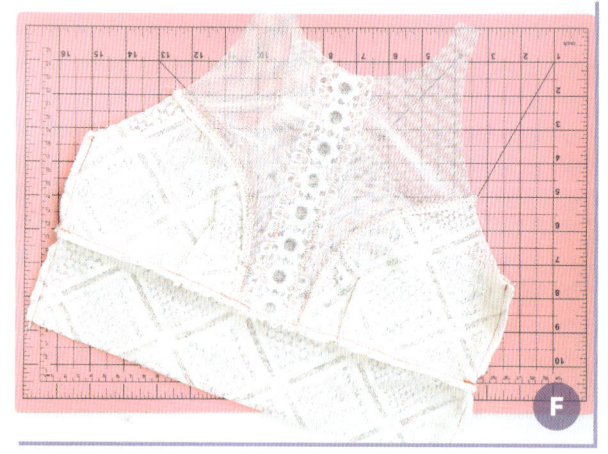

Sew Picot Elastic to Bottom Band

1. Lay the bralette with the wrong side facing up and the seam allowances of the underbust seam facing one direction and bralette facing another. Place the picot elastic on top of the seam allowance with the plush side facing up and the non-picot edge aligned with the seam. **H**

2. Sew along the picot edge of the elastic with a zigzag stitch. I recommend starting approximately ½" (1.2cm) behind the side seam so that when the garment is finished, the start/stop point is not visible when looking at the front of the garment. You should only be stitching through the seam allowances, not the bralette. The zigzag stitch should be adjusted to suit the width of the elastic. Stitch as close to the non-picot edge as possible all the way around the bottom band. Overlap the elastic at ½" (1.2cm). Backstitching is optional. **I**

3. Turn the elastic down towards the bottom band, and sew the opposite (picot) edge of the elastic with a zigzag stitch. Stitch as close to the edge as possible and through all layers (seam allowance and bottom band). **J**

4. With the right side of the bralette facing up, place picot elastic on top of the bottom band at the bottom edge. If the elastic is ¼" (0.6mm) wide, the non-picot edge of the elastic will align with the edge of the fabric (since the seam allowances are ¼" or 0.6cm wide). If the elastic is wider, then it will extend past the edge of the fabric (example: If elastic is ½" or 1.2cm wide, then it will extend past the edge of the fabric ¼" or 0.6cm). Regardless of the width of the elastic, the picot edge should face inward towards the fabric and the plush side should face up.

BRA PROJECTS

RYANN BRALETTE

5. Sew along the picot edge of the elastic with a zigzag stitch. The zigzag stitch width should be adjusted to suit the width of the elastic. Stitch as close to the picot edge as possible all the way around the bottom band. Overlap the elastic at ½" (1.2cm). Backstitching is optional. **K**

6. Turn the elastic to the wrong side of the fabric and sew the opposite (non-picot) edge of the elastic with a zigzag stitch. Stitch as close to the edge as possible. **L**

Sew Fold Over Elastic to Neckline and Racerback

1. With the wrong side of the bralette face up, lay fold over elastic (FOE) on top so that the center of the FOE is aligned with the edge of the fabric. Sew FOE along the racerback, underarm, and front neckline with a zigzag stitch that is approximately ¼" (0.6cm) wide. Zigzag stitches should be as close to the edge of the fold over elastic as possible. **M**

BRA PROJECTS

2. Trim seam allowances as close to the stitches as possible using duck billed scissors. After, turn the fold over elastic to the right side of the fabric and sew a second pass that is approximately ¼" (0.6cm) wide. Zigzag stitches should be as close to the edge of the fold over elastic as possible. **N O**

Make and Attach Shoulder Straps

1. Put rings through strap points, and through the racerback strap point, and turn back ½" (1.2cm). Sew a straight stitch back and forth 3–4 times as close to the ring as possible. Trim the excess close to stitching. **P**

2. Feed one end of the shoulder strap elastic through the bottom of one slider, over the center bar, and then down through the other side. It should look like a belt buckle with one short end and one long end. Fold back ¾" (1.9cm). Repeat for the other strap. **Q**

3. Sew a straight stitch back and forth 3–4 times as close to the slider as possible. It is difficult to sew this step with the slider underneath the presser foot, so if your machine has this setting, move the needle position all the way to the right. This will allow you to butt the edge of the slider against the edge of the presser foot and stitch really close to it.

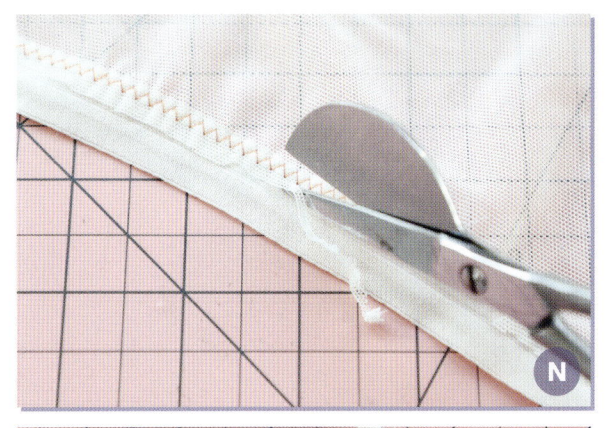

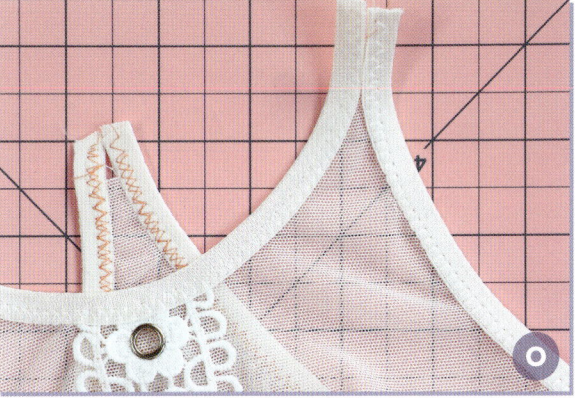

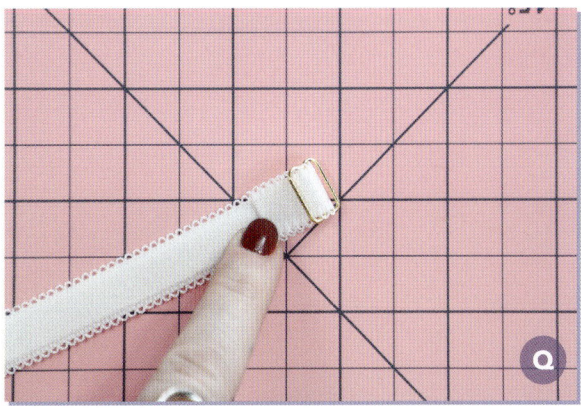

RYANN BRALETTE 121

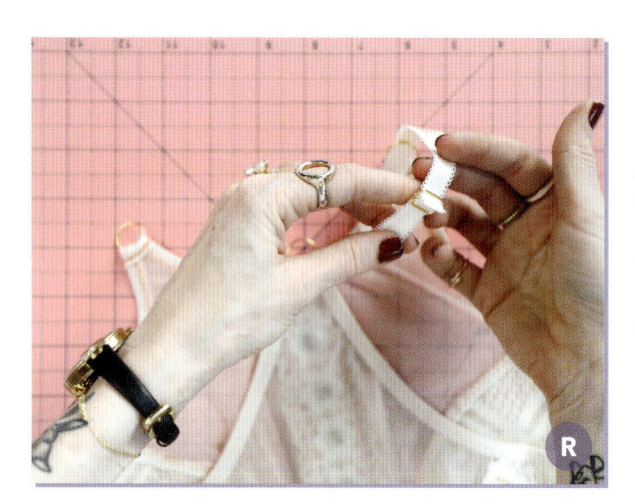

4. Weave the unstitched edge of both strap elastics through the racerback ring from back to front. Then weave up and over the center bar of the slider again just like in Step 2. The "standard" length from slider to ring is approximately 2″ (5cm). **R S**

5. Feed the free ends of the shoulder strap elastic through the rings at the raceback strap point. Turn back ½″ (1.2mm). Sew a straight stitch back and forth 3–4 times as close to the ring as possible. Trim close to stitching. **T**

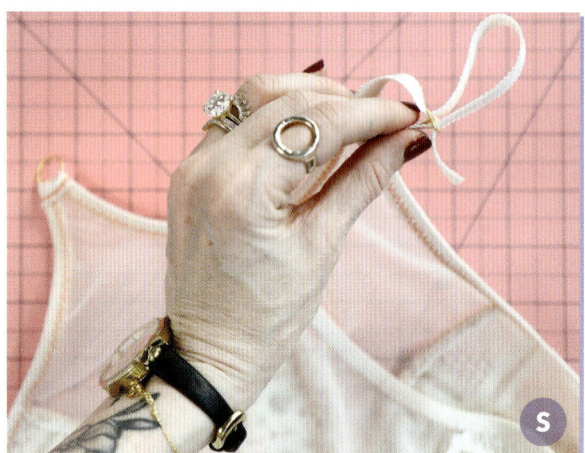

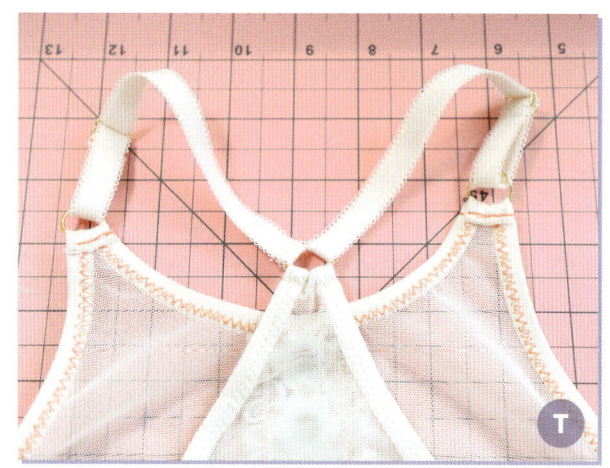

BRA PROJECTS

RYVEN BRALETTE / 123

ADVANCED
REY *underwire bra*

The Rey is a full band underwire bra with a 3-part cup. The bra cups have a top cup with scallop lace along the neckline edge. There are two lower cups that are separated by a vertical seam. The Rey also has a vertical seam on the frame underneath the cups, adjustable shoulder straps, and a hook and eye closure at the center back. Use #reyunderwirebra to share your make!

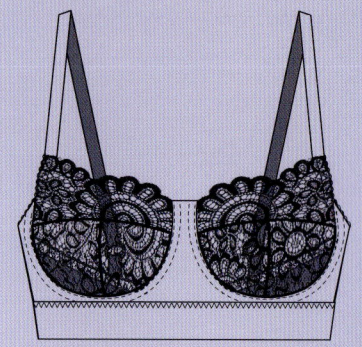

BRA PROJECTS

Fabrics and Notions

MAIN FABRIC: LYCRA, stretch all over lace, or stretch galloon lace at least 9″ (22.9cm) wide

COMBO FABRIC: Non stretch galloon lace at least 9″ (22.9cm) wide

LINING FABRIC #1: Sheer cup lining, 15 denier tricot or bra tulle

LINING FABRIC #2:
- Stretch mesh for band sizes 28–34, cup sizes A–C
- Power net for band sizes 28–34, cup sizes D+ and band sizes 36–44, all cup sizes

PICOT ELASTIC: 3 yards (2.8m) 3/8″ (8mm) wide

BOTTOM BAND ELASTIC: 1½ yards (1.4m) 1 5/8″ (40mm) wide

SHOULDER STRAP ELASTIC:
- 1½ yards (1.4m) ½″ (12mm) wide for band sizes 28–34, cup sizes A–C
- 1½ yards (1.4m) ¾″ (18mm) wide or wider for band sizes 28–34, cup sizes D+ and band sizes 36–44, all cup sizes

RINGS AND SLIDERS: 1 pair, width should match the width of shoulder strap elastic

HOOKS AND EYES: 3 × 3

UNDERWIRE CHANNELING: 1¼ yards (1.2m) 3/8″ (8mm) wide

CLASSIC UNDERWIRE: 1 pair of classic underwires

Tools

SEWING MACHINE WITH STRAIGHT AND ZIGZAG STITCH

BALLPOINT, STRETCH OR MICROTEX NEEDLE (size will depend on the thickness of the fabric, see Needle and Thread, page 36)

POLYESTER THREAD

PINS

ROTARY CUTTER

DUCK BILLED SCISSORS

SPRAY ADHESIVE (optional)

SERGER (optional)

Scan this QR code or visit **tinyurl.com/11531-pattern7-downloads** to download and print the pattern pieces for this project.

FABRIC CHART	XS–L	XL–5X
Main Fabric	¼ yard (23cm)	¼ yard (23cm)
Combo Fabric	¼ yard (23cm)	¼ yard (23cm)
Lining Fabric #1	¼ yard (23cm)	¼ yard (23cm)
Lining Fabric #2	¼ yard (23cm)	¼ yard (23cm)

REY UNDERWIRE BRA

Cutting List

MAIN FABRIC: Center Front Frame (D), Side Front Frame (E), Back Band (F)

COMBO FABRIC: Center Front Cup Lower (A), Side Front Lower Cup (B), Top Cup (C)

LINING FABRIC #1: Center Front Cup Lower (A), Side Front Lower Cup (B), Center Front Frame (D)

LINING FABRIC #2: Side Front Frame (E), Back Band (F)

SHOULDER STRAP ELASTIC (G)

BOTTOM BAND ELASTIC (H)

Notes on Project

Pattern pieces A, B, D, E, F should be lined with sheer cup lining, 15 denier tricot, bra tulle, stretch mesh, or power net. Spray baste the main fabric to the lining using a temporary adhesive before starting to construct the garment for all pattern pieces except A and B. In the instructions, the fabrics and linings are treated as one layer, except pieces A and B. See Temporary Spray Adhesive (page 50). For additional finishing techniques without a serger, see Finishing Seams (page 53). Contrasting color threads are used to clearly show each step.

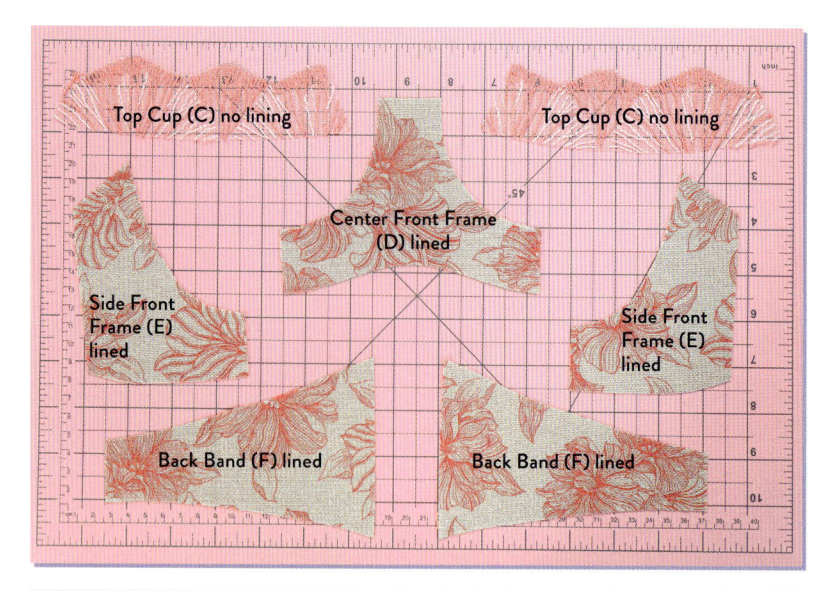

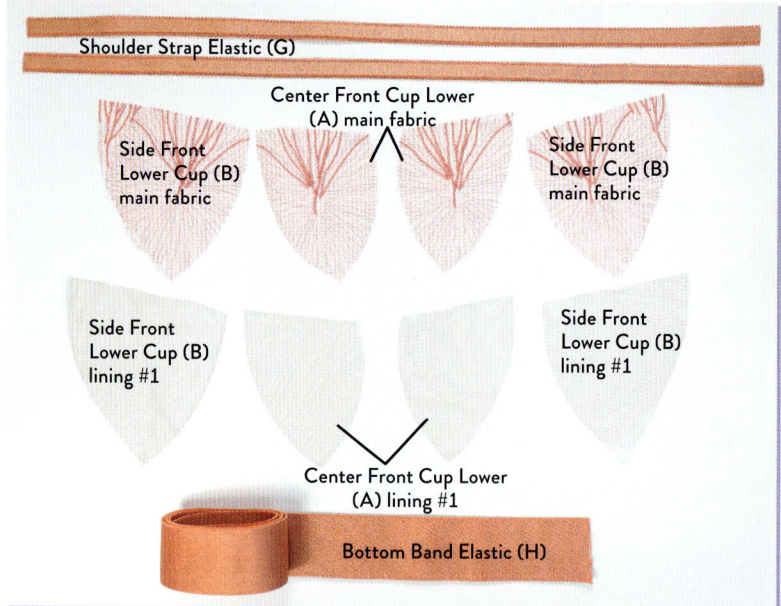

Assemble Bra Cups

1. Instead of using a serger, leaving the edges raw, or sewing down a zigzag stitch on the seam allowances after sewing the cups together, the bra cup seam allowances on the Rey will be "clean finished," as noted in Finishing Seams (page 53).

Sew the lining of the center front cup lower (A) and side front cup lower (B) together. Then, sew the main fabric of (A) and (B) together. Use a straight stitch and backstitch at the beginning and end. These will now be referred to as "lower cups." **Ⓐ**

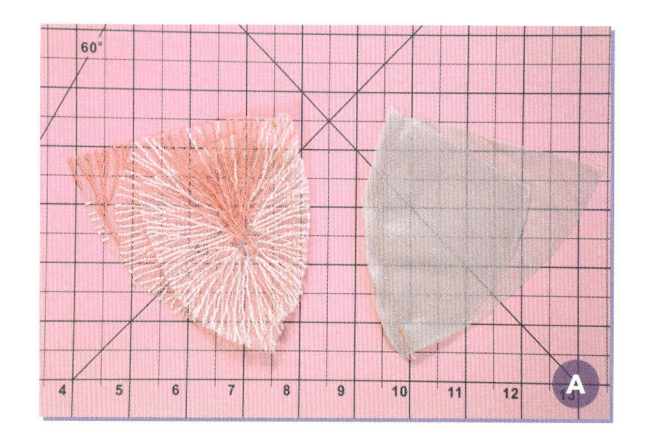

BRA PROJECTS

2. Pin the right side of the top cup to the right side of the lower cups (main fabric). **B**

3. Place the right side of lower cups (lining fabric) on top. Right side of the lower cups (main fabric) should be facing the right side of the lower cups (lining fabric). The top cup should be sandwiched in between the two layers. Repin and sew with a straight stitch. Backstitch at beginning and end.

4. Repeat Steps 2–3 for the second cup. **C**

5. Turn all the pieces right side out. **D** **E**

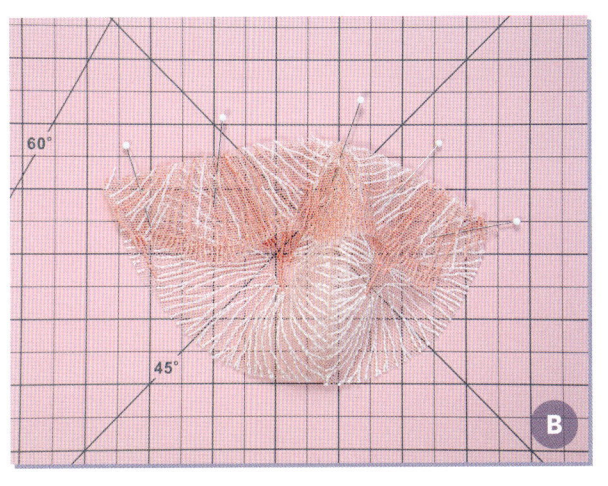

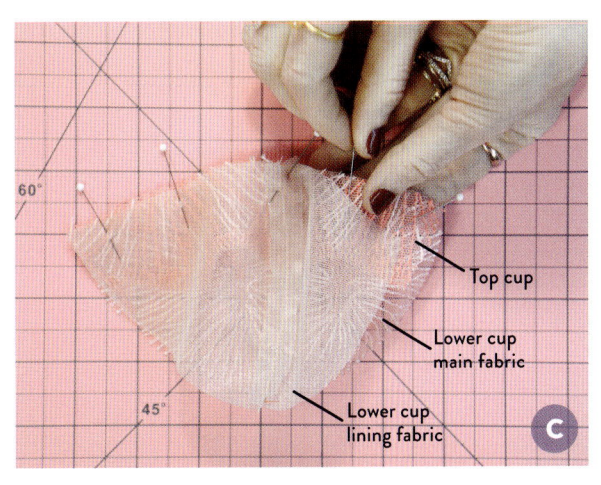

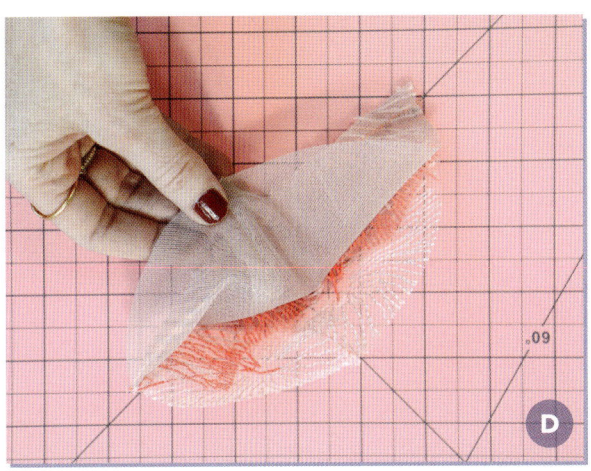

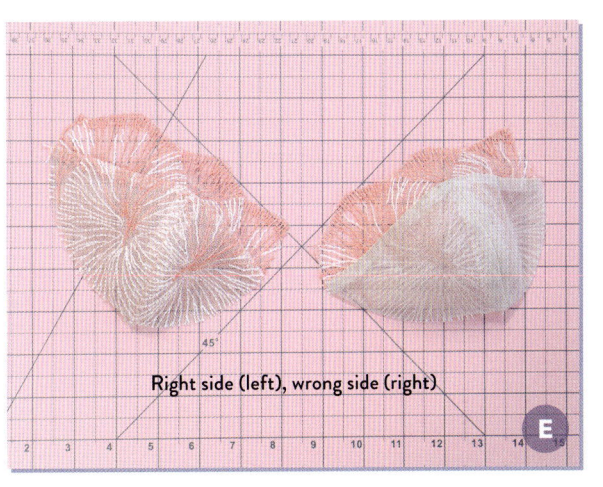

Right side (left), wrong side (right)

REY UNDERWIRE BRA

Assemble Frame

1. Sew a straight stitch ¼" (0.6cm) from the top edge of the center front frame. Do not backstitch at the beginning or end and leave approximately 1" (2.5cm) of thread hanging on either side. **F**

2. Fold down the seam allowance along the stitch line and pin in place. The stitch line is not integral to the bra construction—it's a guide to help fold down the fabric. So, if you find it difficult to make this stitch, you can skip it, and fold down the fabric without sewing first. Sew down the seam allowance with a straight stitch. **G H**

3. With right sides facing, sew the center front frame to the side front frame with a straight stitch. Backstitch at the beginning and end. Repeat on the other side. Press the seams open using an iron set to a synthetic setting, and leave the edges raw. This is the frame. **I**

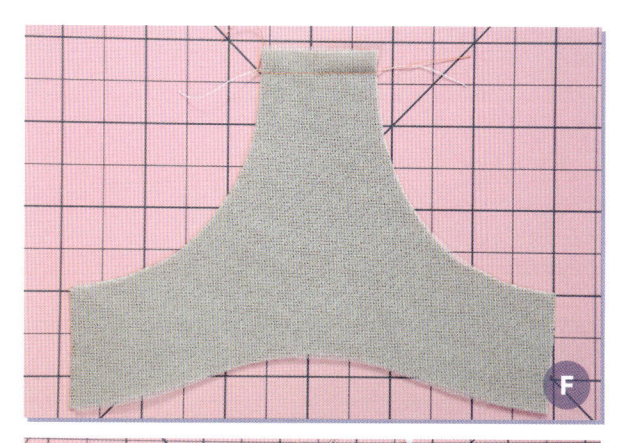

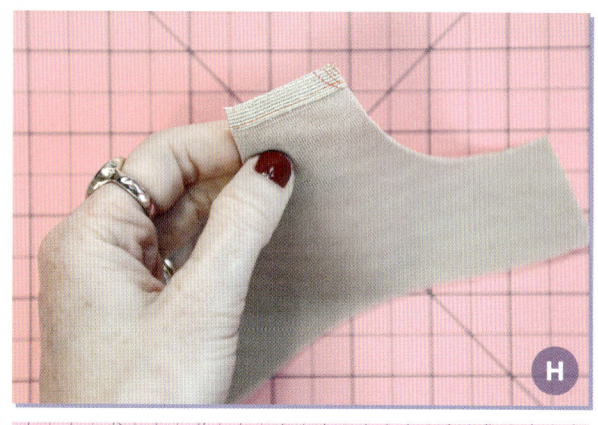

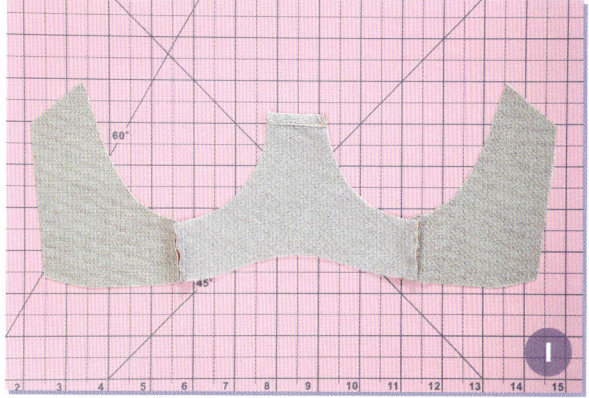

Attach Bra Cups

1. With right sides facing and notches aligned, pin the bra cups to the frame. I find it easiest to start by pinning the bra cup at the center front edge, the underarm edge, and the pattern notch. Then, I pin in between. This prevents pinning all the way in one direction only to realize one edge is shorter/longer than the other. Also, the bra cups are not eased into the frame—they are sewn at a 1:1 ratio, so there shouldn't be any puckers. Sew with a straight stitch, and backstitch at the beginning and end. **J**–**M**

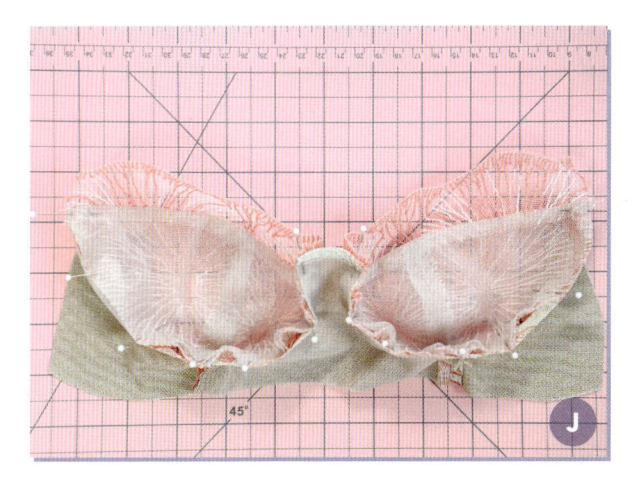

REY UNDERWIRE BRA 129

Sew Front Bra to Back Band

1. With right sides facing, sew the front bra to the back band with a straight stitch. Repeat on the other side. Backstitch at the beginning and end. **N**

Attach Channeling

1. With the wrong side of the bra facing up, fold the bra so that the bra cups seam allowances are pointing in one direction and the bra cups and frame are pointing in the other direction. **O**

2. Place the channeling over the bra cup seam allowance with the left edge of the channeling extending past the wire seam line ⅛″ (0.3cm). Before sewing, do a quick check and make sure that the channeling is oriented so that it will be flipped down towards the frame. This is the correct orientation. **P Q**

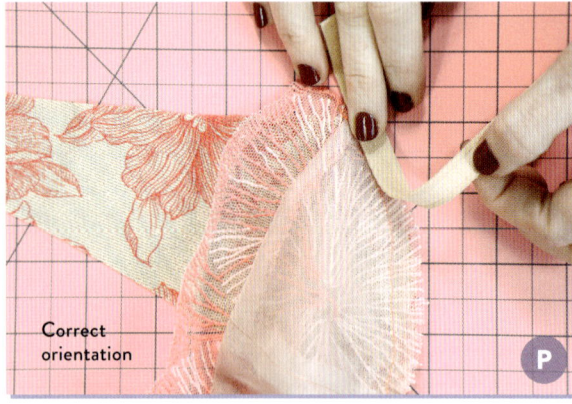

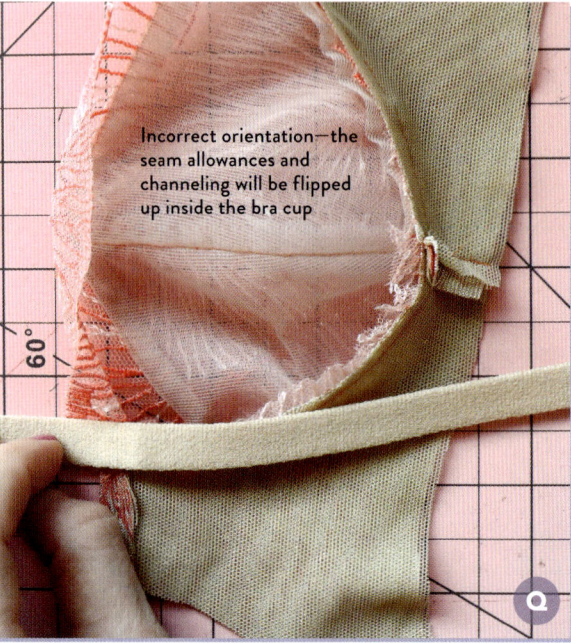

Correct orientation

Incorrect orientation—the seam allowances and channeling will be flipped up inside the bra cup

130 SEW LINGERIE

BRA PROJECTS

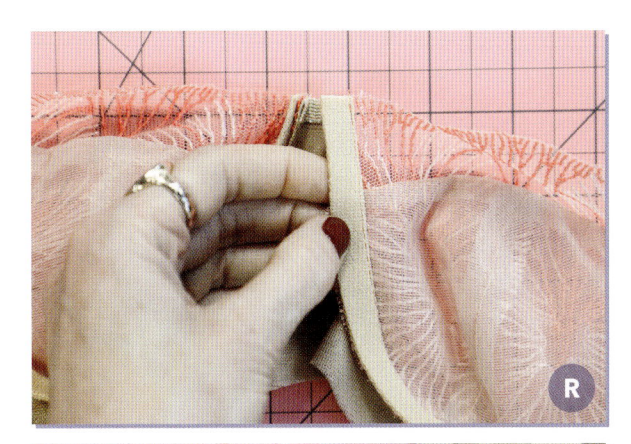

3. Sew the channeling to the cup seam allowances approximately ⅛" (0.3cm) from the left edge of the channeling with a straight stitch. When sewing scant seam allowances, the best tip is to go slow. So, you should be stitching **on the wire seam line**. Stop stitching ¾" (18mm) from the underarm edge to allow for elastic to be sewn in the next steps. Stitch all the way to the center front and back stitch. **R**

4. Trim seam allowances to ⅛" (0.3cm). Fold channeling down towards the frame and sew ⅛" (0.3cm) from the right edge. For this step, sew through all layers. Backstitch at the beginning and end. **S**

5. Sew channeling to the side seam using the same method. Backstitch at the beginning and end, and cut channeling so that it is ⅜" (0.9cm) below the top of the side seam. **T**

REY UNDERWIRE BRA

Sew Picot Elastic at Underarm

1. With the right side of the bra facing up, place the picot elastic on top so that there is ¼" (0.6cm) of overlap between the bra and elastic. If the picot elastic is ⅜" (0.9cm) wide, align the edge of the elastic to extend ⅛" (0.3cm) past the edge of the fabric. If the picot elastic is wider, then it should extend past the edge of the fabric more (i.e. if the picot elastic is ½" or 1.2cm wide, then it will extend past the edge of the fabric ¼" or 0.6cm). Regardless of the width of the picot elastic, the picot edge should face inward towards the fabric and the plush side should face up.

2. Sew along the picot edge of the elastic with a zigzag stitch approximately ¼" (0.6cm) wide. Zigzag stitches should be as close to the picot edge as possible. **U**

3. Flip the picot elastic to the inside of the bra and sew along the flat edge of the elastic with a zigzag stitch approximately ¼" (0.6cm) wide. Zigzag stitches should be as close to the flat edge as possible. **V**

Serge Bottom of Bra

1. Serge (overlock) the bottom edge of the bra. If you do not have a serger, you can skip this step and leave the edges unfinished or you can sew the edge with a zigzag stitch that is ¼" (0.6cm) wide. If you do serge, insert plastic boning inside channeling at the side seam before serging.

Sew Bottom Band Elastic to Bottom of Bra

1. Overlap the bottom band elastic and the bottom of the bra ¼" (0.6cm). The bottom band elastic should be on top. **W**

2. Sew the wide band elastic to the bottom of the bra with a zigzag stitch that is approximately ¼" (0.6cm) wide. You will be sewing over the channeling at the side seam. **X**

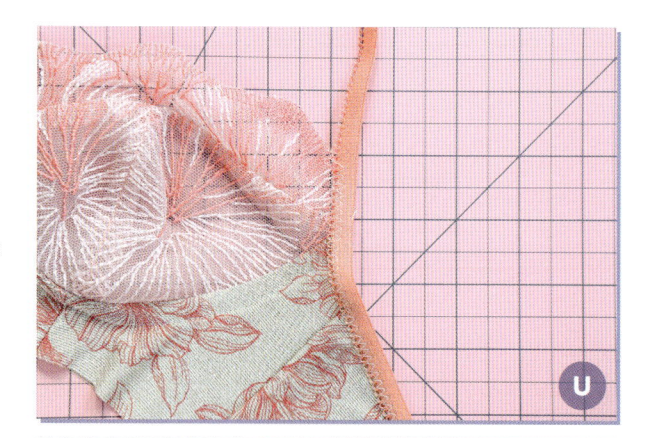

BRA PROJECTS

Insert and Secure Channeling At Center Front

1. Insert underwires into channeling around the cups. **Y**

2. With the right or wrong side of the bra facing up, stitch back and forth 3–4 times with a straight stitch approximately ⅛″ (0.3cm)–¼″ (0.6cm) below the center front edge to close off the channeling and prevent the underwires from coming out.

3. Trim channeling so it is flush with the center front edge. **Z**

Attach Hook and Eye

Eyes go on the left side of the bra, as if you were fastening it on someone else, and hooks go on the right side.

1. Open tape on the eyes and wrap it around the raw edge at the center back. Sew with a straight stitch ⅛″ (0.3mm) from the edge of the tape. **A**

2. For the hook side, wrap the tape around the raw edge at the center back, and sew ⅛″ (0.3cm) from the edge of the hook. When sewing the hook, you must sew with the hooks facing up to avoid damage to your machine. If your machine has this setting, move the needle position all the way to the right so that you can put the tape underneath the presser foot and still sew close to the hooks. **B**

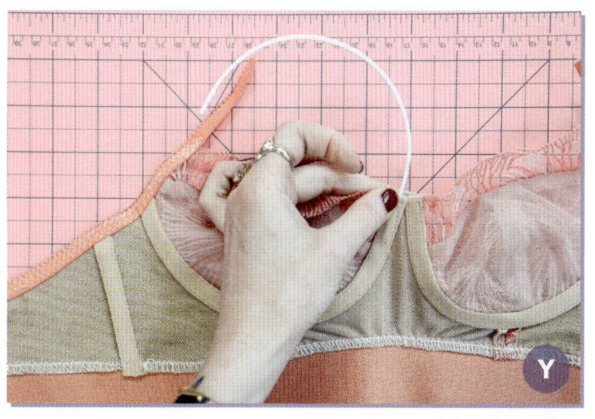

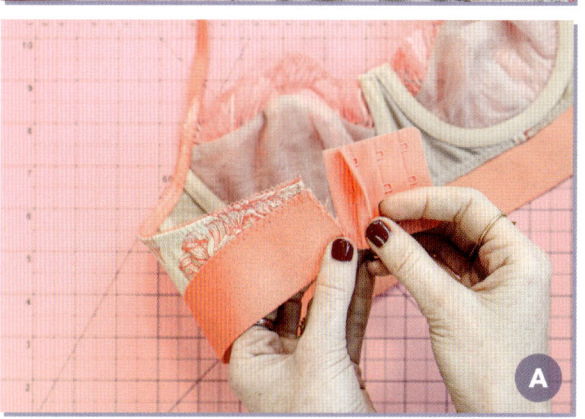

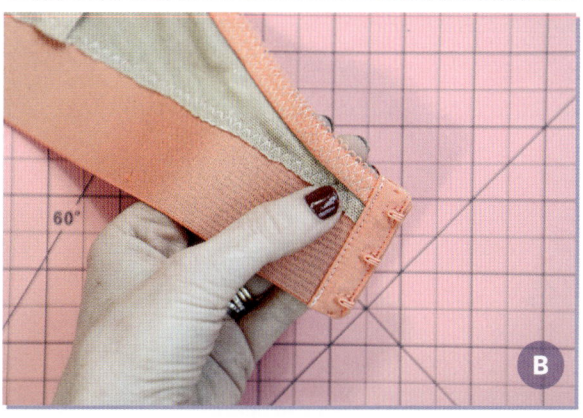

REY UNDERWIRE BRA 133

Make and Attach Shoulder Straps

1. Feed one end of the shoulder strap elastic through the bottom of one slider, over the center bar, and then down through the other side. It should look like a belt buckle with one short end and one long end. Fold back ¾" (1.9cm). Repeat for the other strap. **C**

2. Sew a straight stitch back and forth 3–4 times as close to the slider as possible. It is difficult to sew this step with the slider underneath the presser foot, so if your machine has this setting, move the needle position all the way to the right. This will allow you to butt the edge of the slider against the edge of the presser foot and stitch really close to it. **D**

3. Cut a strip of shoulder strap elastic that is 4" (10.2cm) long and feed through a ring. With the wrong side of the back band face up, lay strap elastic on top. Refer to the pattern notches for placement. The shoulder strap elastic should extend down to where the back band meets the bottom band elastic, and it should extend above the top edge of the back band ½" (1.2cm). Stitch back and forth 3–4 times approximately ¼" (0.6cm) from top edge. Then, stitch at the bottom, attaching it to the back band. Trim excess at the bottom. Repeat on the other side. **E**

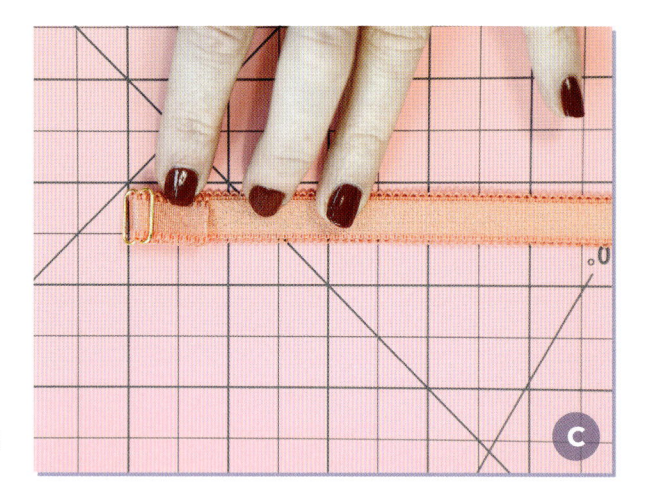

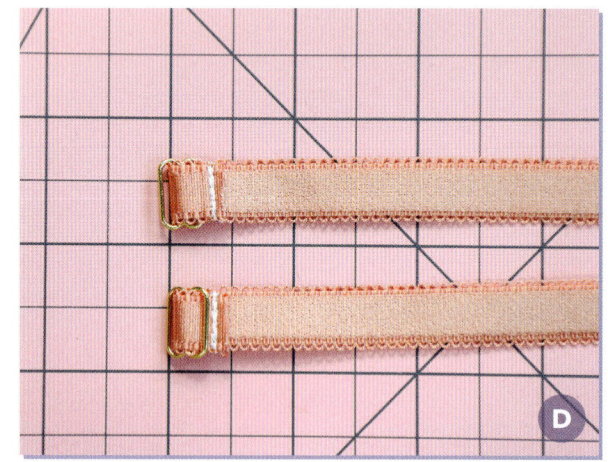

4. Weave the unstitched sides of the strap elastics through rings from back to front. Then weave up and over the center bar of the slider again just like in Step 1. The "standard" length from slider to ring is approximately 2″ (5cm). Repeat on the other side. **F G**

5. With the wrong side of the bra cups face up, lay strap elastic on top of strap points so that it is overlapping ½″ (1.2cm). The right side of the shoulder strap elastic should face the wrong side of the bra cup. Stitch back and forth 3–4 times with a straight stitch approximately ¼″ (0.6cm) from the top edge of the bra cup. For extra security, stitch back and forth 3–4 with straight stitch times approximately ¼″ (0.6cm) below the previous stitch. If there is any elastic hanging below the stitch, trim it close to stitching. **H**

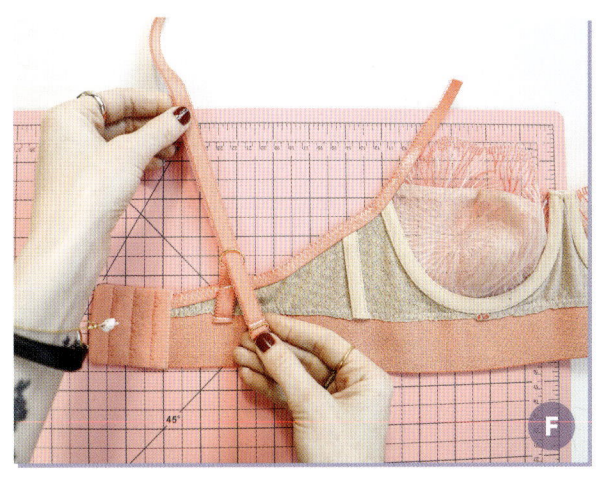

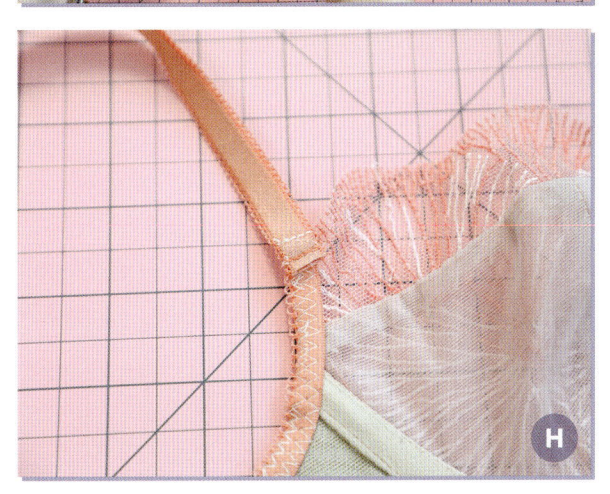

· INTERMEDIATE ·

KENNEDY *sports bralette*

The Kennedy Sports Bralette is a low-impact style that is perfect for yoga, daily stretching, walking, weight lifting, indoor cycling, and the elliptical. The bralette features a vertical seam on the bra cups, mesh panels, adjustable shoulder straps and a wide bottom band for more support. Use #kennedysportsbralette to share your make!

BRA PROJECTS

Fabrics and Notions

MAIN FABRIC: LYCRA or other activewear fabric

COMBO FABRIC: Stretch mesh or LYCRA

LINING FABRIC:
- Stretch mesh for sizes XS–M
- Power net for sizes L–4X

FOLD OVER ELASTIC: 2½ yards (2.3m) ⅝″ (16mm) wide (⅜″ or 8mm when folded)

WIDE BAND ELASTIC: 1½ yards (1.4m) 1½″ (38mm) wide or wider

SHOULDER STRAP ELASTIC:
- 1 yard (1m) ½″ (12mm) wide for sizes XS–M
- 1 yard (1m) ¾″ (18mm) wide for sizes L–4X

3 RINGS, 2 SLIDERS: Width should match the width of the shoulder strap elastic

Tools

SEWING MACHINE WITH STRAIGHT AND ZIGZAG STITCH

POLYESTER THREAD

PINS

ROTARY CUTTER

DUCK BILLED SCISSORS

SPRAY ADHESIVE *(optional)*

SERGER *(optional)*

Scan this QR code or visit **tinyurl.com/11531-pattern8-downloads** to download and print the pattern pieces for this project.

FABRIC CHART	XS–L	XL–5X
Main Fabric	¼ yard (23cm)	⅓ yard (31cm)
Combo Fabric	¼ yard (23cm)	¼ yard (23cm)
Lining Fabric	¼ yard (23cm)	⅓ yard (31cm)

KENNEDY SPORTS BRALETTE 137

Cutting List

MAIN FABRIC: Center Front Bralette (B), Side Front Bralette (C), Bottom Band Casing (E)

COMBO FABRIC: Upper Bralette (A), Center Back Bralette (D)

LINING FABRIC: Center Front Bralette (B), Side Front Bralette (C)

BOTTOM BAND ELASTIC (F)

SHOULDER STRAP ELASTIC (G)

Notes on Project

Pattern pieces B and C should be lined with a stretch mesh or power net. Spray baste the main and combo fabric to the lining using a temporary adhesive before starting to construct the garment. In the instructions, the fabrics are treated as one layer. See Temporary Spray Adhesive (page 50). For additional finishing techniques without a serger, see Finishing Seams (page 53). Contrasting color threads are used to clearly show each step.

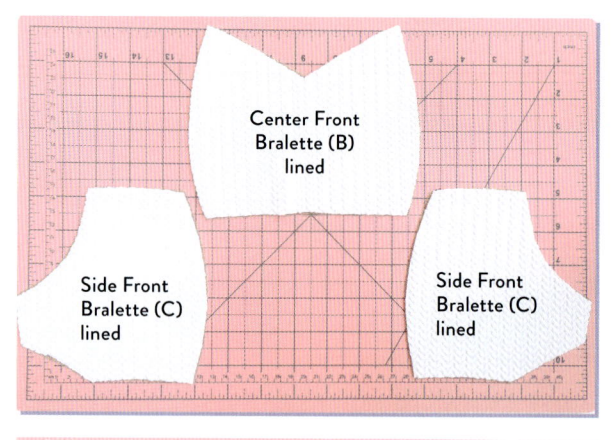

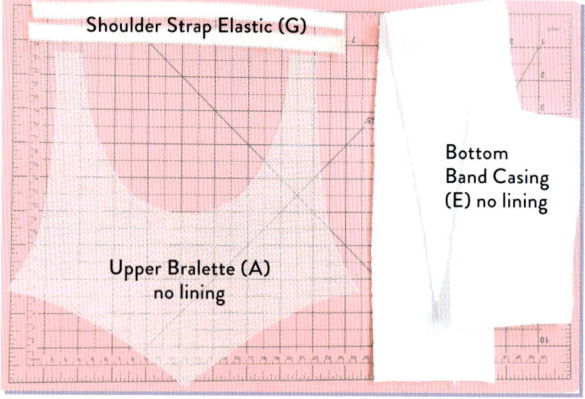

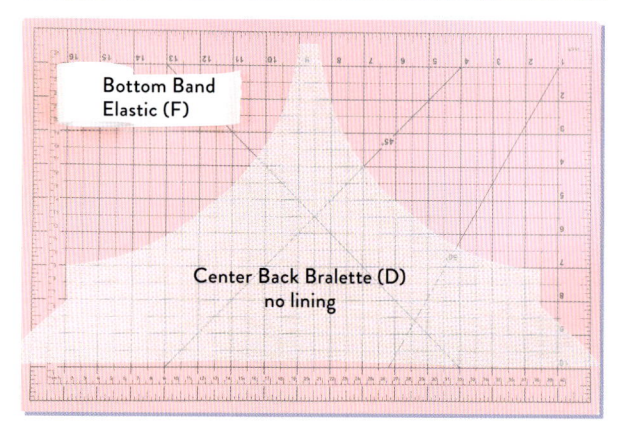

138 SEW LINGERIE

BRA PROJECTS

Sew Front Bralette Cups Together

1. With right sides facing, sew center front bralette to side front bralette with a straight stitch. Backstitch at the beginning and end. Serge (overlock) seam allowances. Repeat for the other side. **A**

Sew Lower Front Bralette Cups to Upper Bralette

1. With right sides facing, sew lower front bralette cups to upper bralette with a straight stitch. Backstitch at beginning and end. Serge (overlock) seam allowances. If you do not have a serger, you can skip this step and leave the edges unfinished or push seam allowances to one side and sew down with a zigzag stitch that is ¼″ (0.6mm) wide. **B**

Sew Front Bralette to Center Back Bralette

1. With right sides facing, sew front bralette to center back bralette with a straight stitch. Start sewing down from the underarm, then put the needle down in the fabric, lift up the presser foot and pivot to sew the diagonal portion of the seam. Backstitch at beginning and end. Serge (overlock) seam allowances. **C D**

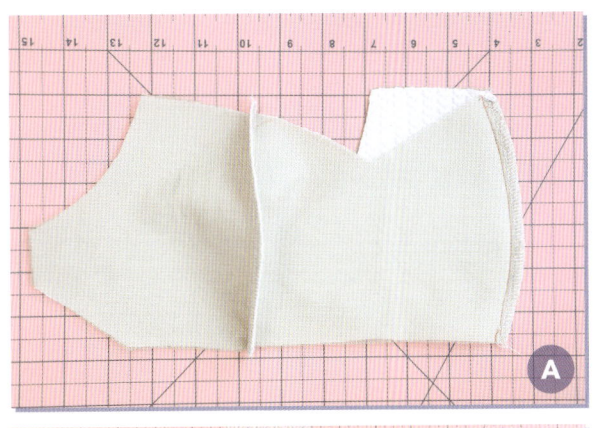

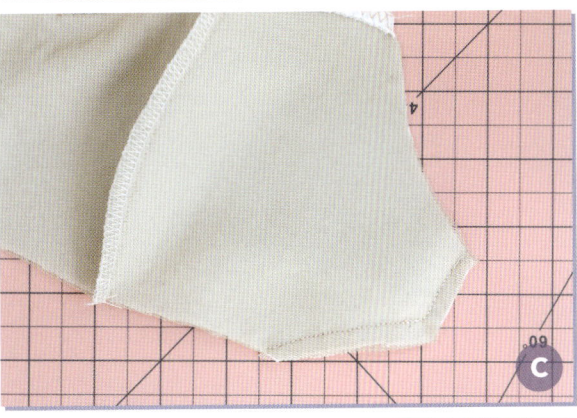

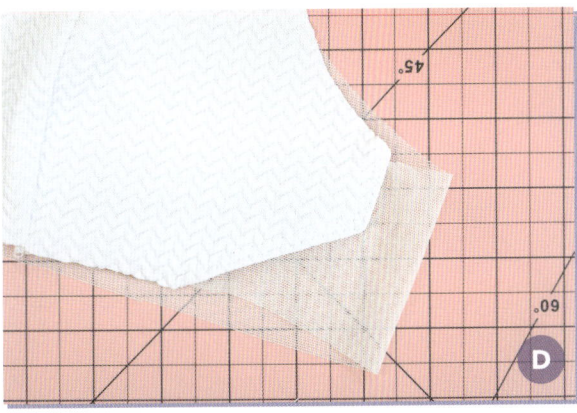

KENNEDY SPORTS BRALETTE

Sew Fold Over Elastic

1. With the wrong side of the bralette face up, lay fold over elastic (FOE) on top so that the center of the FOE is aligned with the edge of the fabric. Sew FOE along the racerback, underarm and front neckline with a zigzag stitch that is approximately ¼" (0.6cm) wide. Zigzag stitches should be as close to the outer edge of the fold over elastic as possible. **E**

2. Trim seam allowances as close to stitches as possible using duck billed scissors. After, turn the FOE to the right side of the fabric and sew a second pass that is approximately ¼" (0.6mm) wide. Zigzag stitches should be as close to the edge of the FOE as possible. **F G**

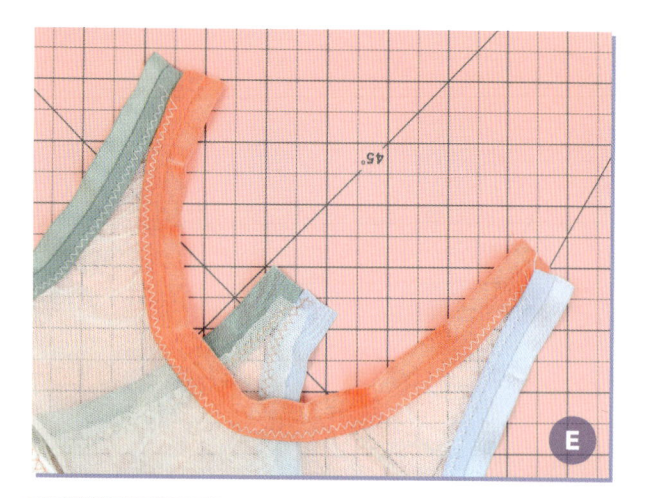

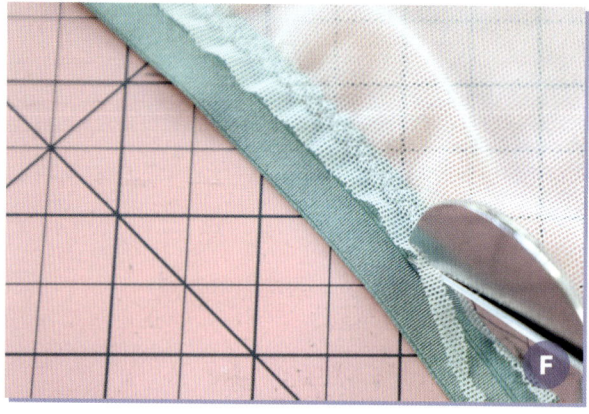

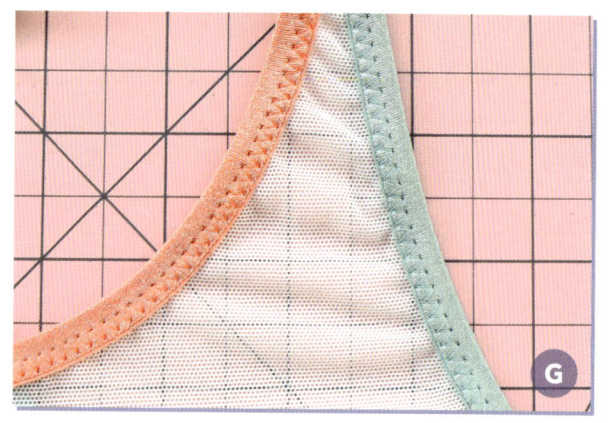

SEW LINGERIE

BRA PROJECTS

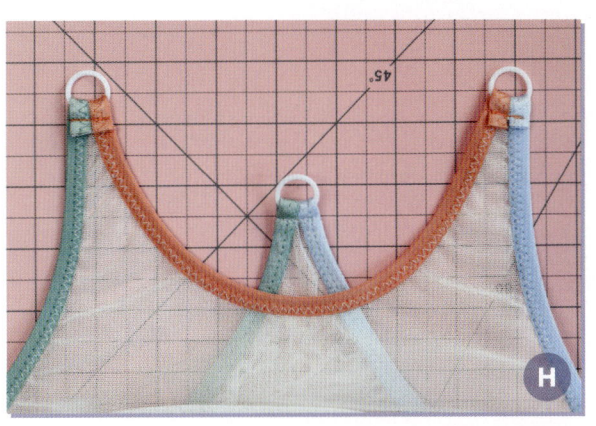

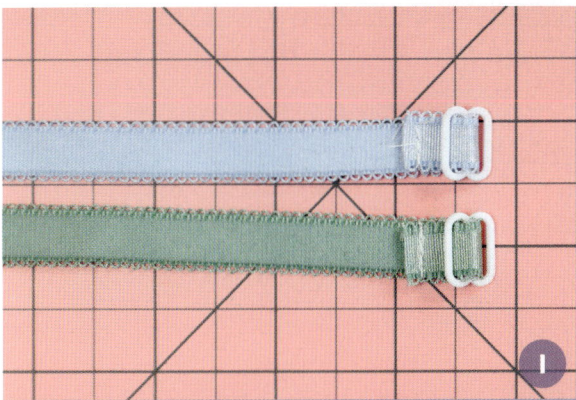

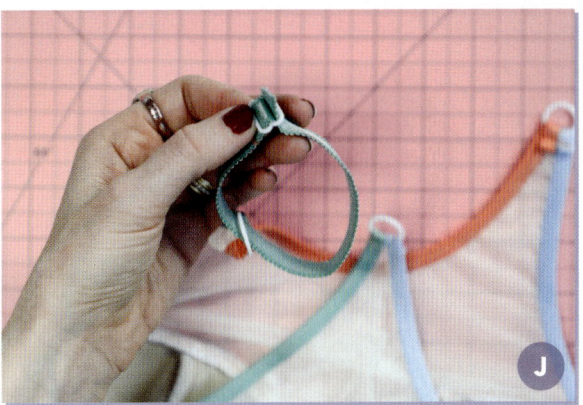

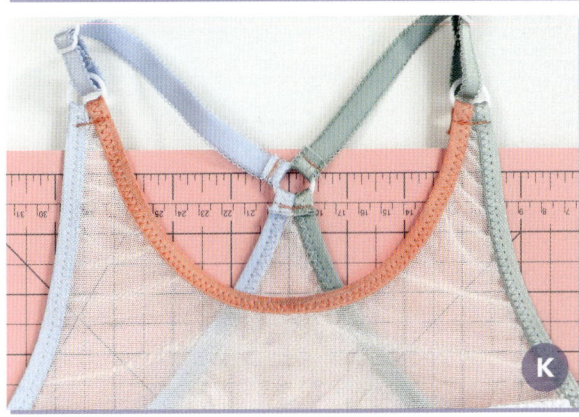

Make and Attach Shoulder Straps

1. Put rings through the strap points and racerback strap point and turn back ½″ (1.2cm). Sew a straight stitch back and forth 3–4 times as close to the ring as possible. Trim close to stitching. **H**

2. Feed one end of the shoulder strap elastic through the bottom of one slider, over the center bar, and then down through the other side. It should look like a belt buckle with one short end and one long end. Fold back ¾″ (1.9cm). Repeat for the other strap.

3. Sew a straight stitch back and forth 3–4 times as close to the slider as possible. It is difficult to sew this step with the slider underneath the presser foot, so if your machine has this setting, move the needle position all the way to the right. This will allow you to butt the edge of the slider against the edges of the presser foot and stitch really close to it. **I**

4. Weave each unstitched side of the strap elastic through each of the front strap points from back to front. Then, weave up and over the center bar again just like in Step 2. The "standard" length from slider to ring is approximately 2″ (5cm). **J**

5. Feed free ends of the shoulder strap elastic through the racerback ring. Turn back ½″ (1.2cm). Sew a straight stitch back and forth 3–4 times as close to the ring as possible. Trim close to stitching. **K**

KENNEDY SPORTS BRALETTE **141**

Make and Attach Bottom Band

1. Sew the short ends of the elastic and the casing together with a straight stitch. Backstitch at beginning and end. **L**

2. Fold the casing in half lengthwise and insert the elastic inside, with the seams on the elastic and casing aligned. **M**

3. Pin the elastic band in casing to the wrong side of the bottom of the bralette, overlapping the two by ¼" (0.6cm). The seam on the casing should align with one side seam on the bralette. Sew the elastic band all the way around the bralette with a lightning stitch. Overlap the stitches at beginning and end. Serge (overlock) seam allowances. **N**

4. Sew vertical straight stitches the width of the casing back and forth 3–4 times at the center front and both sides to prevent the elastic from rolling or twisting inside the casing.

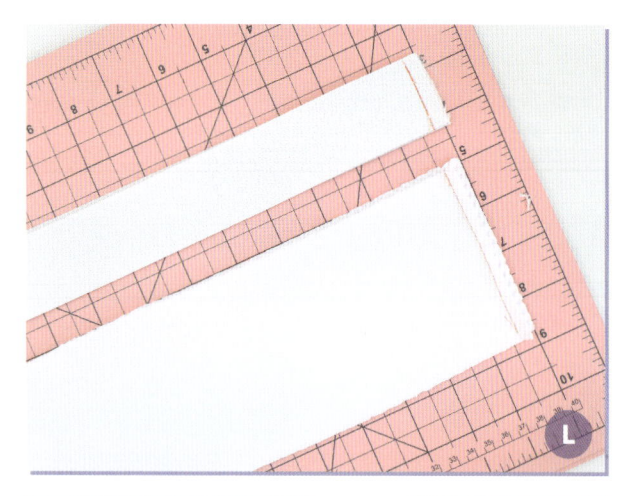

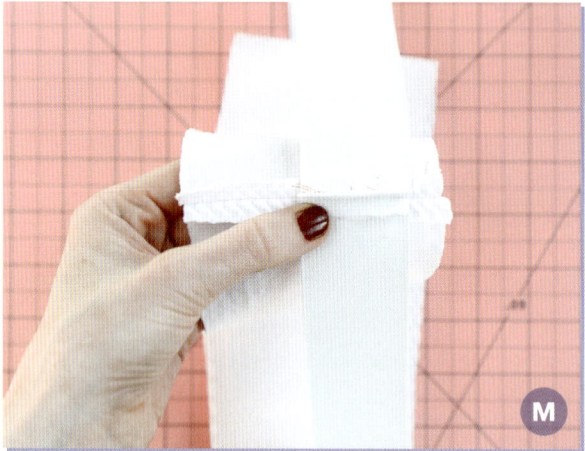

BRA PROJECTS

KENNEDY SPORTS BRALETTE **143**

swim PROJECTS

To access each pattern, scan the QR code in each individual project. You can then download the pattern at full size, or in print-at-home format.

All seam allowances are included in patterns and ¼" (0.6cm), unless otherwise noted. Whenever instructed to serge a seam allowance, if you do not have a serger, you can skip this step and leave the edges unfinished or push seam allowances to one side and sew them down with a zigzag stitch that is ¼" (0.6cm) wide.

Bra Band Size (Numerical)

Size	28	30	32	34	36
Underbust (Ribcage)	28"–30" (71.1–76.2cm)	30"–32" (76.2–81.3cm)	32"–34" (81.3–86.4cm)	34"–36" (86.4–91.4cm)	36"–38" (91.4–96.5cm)

Size	38	40	42	44
Underbust (Ribcage)	38"–40" (96.5–101.6cm)	40"–42" (101.6–106.7cm)	42"–44" (106.7–111.8cm)	44"–46" (111.8–116.8cm)

Bra Size (Alpha)

Size	XS	S	M	L	XL
Full Bust	28″–30″ (71.1–76.2cm)	30″–32″ (76.2–81.3cm)	32″–34″ (81.3–86.4cm)	34″–36″ (86.4–91.4cm)	36″–38″ (91.4–96.5cm)

Size	2X	3X	4X	5x
Full Bust	38″–41″ (96.5–104.1cm)	41″–44″ (104.1–111.8cm)	44″–47″ (111.8–119.4cm)	47″–50″ (119.4–127cm)

Cup Size

Size	A	B	C	D	E	F	G	H	I	J
Difference between full bust and underbust/ribcage	1″ (2.5CM)	2″ (5cm)	3″ (7.5cm)	4″ (10cm)	5″ (13cm)	6″ (15cm)	7″ (18cm)	8″ (20cm)	9″ (23cm)	10″ (25.5cm)

Panty Size

Size	XS	S	M	L	XL
Waist	23″–25″ (58.4–63.5cm)	25″–27″ (63.5–68.6cm)	27″–29″ (68.6–73.7cm)	29″–31″ (73.7–78.4cm)	31″–34″ (78.4–86.4cm)
Hip	33–35″ (83.8–88.9cm)	35″–37″ (88.9–94cm)	37″–39″ (94–99.1cm)	39″–41″ (99.1–104.1cm)	41″–44″ (104.1–111.8cm)

Size	2X	3X	4X	5x
Waist	34″–37″ (86.4–94cm)	37″–41″ (94–104.1cm)	41–45″ (104.1–114.3cm)	45″–49″ (114.3–124.5cm)
Hip	44″–47″ (111.8–119.4cm)	47″–51″ (119.4–129.5cm)	51″–55″ (129.5–139.7cm)	55″–59″ (139.7–149.7cm)

HENRIETTA *one piece*

·BEGINNER·

The Henrietta is a one piece swimsuit that features a surplice, or cross over front, with the potential for a lot of color blocking and pattern mixing! All edges are finished with rubber elastic. Use #henriettaonepiece to share your make!

SWIM PROJECTS

Fabrics and Notions

MAIN FABRIC: LYCRA or other swimwear fabric
LINING FABRIC: Stretch mesh, power net, or Helenca
RUBBER ELASTIC: 6 yards (5.5m) ⅜″ (8mm) wide

FABRIC CHART	XS–L	XL–5X
Main Fabric	1 yard (1m)	1⅓ yards (1.2m)
Lining Fabric	1 yard (1m)	1⅓ yard (1.2m)s

Tools

SEWING MACHINE WITH STRAIGHT, ZIGZAG, AND LIGHTNING STITCH
POLYESTER THREAD
PINS
ROTARY CUTTER
SPRAY ADHESIVE *(optional)*
SERGER *(optional)*

Scan this QR code or visit
tinyurl.com/11531-pattern9-downloads
to download and print the pattern pieces for this project.

Cutting List

MAIN FABRIC: Front Bodice (A), Back Bodice (B), Swimsuit Front Bottom (C), Swimsuit Back Bottom (D)

LINING FABRIC: Front Bodice (A), Back Bodice (B), Swimsuit Front Bottom (C), Swimsuit Back Bottom (D)

Notes on Project

All pattern pieces should be lined. Spray baste the main fabric to the lining using a temporary adhesive before starting to construct the garment. In the instructions, the fabrics are treated as one layer. See Temporary Spray Adhesive (page 50). For additional finishing techniques without a serger, see Finishing Seams (page 53). Contrasting color threads are used to clearly show each step.

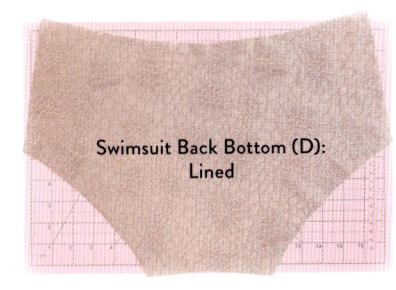

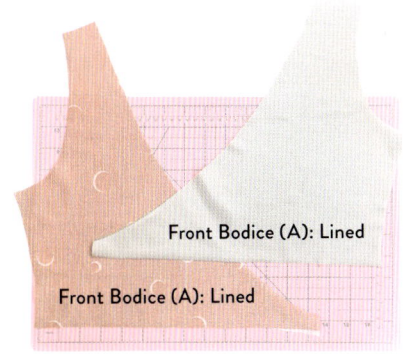

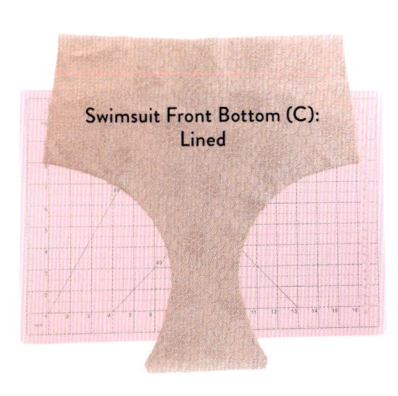

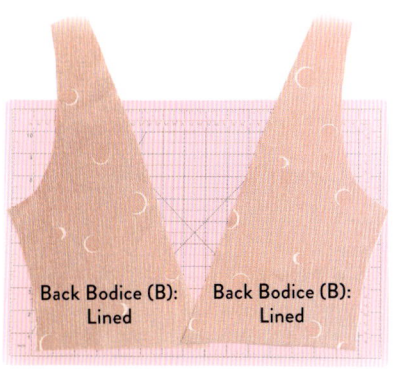

Swimsuit Back Bottom (D): Lined
Front Bodice (A): Lined
Front Bodice (A): Lined
Swimsuit Front Bottom (C): Lined
Back Bodice (B): Lined
Back Bodice (B): Lined

HENRIETTA ONE PIECE 147

Assemble Bodice + Bottoms

1. With right sides facing, sew front bodice to back bodice at shoulder seam, and sew swimsuit front bottom to swimsuit back bottom at side seam and crotch seam. Backstitch at beginning and end. Serge (overlock) seam allowances. **A B**

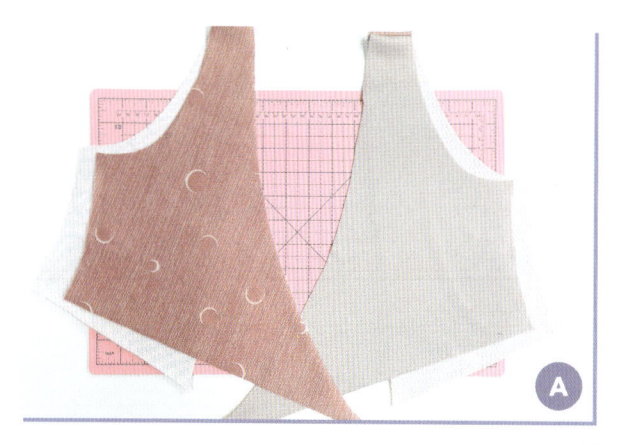

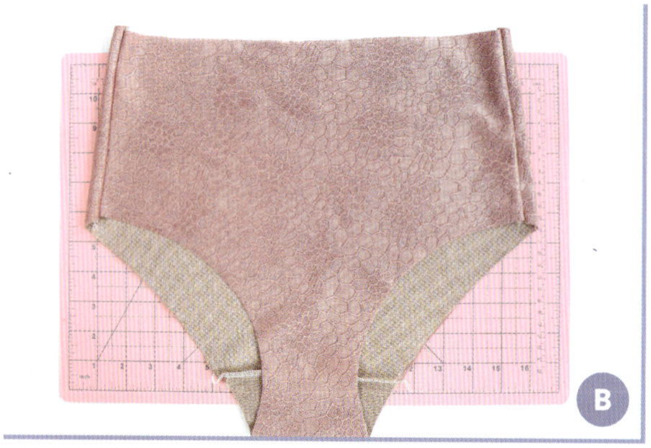

Sew Rubber Elastic

1. With the wrong side of the swimsuit bodice and bottom face up, lay rubber elastic on top so that the outer edge of the rubber elastic is aligned with the edge of the fabric. Serge (overlock) at armhole edges, front and back necklines, and leg openings. On armhole and leg openings, overlap the elastics ½″ (1.2cm) at the beginning and end. If you do not have a serger, you can sew the elastic down with a zigzag stitch approximately ⅜″ (0.9cm) wide. **C D**

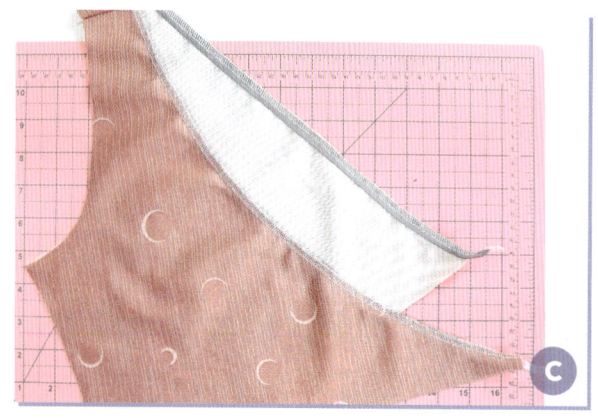

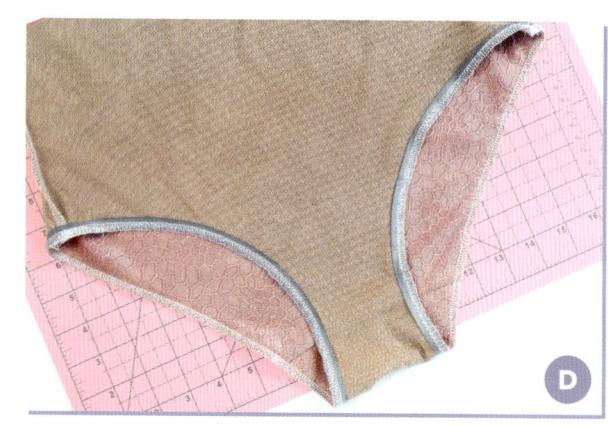

2. After, turn the rubber elastic to the wrong side of the fabric and sew a second pass using a zigzag stitch that is approximately ⅜″ (0.9mm) wide. **E F**

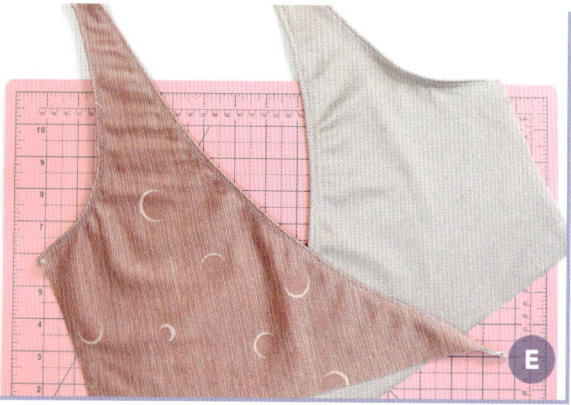

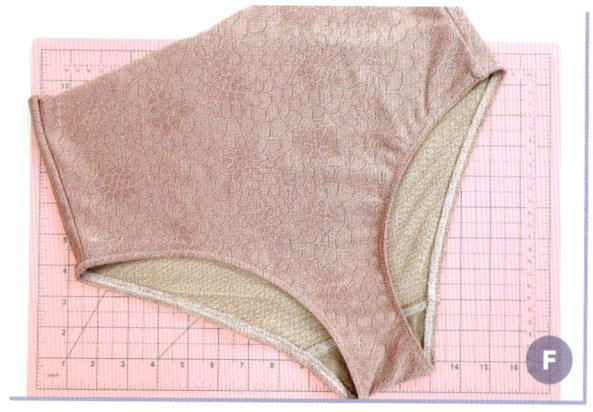

148   SEW LINGERIE

SWIM PROJECTS

Finish Assembling Bodice

1. With right sides facing, sew front bodice to back bodice at side seam. Serge (overlock) seam allowances. At this step, the two sides of the bodice (left and right) are not connected. They will be connected in the next steps when the bodice is attached to the bottom. **G**

Attach Bodice to Bottoms

1. With right sides facing and side seams aligned, pin bodice to bottoms. Sew together with a lightning stitch. Overlap stitches at beginning and end. Serge (overlock) seam allowances.

2. Sew down surplice (crossover) and center back opening to secure in place with a zigzag stitch that is ¼″ (6mm) wide. **H** **I**

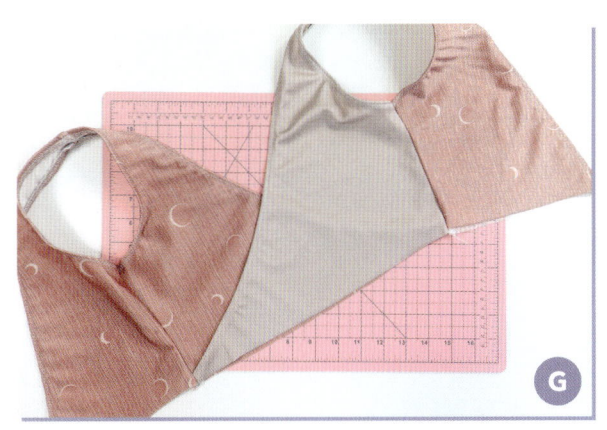

Sewing down front surplice

Sewing down back opening

HENRIETTA ONE PIECE

HALLIE *bikini*
· INTERMEDIATE ·

The Hallie bikini is a two piece swimsuit that features a scoop neckline with a V opening at the center front, and high waisted bikini bottoms. The edges are finished with FOE, and the bottom edge of the bikini top and the waistline edge of the bikini bottoms are finished with an elastic band. Use #halliebikini to share your make!

SWIM PROJECTS

Fabrics and Notions

MAIN FABRIC: LYCRA or other swimwear fabric

LINING FABRIC #1: Stretch mesh, power net, or Helenca

LINING FABRIC #2 SHEER CUP LINING

FOLD OVER ELASTIC: 5 yards (4.6m) 3/8″ (8mm) wide

WIDE BAND ELASTIC: 1½ yards (1.4m) 1″ (20mm) wide or wider

UNDERWIRE CHANNELING: ½ yard (46cm) 3/8″ (8mm) wide

V WIRE OPENING

FABRIC CHART	XS–L	XL–5X
Main Fabric	¾ yard (69cm)	1 yard (1m)
Lining Fabric #1	¾ yard (69cm)	1 yard (1m)
Lining Fabric #2	¼ yard (23cm)	¼ yard (23cm)

Tools

SEWING MACHINE WITH STRAIGHT AND ZIGZAG STITCH

POLYESTER THREAD

PINS

DUCK BILLED SCISSORS

ROTARY CUTTER

SPRAY ADHESIVE

SERGER *(optional)*

Scan this QR code or visit
tinyurl.com/11531-pattern10-downloads
to download and print the pattern pieces for this project.

HALLIE BIKINI

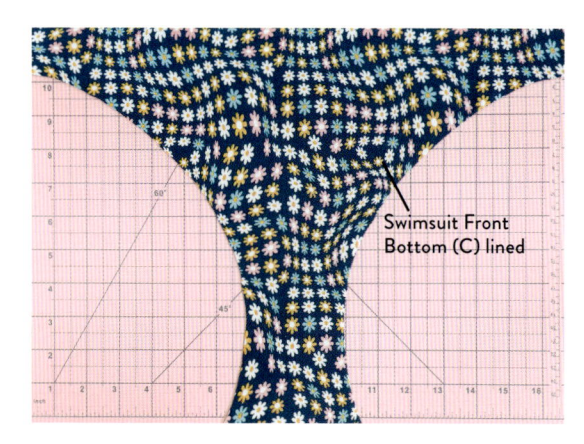

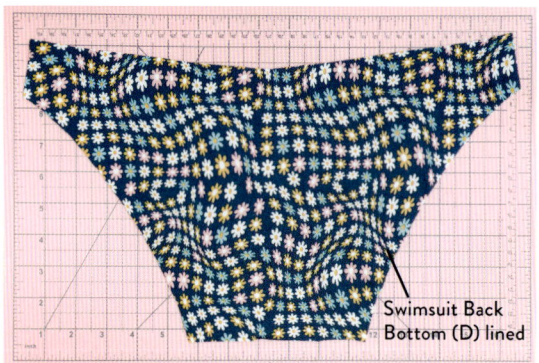

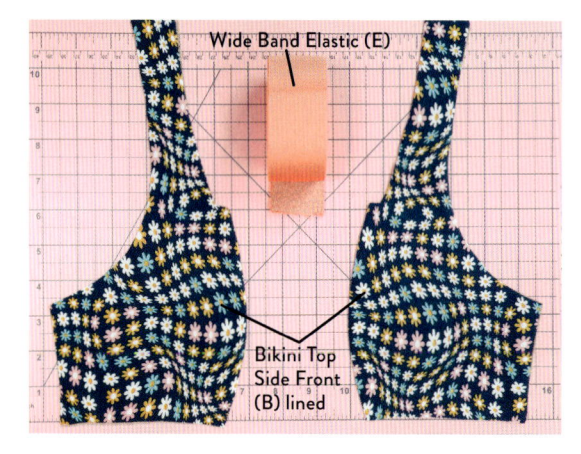

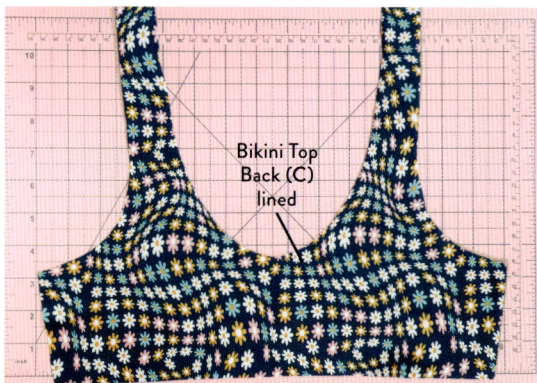

Cutting List

MAIN FABRIC: Bikini Top—Center Front (A), Bikini Top—Side Front (B), Bikini Top—Back (C), Bikini Bottom—Center Front (D), Bikini Bottom—Center Back (E)

LINING FABRIC #1: Bikini Top—Center Front (A), Bikini Top—Side Front (B), Bikini Top—Back (C), Bikini Bottom—Center Front (D), Bikini Bottom—Center Back (E)

LINING FABRIC #2: Bikini Top—Center Front (A)

TOP WIDE BAND WAISTBAND (F)

BOTTOM WIDE BAND WAISTBAND (G)

Notes on Project

All pattern pieces should be lined. Spray baste the main fabric to the lining fabric #1 using a temporary adhesive before starting to construct the garment. In the instructions, the fabrics are treated as one layer. Lining fabric #2 should remain separate. See Temporary Spray Adhesive (page 50). For additional finishing techniques without a serger, see Finishing Seams (page 53). Contrasting color threads are used to clearly show each step.

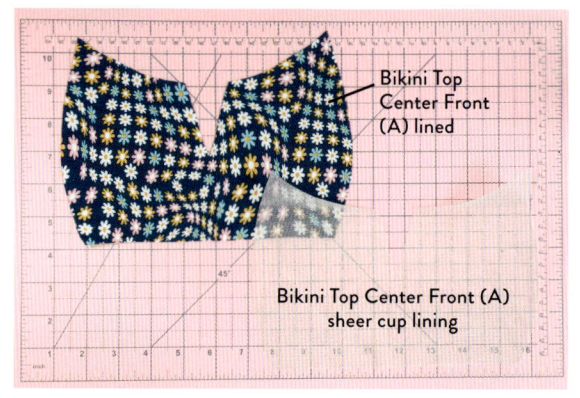

152 SEW LINGERIE

Sew V Opening

1. With right sides of front bodice main fabric and lining fabric #1 (which are spray basted together) and lining #2 facing, sew along the edges of the V opening using a straight stitch. When you get close to the "V" (about ½" or 1.2cm), reduce stitch length slightly (approximately 1.5mm). **A**

2. Use scissors to clip to, but not through, where the stitches intersect at the "V". Sew an edge stitch along either side of the "V". **B C**

3. Flip lining fabric #2 to the wrong side. Use an iron on a synthetic setting and with steam to press in place. **D**

HALLIE BIKINI

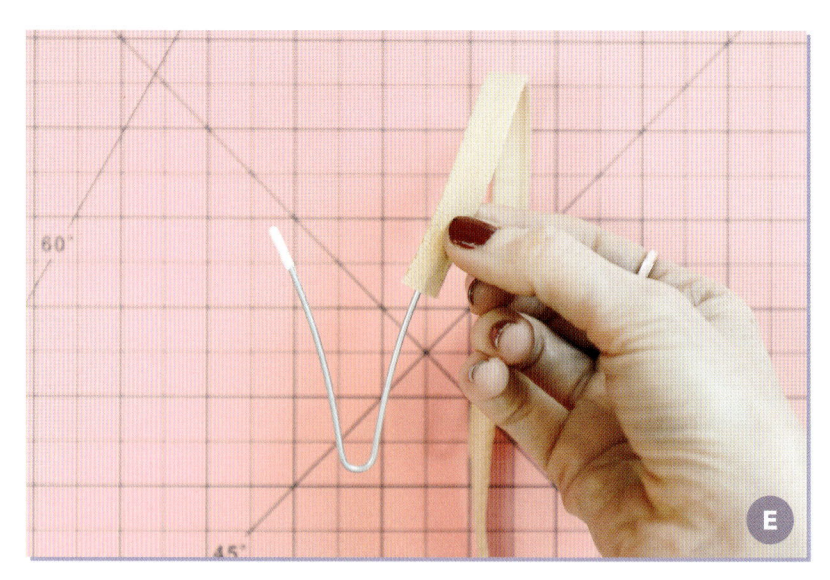

4. Insert "V" underwire into underwire channeling. There should be extra space at top of the channeling. Then place "V" underwire and channeling in between lining #2 and lining #1 and main fabric. Pin in place. Optional: Sew a small tack at the top edge through all layers to keep it in place. Spray adhesive in between sheer cup lining and main fabric layers to adhere them together so that the fabric layers lay flat and do not shift. **E**–**G**

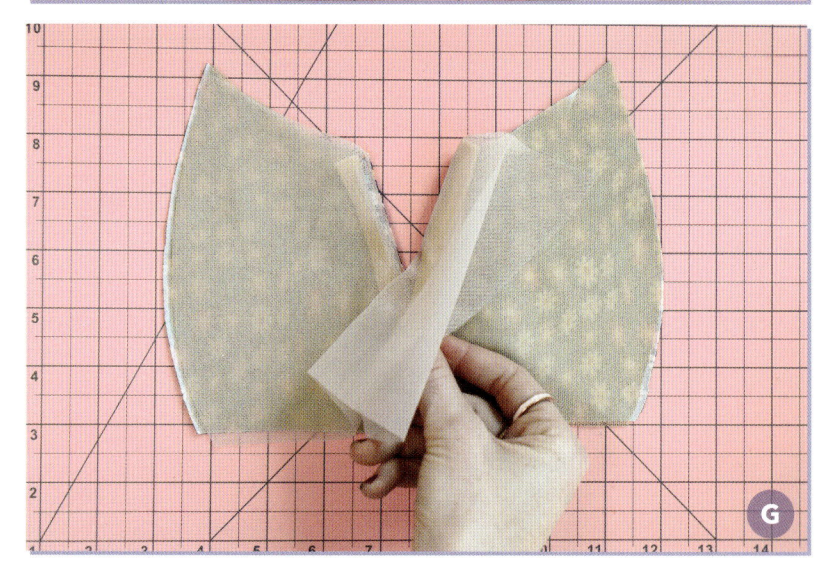

154 SEW LINGERIE

SWIM PROJECTS

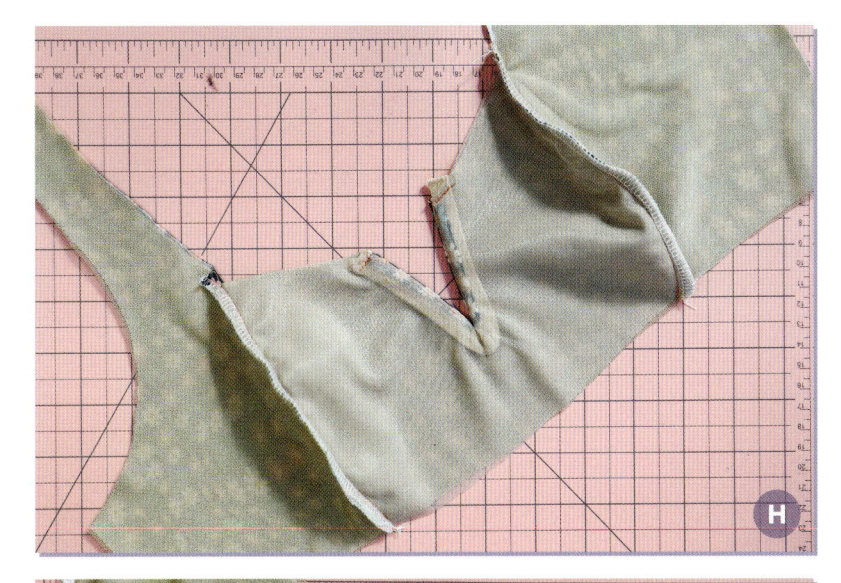

Assemble Bikini Top and Bottom

1. With right sides facing, sew bikini top—center front (A) to bikini top—side front (B). With right sides facing, sew bikini bottom—center front (D) to bikini bottom—center back (E) at side seam and crotch seam. Backstitch at beginning and end. Serge (overlock) seam allowances. **H I**

2. Sew bikini top front to bikini top—back (C) at shoulder seam and side seam using the same method as in Step 1. **J**

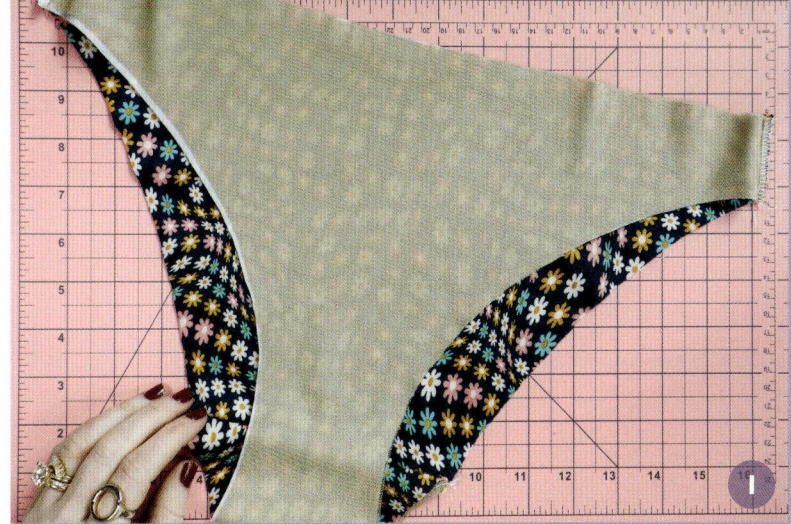

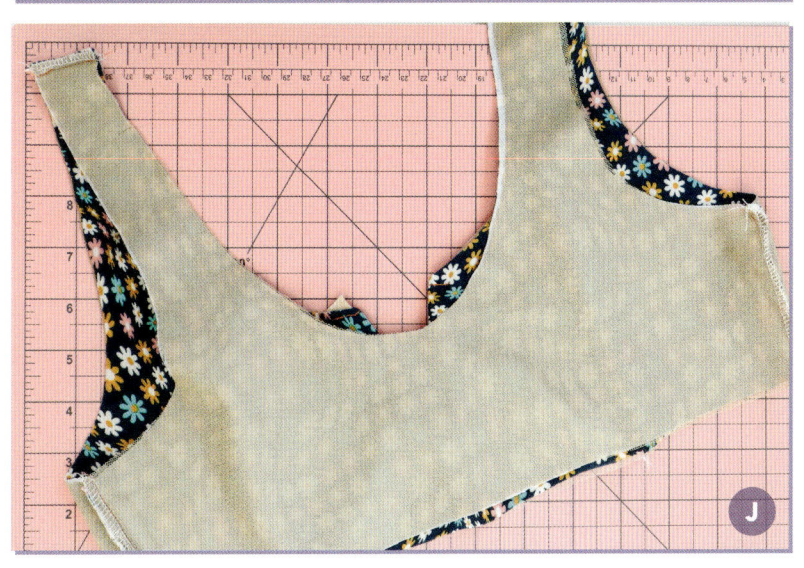

HALLIE BIKINI   155

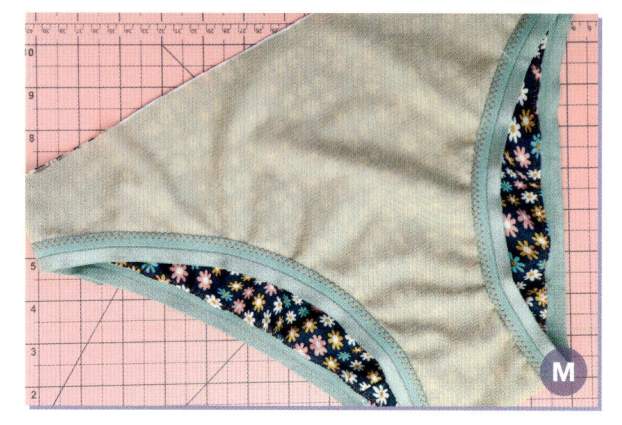

Sew Fold Over Elastic

1. With the wrong side of the bikini face up, lay fold over elastic (FOE) on top so that the center of the FOE is aligned with the edge of the fabric. Sew FOE to armhole and neckline edges on bikini top and leg openings on bikini bottom using a zigzag stitch that is approximately ¼″ (0.6cm) wide. Zigzag stitches should be as close to the outer edge of the FOE as possible. Overlap zigzag stitches ½″ (1.2cm) at beginning and end on armhole and legs. On the front neckline, wrap the FOE around the edge to the front side and stitch down. **K**–**M**

2. Trim seam allowances as close to stitches as possible using duck billed scissors. After, turn the FOE to the right side of the fabric and sew a second pass that is approximately ¼″ (0.6cm) wide. Zigzag stitches should be as close to the outer edge of the FOE as possible. **N O**

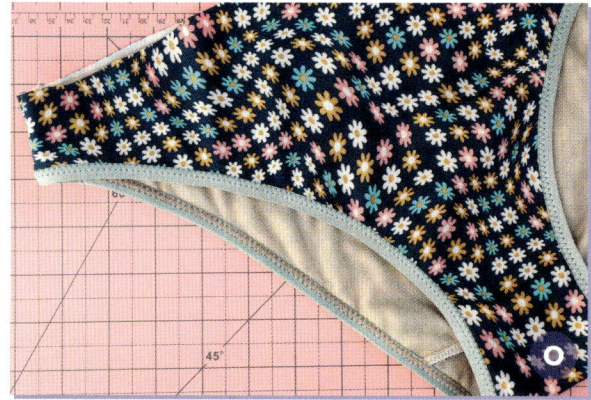

156 SEW LINGERIE

Sew Wide Band Elastic and Attach to Bikini

1. Serge (overlock) bottom edge of the bikini top and the waistline on bikini bottom.

2. With right sides facing, sew the short ends of wide band elastics with a straight stitch. Backstitch at beginning and end. Wide band elastic should now be a circle.

3. Finger press seams open and on one edge, sew a straight stitch back and forth 3–4 times. This side will not be sewn to the bikini, so its purpose is to keep seam allowance secure and in place. **P**

4. Overlap the wide band elastic and the bottom edge of the bikini top ¼″ (6mm). The wide band elastic should be on top. Pin together all the way around. Repeat on the bikini bottom waistband.

5. Sew wide band elastic to bottom of bikini top and waistband of bikini bottom with a zigzag stitch that is approximately ¼″ (6mm) wide. Overlap zigzag ¼″ (0.6cm)–½″ (1.2cm) at beginning/end. **Q**

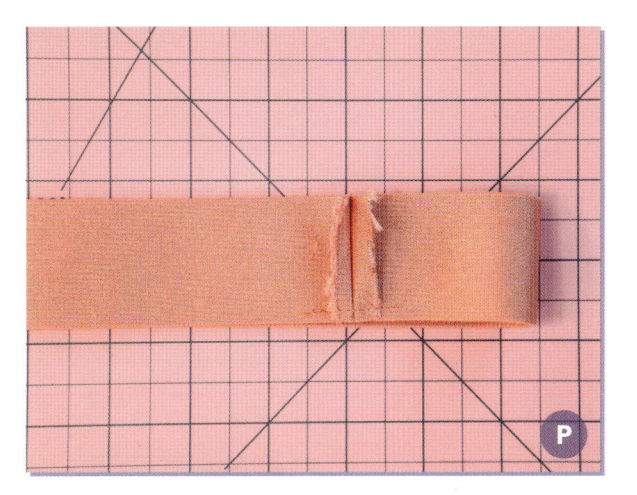

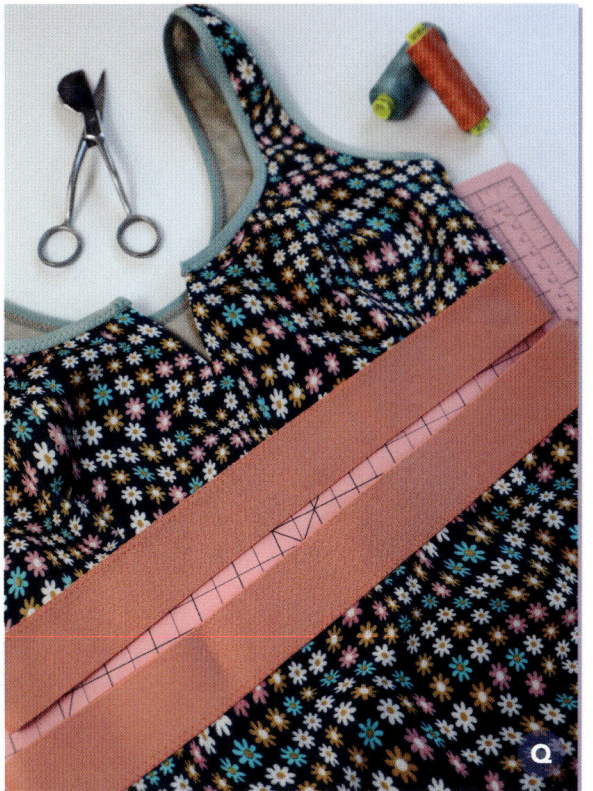

ADVANCED

GODIVA *underwire bodysuit*

The Godiva is a thong bodysuit with a full band underwire bra. The bra cups and the frame are the same as the Rey, showing that you can easily use your bra patterns as a base to make other designs. The Godiva also has paneling on the front bodysuit, great for fun color blocking and pattern mixing. A sheer, mesh back provides a flexible, comfortable fit. Use the size charts on page 145 to select your size. Use #godivaunderwirebodysuit to share your make!

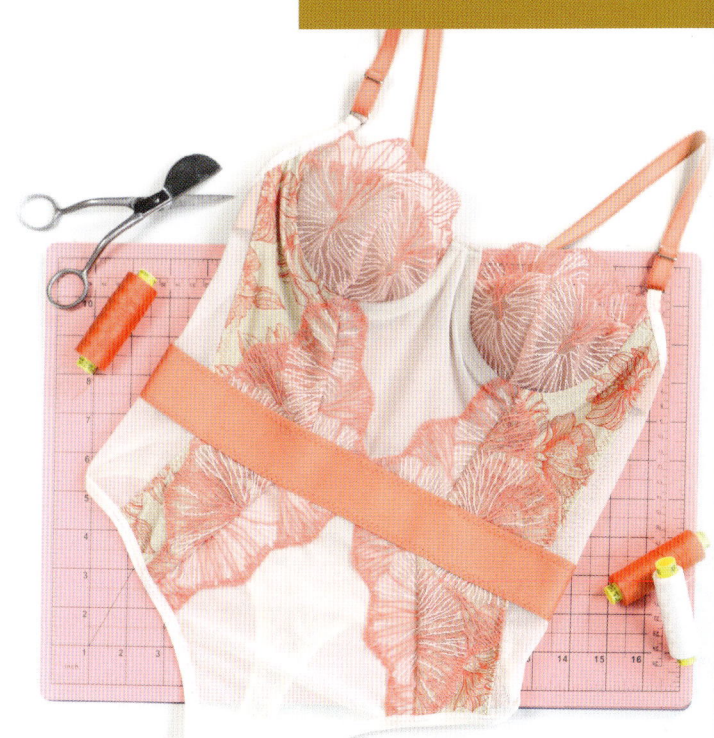

BODYSUIT PROJECT

Fabrics and Notions

MAIN FABRIC: LYCRA, stretch all over lace, or stretch galloon lace at least 9″ (22.9cm) wide

COMBO FABRIC #1: Non stretch galloon lace at least 9″ (22.9cm) wide

COMBO FABRIC #2: Stretch mesh

LINING FABRIC #1: Sheer cup lining, 15 denier tricot or bra tulle

LINING FABRIC #2:
- Stretch mesh for band sizes 28–34, cup sizes A–C
- Power net for band sizes 28–34, cup sizes D+ and band sizes 36–44, all cup sizes

FOLD OVER ELASTIC: 6 yards (5.5m) ⅝″ (16mm) wide (⅜″ or 8mm when folded)

WAISTBAND ELASTIC: 1½ yards (1.4m) 1⅝″ (40mm) wide

SHOULDER STRAP ELASTIC:
- 1½ yards (1.4m) ½″ (12mm) wide for band sizes 28–34, cup sizes A–C
- 1½ yards (1.4m) ¾″ (18mm) wide or wider for band sizes 28–34, cup sizes D+ and band sizes 36–44, all cup sizes

RINGS AND SLIDERS: 1 pair, width should match the width of shoulder strap elastic

UNDERWIRE CHANNELING: 1¼ yards (1.2m) ⅜″ (8mm) wide

CLASSIC UNDERWIRE: 1 pair of classic underwires

PLASTIC BONING: ½ yard (46cm) ⅛″ (4mm)

COTTON JERSEY SWATCH FOR GUSSET

FABRIC CHART	XS–L	XL–5X
Main Fabric	¾ yard (69cm)	1 yard (1m)
Combo Fabric #1	3 yards (2.8m)	3½ yards (3.3m)
Combo Fabric #2	⅞ yard (80cm)	1 yard (1m)
Lining Fabric #1	⅓ yard (31cm)	½ yard (46cm)
Lining Fabric #2	⅞ yard (80cm)	1 yard (1m)

Tools

SEWING MACHINE WITH STRAIGHT AND ZIGZAG STITCH

BALLPOINT, STRETCH OR MICROTEX NEEDLE (size will depend on the thickness of the fabric)

POLYESTER THREAD

PINS

ROTARY CUTTER

DUCK BILLED SCISSORS

SPRAY ADHESIVE *(optional)*

SERGER *(optional)*

Scan this QR code or visit
tinyurl.com/11531-pattern11-downloads
to download and print the pattern pieces for this project.

GODIVA UNDERWIRE BODYSUIT

Cutting List

MAIN FABRIC: Side Front Frame (E), Panty Side Panel (G)

COMBO FABRIC #1: Center Front Cup Lower (A), Side Front Cup Lower (B), Top Cup (C), Side Lace Panel—Panty (M), Center Front Lace Panel—Panty (N), Side Lace Panel—Top (O), Center Front Lace Panel—Top (P)

COMBO FABRIC #2: Center Front Frame (D), Center Front Panty (F), Back Band (I), Center Back Panty (H)

LINING FABRIC #1: Center Front Cup Lower (A), Side Front Cup Lower (B), Center Front Frame (D)

LINING FABRIC #2: Side Front Frame (E), Panty Side Panel (G), Center Front Panty (F)

COTTON JERSEY: Gusset (L)

SHOULDER STRAP ELASTIC (K)

BAND ELASTIC (J)

Notes on Project

Pattern pieces A, B, D, E, G, and F should be lined with sheer cup lining, 15 denier tricot, bra tulle, stretch mesh, or power net. Spray baste the main fabric to the lining using a temporary adhesive before starting to construct the garment for all pattern pieces except A and B. In the instructions, the fabrics and linings are treated as one layer, except pieces A and B. See Temporary Spray Adhesive (page 50). Whenever instructed to serge a seam allowance, if you do not have a serger, you can skip this step and leave the edges unfinished or push seam allowances to one side and sew them down with a zigzag stitch that is ¼″ (0.6cm) wide. For additional finishing techniques without a serger, see Finishing Seams (page 53). Contrasting color threads are used to clearly show each step.

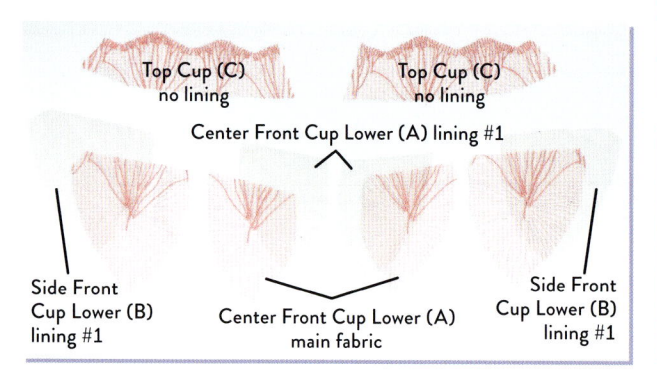

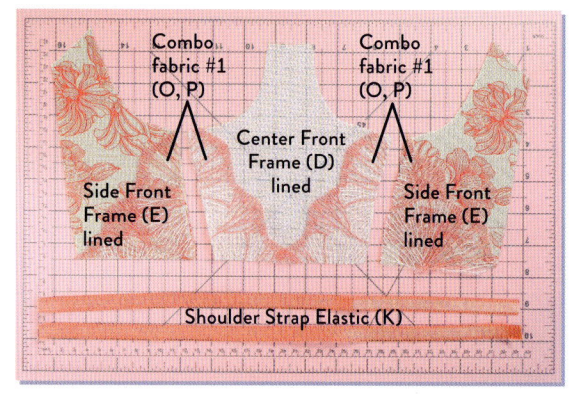

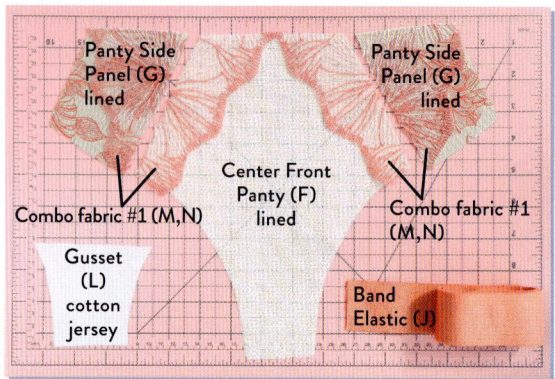

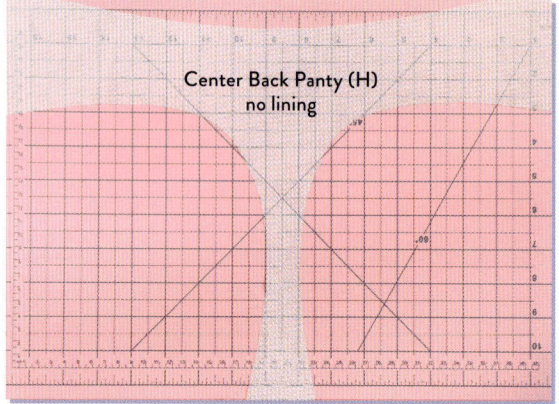

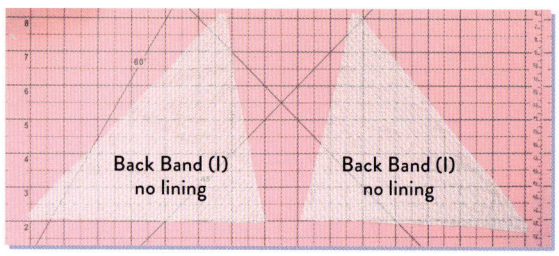

160 SEW LINGERIE

BODYSUIT PROJECT

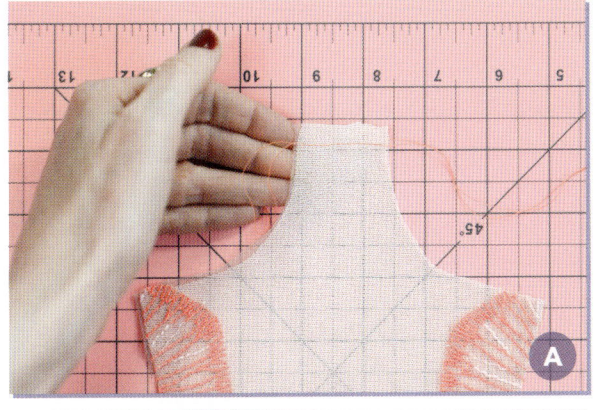

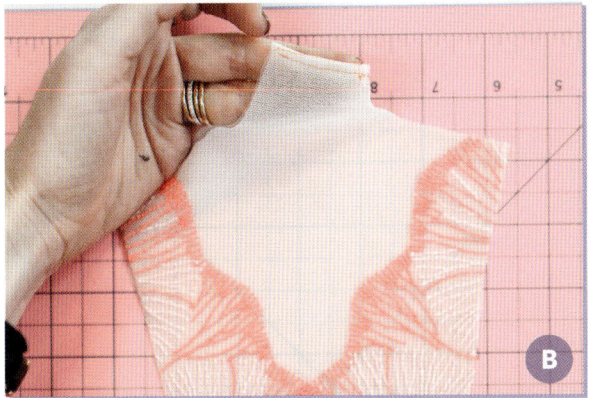

Combo Fabric

1. Lay Side Lace Panel—Panty (M), Center Front Lace Panel—Panty (N), Side Lace Panel—Top (O), Center Front Lace Panel—Top (P) on top of the main fabric. Spray baste to the right side of the main fabric. Refer to images of the cutting list.

Lace can be sewn down before construction begins, or after the front frame and the front panty are assembled. Whether sewing lace before construction begins or after the front frame and the front panty are assembled, follow the directions in Place Lace Side Panel from the Millie Panty (page 84).

Assemble Bra Cups

1. Follow the instructions in the Rey Underwire Bra project to Assemble Bra Cups (page 126).

Assemble Front Frame and Front Panty

1. Sew a straight stitch ¼″ (0.6cm) from the top edge of the center front frame at the center front. Do not backstitch at beginning or end and leave approximately 3″ (8cm) of thread hanging on either side. **A**

2. Fold down the seam allowance along the stitch line and pin in place. The stitch line is not integral to the bra construction—it's a guide to help fold down the fabric. So, if you find it difficult to make this stitch, you can skip it, and fold down the fabric without sewing first. Sew down the seam allowance with a straight stitch. **B**

3. With right sides facing, sew the center front frame to both side front frames, and the center front panty to both panty side panels with a straight stitch. Backstitch at the beginning and end. Press seams open using an iron set to a synthetic setting and leave the edges raw. **C**

GODIVA UNDERWIRE BODYSUIT

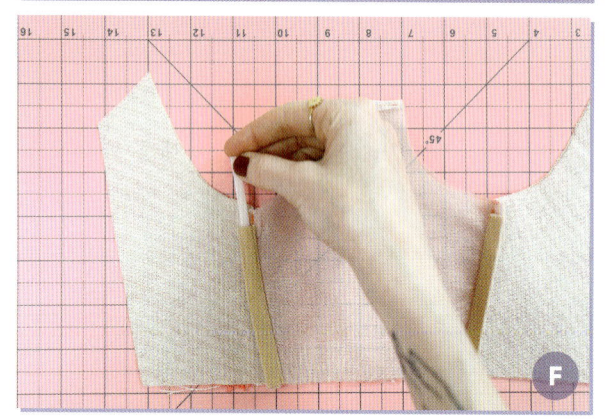

4. With the wrong side of the front frame and the front panty facing up, fold both so that the seam allowances are pointing in one direction and the bodysuit is pointing in the other direction. Place channeling over seam allowance with the left edge of the channeling extending past the seam line ⅛″ (0.3cm). Before sewing, do a quick check and make sure that the channeling is oriented in a way that it will be flipped towards the side seam, not flipped towards the center front. **D**

5. Sew the channeling to the seam allowances approximately ⅛″ (0.3cm) from the left edge of the channeling with a straight stitch So, you should be stitching **on the seam line only**. Stop stitching ⅜″ (8cm) below the bra cups to allow for channeling to be sewn in a later step. Stitch all the way to the end on all other edges. Insert plastic boning into channeling on the frame only. Plastic boning should be ¼″ (0.6cm) shorter at the top and the bottom edges. Plastic boning goes inside the channeling, not in between the channeling and the fabric. **E F G**

Attach Bra Cups and Channeling

Next, follow the instructions in *only* Attach Bra Cups (page 129) and Attach Channeling (page 130) in the Rey Underwire Bra, as the steps are the same. Then, return here to continue the Godiva. **H**

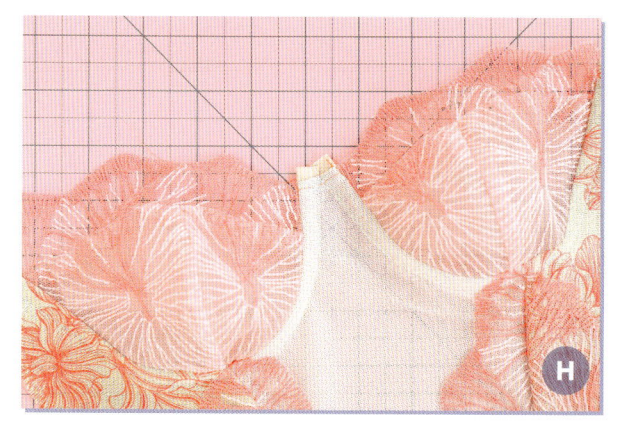

SEW LINGERIE

BODYSUIT PROJECT

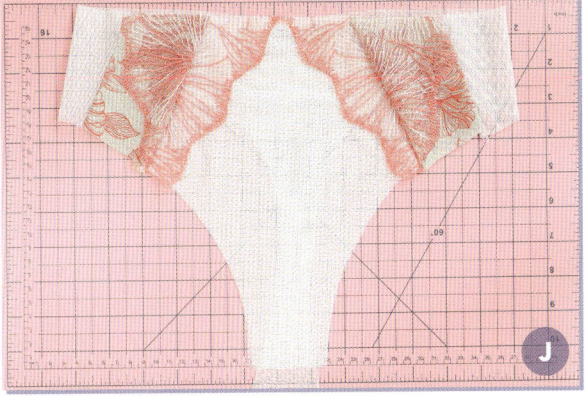

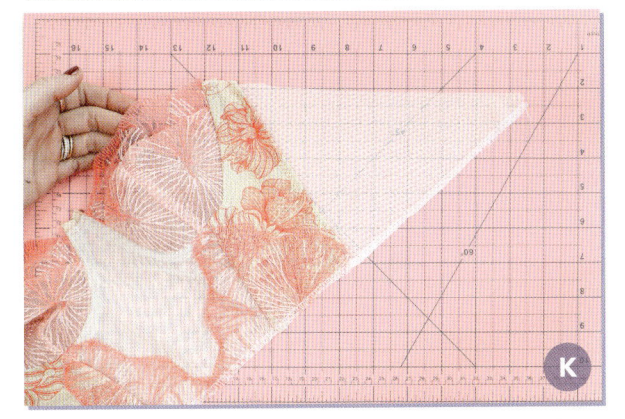

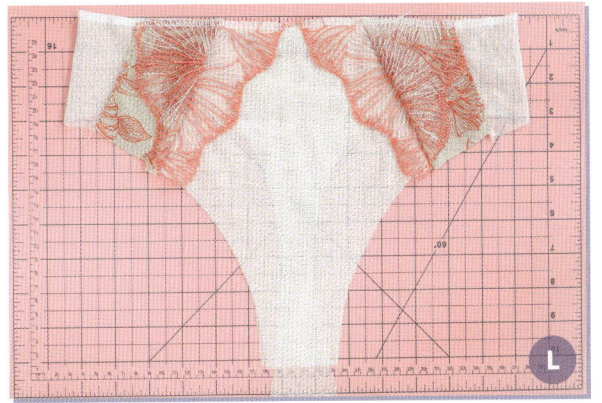

Sew Front Frame to Back Band and Front Panty to Back Panty

1. With right sides facing, sew the front frame to the back band. Repeat on the other side. With the right sides facing, sew the front panty to the back panty at the side seam with a straight stitch. Backstitch at beginning and end. Serge (overlock) seam allowances. **I J**

2. Serge (overlock) the bottom edge of the top and the waistline on the panty. If you do not have a serger, you can skip this step and leave the edges unfinished. **K L**

Sew Fold Over Elastic

1. With the wrong side of the frame and the back band face up, lay fold over elastic (FOE) on top of the back hand and edge of the front frame so that the center of the FOE is aligned with the edge of the fabric. Sew FOE with a zigzag stitch that is approximately ¼" (0.6cm) wide. Zigzag stitches should be as close to the edge of the FOE as possible. At the strap points, the FOE should extend past the fabric 1" (2.5cm). **M**

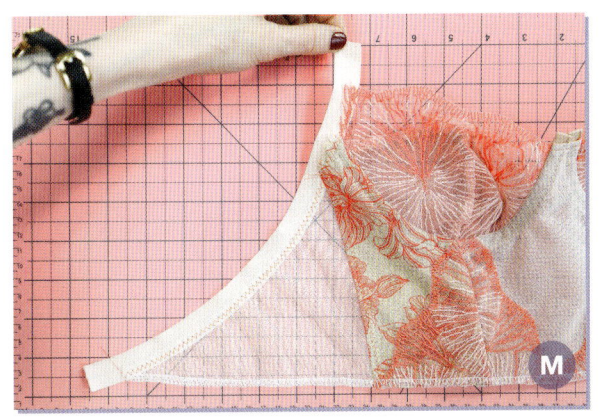

GODIVA UNDERWIRE BODYSUIT 163

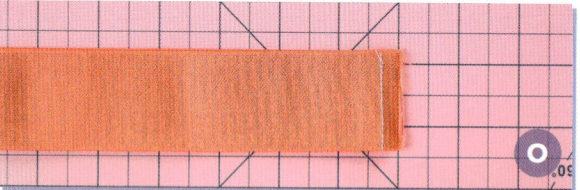

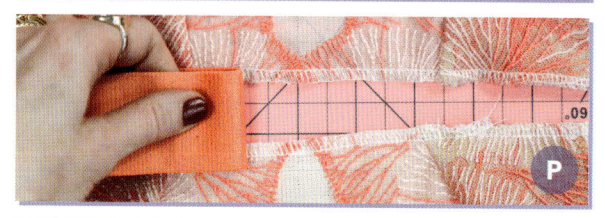

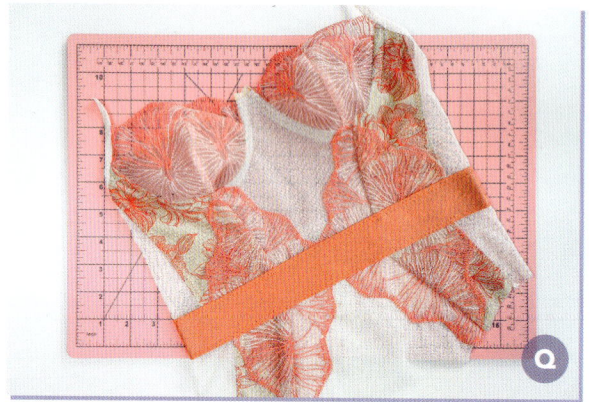

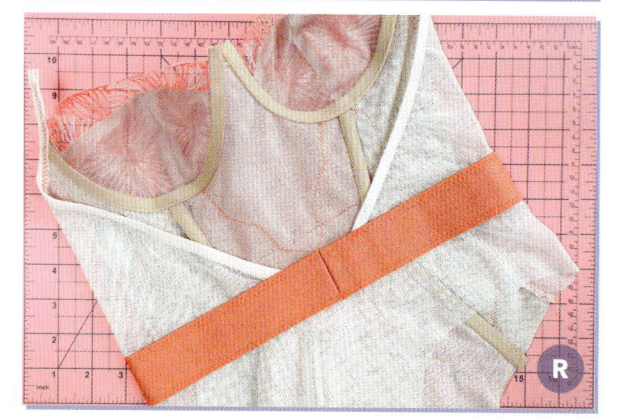

2. After sewing the first "pass", or line of zigzag stitches, trim seam allowances as close to stitches as possible using duck billed scissors. After, turn the FOE to the right side of the fabric and sew a second pass that is approximately ¼" (0.6cm) wide. Just like the first pass, zigzag stitches should be as close to the edge of the FOE as possible. **N**

Attach Band Elastic

1. With right sides facing, sew short ends of band elastic with a straight stitch. Backstitch at beginning and end. Wide band elastic should now be a circle. **O**

2. Finger press seams open and on one edge, sew a straight stitch back and forth 3–4 times. This side will not be sewn to bodysuit, so its purpose is to keep seam allowance secure and in place.

3. With the seam on the band elastic aligned with center back panty, overlap the band elastic with both the frame/back band and the panty ¼" (0.6cm) on each side. The band elastic should be on top. Pin together all the way around. The back band will not extend all the way to the center back. **P**

4. Sew the band elastic with a zigzag stitch that is approximately ¼" (0.6mm) wide and close to top and bottom edges. Overlap zigzag the ¼" (0.6cm)–½" (1.2cm) at the beginning/end. **Q**–**S**

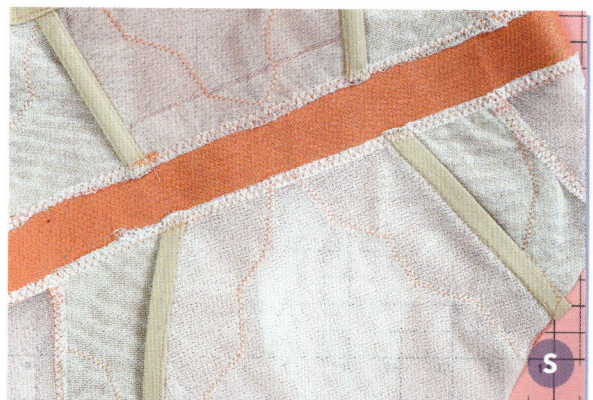

164 SEW LINGERIE

BODYSUIT PROJECT

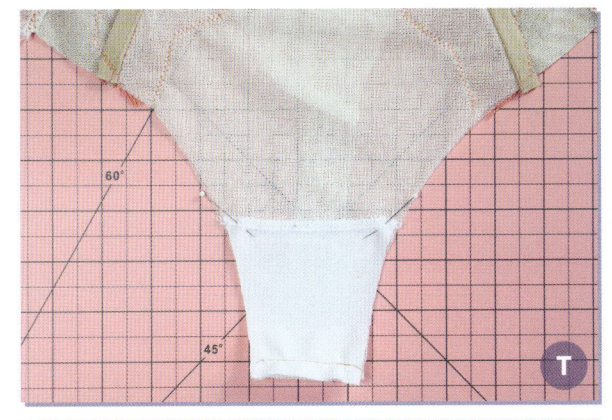

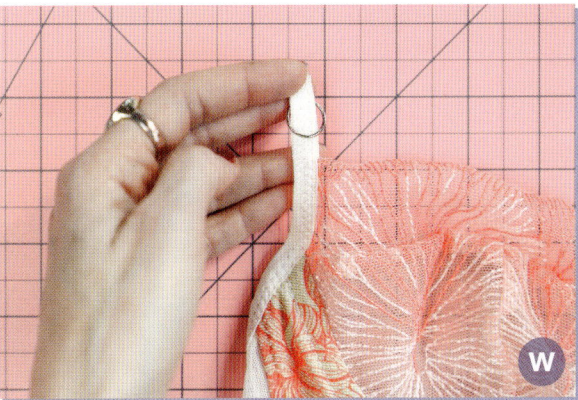

Serge and Place Gusset

1. Serge front edge of gusset. If you do not have a serger, you can skip this step and leave the edges unfinished.

2. With the wrong side of the gusset facing the wrong side of the front panty, pin in place. Sew front panty to back panty with a straight stitch. Backstitch at beginning and end. **T**

Sew FOE at Leg Opening

1. With the wrong side of the bodysuit face up, lay FOE on top so that the center of the FOE is aligned with the edge of the fabric. Sew FOE with a zigzag stitch that is approximately ¼" (0.6cm) wide. Zigzag stitches should be as close to the edge of the FOE as possible. Overlap elastics ½" (1.2cm) at the beginning and end. **U**

2. After sewing the first "pass", or line of zigzag stitches, trim seam allowances as close to stitches as possible using duck billed scissors. After, turn the FOE to the right side of the fabric and sew a second pass that is approximately ¼" (0.6cm) wide. Just like the first pass, zigzag stitches should be as close to the edge of the FOE as possible. **V**

Make and Attach Shoulder Straps

1. Put rings through strap points and turn back ½" (1.2cm). Sew a straight stitch back and forth 3–4 times as close to the ring as possible. Then sew another line of stitching ¼" (0.6cm) below using the same method. Trim close to stitching. **W** **X**

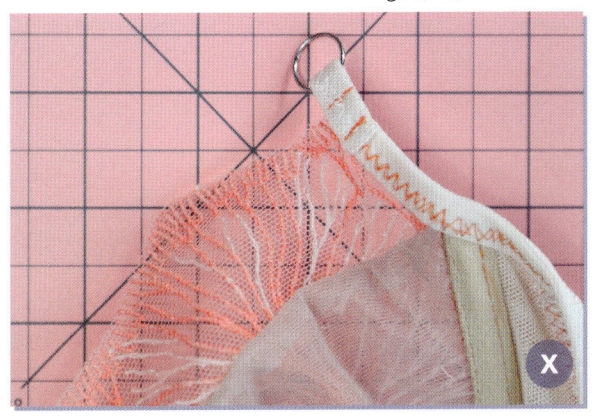

GODIVA UNDERWIRE BODYSUIT 165

2. Feed one end of the shoulder strap elastic through the bottom of one slider, over the center bar, and then down through the other side. It should look like a belt buckle with one short end and one long end. Pull the strap flat in the slider, and fold ¾″ (1.9cm) of elastic around the back of the slider to touch the long elastic on the other side. Repeat for the other strap. **Y**

3. Sew a straight stitch back and forth 3–4 times as close to the slider as possible. It is difficult to sew this step with the slider underneath the presser foot, so if your machine has this setting, move the needle position all the way to the right. This will allow you to butt the edge of the slider against the edges of the presser foot and stitch really close to it. **Z**

4. Weave unstitched sides of the strap elastics through rings from back to front. Then weave up and over the center bar of the slider again just like in Step 2. The "standard" length from slider to ring is approximately 2″ (5cm). **A**

5. With the back of the bodysuit right side face up, lay shoulder strap elastic underneath the band elastic at center back. Strap elastics should be on top of one another. Sew shoulder straps to band elastic with a straight stitch. Stitch back and forth 3–4 times. If there is any elastic hanging below the stitch, trim it close to stitching. **B**

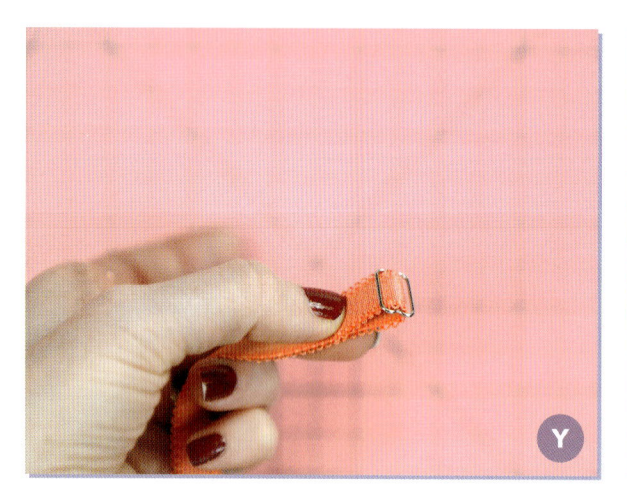

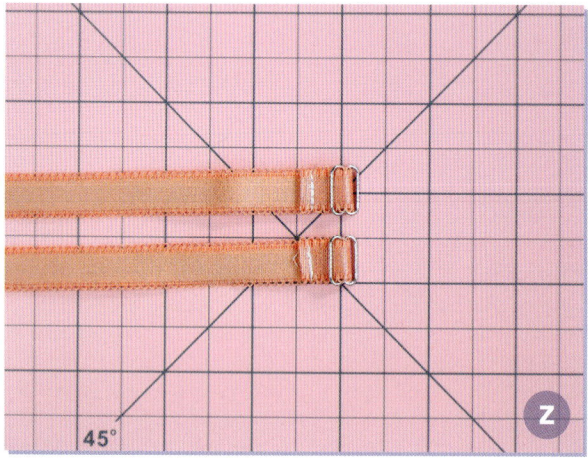

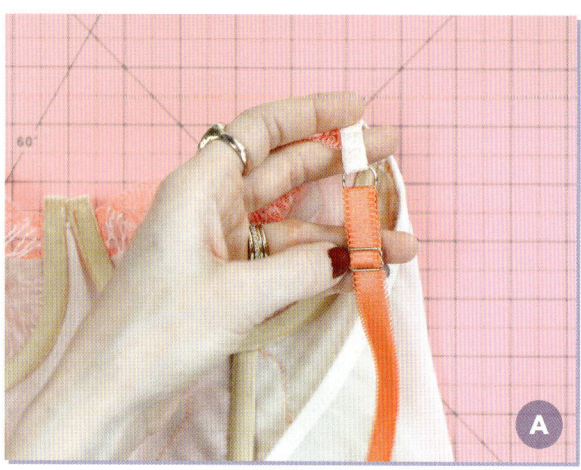

166 SEW LINGERIE

BODYSUIT PROJECT

Insert and Secure Channeling At Center Front

1. Insert underwires into channeling on the cups. **C**

2. With the right or wrong side of the bra facing up, stitch back and forth 3–4 with straight stitch times approximately ⅛″ (0.3cm)–¼″ (0.6cm) below the center front edge to close off the channeling and prevent the underwires from coming out. Trim the channeling so it is flush with the center front edge. **D**

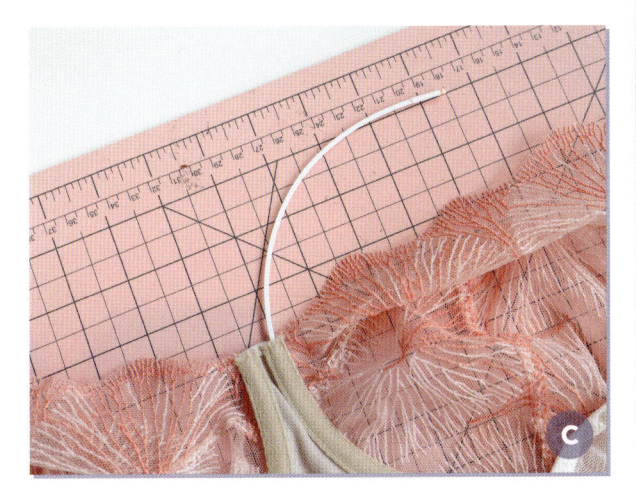

NURSING AND MASTECTOMY BRAS

Nursing and mastectomy bras are two niches within bra making. The great thing about both is that they can easily be achieved with simple alterations to your me-made bras and the patterns in this book.

Nursing Bras

Nursing bras unclip or pull open to make it easy for mothers to bring their baby to their breasts to feed. There are several different styles of nursing bralettes, and each mother has their own preference. Fiber content can make a nursing bra incredibly resilient and less likely to stretch out, removable pads can prevent leakage, and slings can help with keeping a bra in place while a mother is feeding. There are so many options for moms!

What to Look For

When it comes to nursing, breastfeeding and pumping, there are a lot of ups and downs—literally. You may experience discomfort and engorgement a few days after birth, and you may feel sore once you start breastfeeding. You may be tempted to purchase a store-bought bra in a larger size, but nursing and pumping bras are worth the investment. Not only do they allow for easy maneuvering, they also have special features that are designed with new moms in mind.

Flexibility: You can go up and down a cup size before and after feeding, so having stretch fabric is essential. They will accommodate these fluctuations as opposed to a bra made with a non stretch fabric.

Comfort and Sizing: If you're one of those people whose breasts take on a new shape before and after nursing, then having a pattern that fits a wide range of sizes will come in handy. One of the many things I love about bra making is that it only takes a few hours to sew a bra. So after you stop breastfeeding, you can whip up a new bra (maybe even a new lingerie wardrobe!) in no time.

Leak Protection: Many moms will say that they went from washing their bras once a week or once every two weeks to almost every day. Between feeding, spit up, and throw up, there's often some sort of liquid on new moms. Adding foam cups can help with leakage so that breast milk doesn't show through your clothes.

SEW LINGERIE

Types of Nursing Bras

Drop Down Cups (or Feeding): The most common type. The bra cups have clips, poppers or hooks at the top so you can drop them down from the strap to feed your baby easily. Many have slings as well to keep the bra upright while feeding. Some styles have flaps, so only part of the cup comes off the strap, which is ideal if you prefer more privacy while breastfeeding in public.

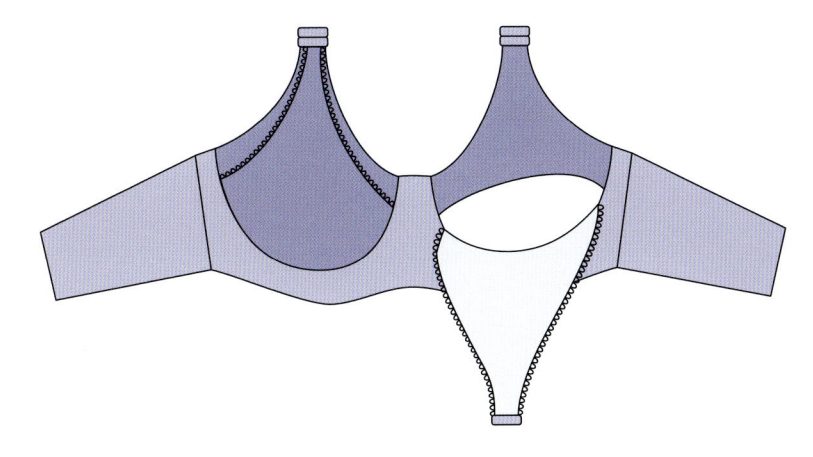

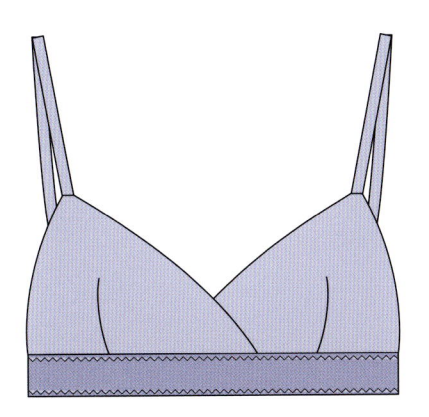

Cross Over: This kind of nursing bra has cups that cross over each other at the center front so you can pull the cup to one side.

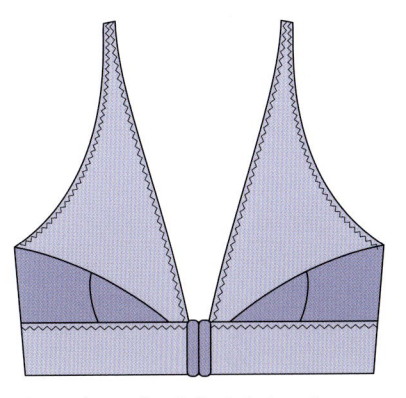

Front Closure: This kind of nursing bra has a closure at the center front—the Margo bralette is a perfect example. The front closure is the same concept as clips on a drop down bra—it allows a person to unhook the bralette and push it to the side to feed their baby. A horizontal sling can be added using strap elastics from side seam to side seam, which act as a sling. Without a sling, this type of nursing bra doesn't make for discreet nursing, because breasts can feel exposed when the bra opens.

No hardware

Night Bra: A night bra (or sleep bra) is a lighter bra with no hooks or hard seams. It might have a crossover front design so you can slip your breast out easily for a night feed.

PREGNANCY, NURSING, AND PUMPING BRAS—WHAT'S THE DIFFERENCE?

The primary difference between a nursing and pregnancy bra is that a nursing bra comes with special openings for quick, easy breastfeeding accessibility. Pumping bras allow you to keep the breast pump in place while using it; they attach to your breast, leaving your hands free. These are typically made with some sort of "X" structure, which allows you to pull away the fabric to provide pumping access.

NURSING AND MASTECTOMY BRAS

When to Buy a Nursing Bra

The best time to buy or make a nursing bra is around 36 weeks, because it is usually when you are the largest. As your size decreases after the birth, the bra should be fitted to its widest setting so you can use its tighter settings after birth. A set of (or more) hooks in the band is ideal because it allows for flexibility.

Adding Foam Cups

There could be several reasons for adding foam cups to a bralette, even if they aren't for nursing. They can provide a nice shape, add support/comfort/coverage, or prevent nipples from showing through.

What is Polylaminate Foam?

There are different names and types of foam that you can use, including bra foam, foam bra padding, cut and sew sheet foam, or sheet foam. Generally speaking, polylaminate foam is a layer of foam that has been laminated with fabric on one or both sides. The thicknesses, qualities, and types of fabric lamination can vary—my favorite is 1/8" thick polylaminate foam.

Using Polylaminate Foam

The number one thing to keep in mind with foam is bulk. Polylaminate foam is bulky! So, you want to eliminate seam allowances when possible. You may be asking, "If you eliminate the seam allowances, how the heck do you sew it?" Great question. The answer is, polylaminate foam usually isn't seamed in the traditional way. It is normally butted together and sewn with a zig-zag stitch.

Polylaminate Versus Pre Molded Cups

By drafting and sewing foam cup pattern pieces, you are guaranteed that the shape of the foam is going to match the shape of the bra cup. If you purchase a pre molded cup, you run the risk that it won't be the same shape or size. However, molded cups provide a non-permanent solution. So if you're looking for something to use just while nursing, this would be a good option.

Drafting and Sewing Foam Cups for the Brooklyn Bralette

The following instructions will replace Attach Pattern Pieces (page 98). After completing these steps, proceed to Sew Fold Over Elastic (FOE) (page 99).

1. Cut main fabric, lining fabric, and polylaminate foam for the center front and side front bralette pieces. Remove seam allowances from the vertical seam on the polylaminate foam only. **A**

2. With right sides facing, sew center front bralette to side front bralette with a straight stitch. Backstitch at the beginning and end. Leave seam allowances unfinished. **B**

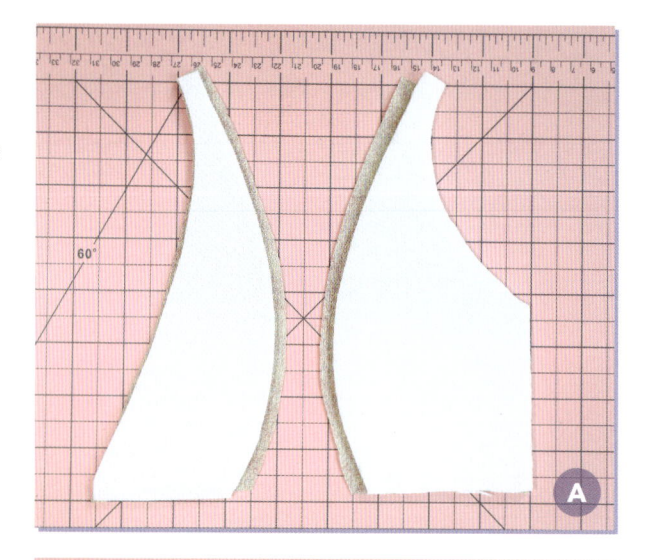

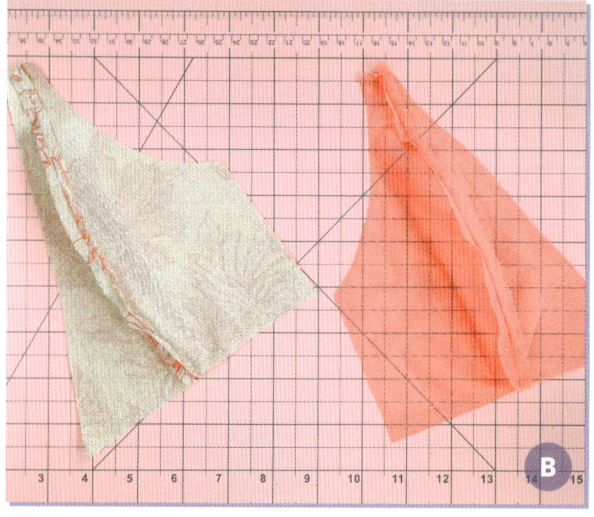

170 SEW LINGERIE

3. Butt the edges of the vertical seam on the polylaminate foam cups and sew together using a wide zig zag stitch that is at least ½" (12mm) or wider. **C D**

4. Place polylaminate foam cups in between the main fabric and lining fabric. Spray adhesive such as Odif 505 to keep the layers in place and prevent shifting. Proceed with constructing the remainder of the Brooklyn bralette according to the instructions. **E–G**

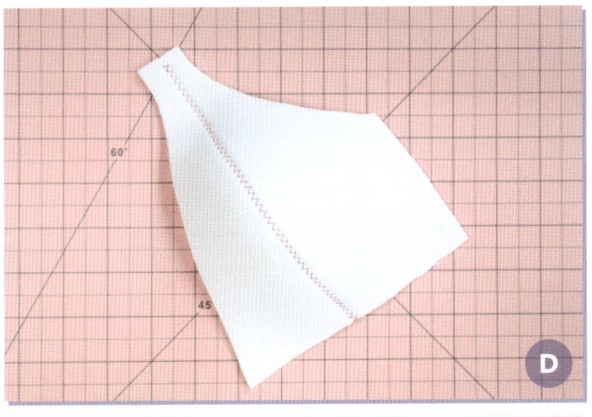

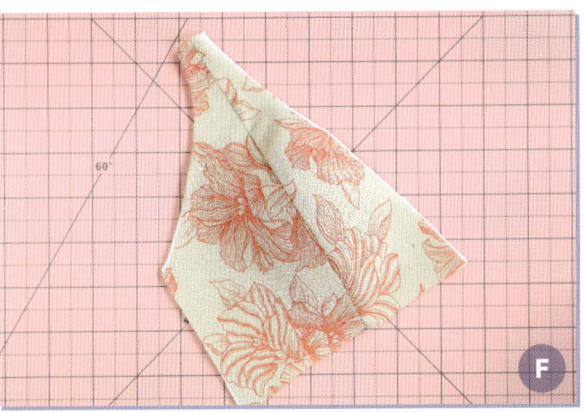

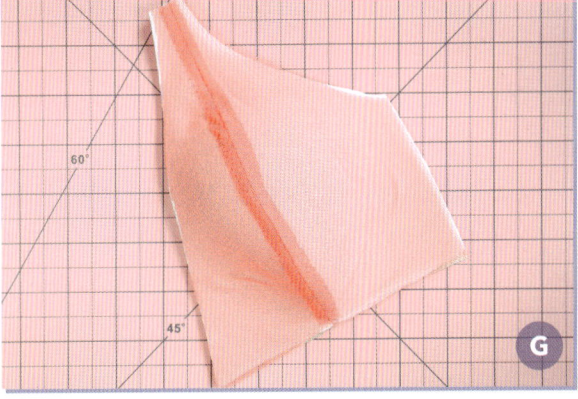

NURSING AND MASTECTOMY BRAS 171

Anatomy of a Nursing Bra with Nursing Clips

If you want a bra with nursing clips or an internal sling, I suggest looking at a ready made nursing bra and finding one that fits and suits your nursing lifestyle. Look at the fabric used for the main fabric, the lining, and the sling. Examine how the nursing clips are sewn and where the sling is placed. Are there any other elements that you like? Ready to wear can serve as an inspiration and example to make your own.

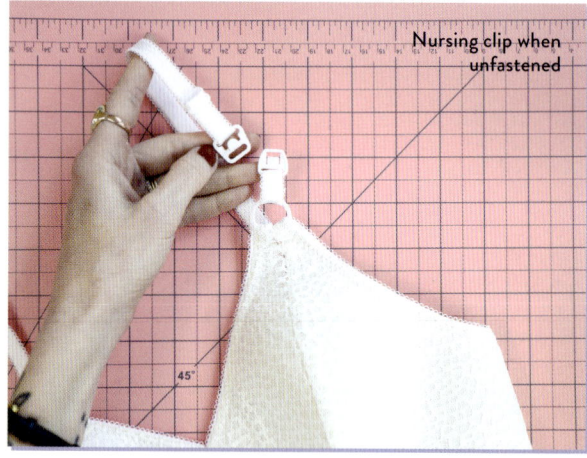

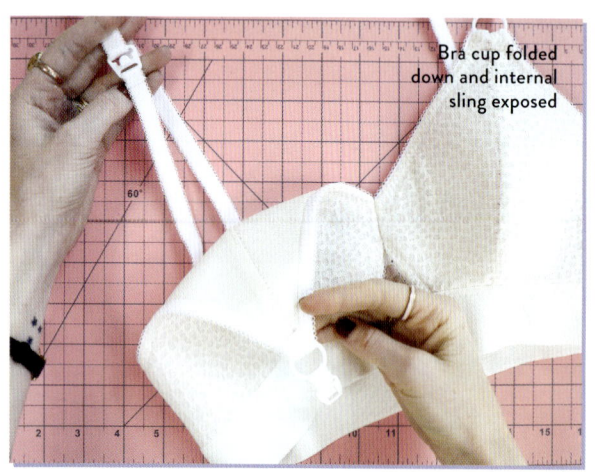

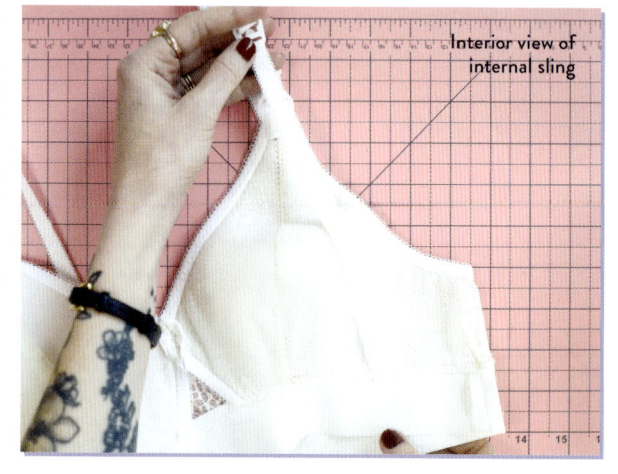

Nursing clip when fastened

Nursing clip when unfastened

Bra cup folded down and internal sling exposed

Interior view of internal sling

172 SEW LINGERIE

Mastectomy Bras

A mastectomy bra is designed to accommodate the issues a person faces after having breast removal surgery. Mastectomy bras can have bra cups with fabric pockets inside that hold a prosthesis. Some need a bra where the curve of the cups have been decreased for a flat chest. Not everyone opts for a prosthesis however, and some choose to get reconstructive surgery so they wouldn't need a mastectomy bra.

Just like nursing bras, if you want to get started making your own mastectomy bra by adding a pocket or adjusting the curve of the bra cups, I recommend looking for a ready to wear style and finding one that fits and feels comfortable. Look at the fabric used. Examine how the pocket is sewn and where it is placed. Are there any other elements that you like? Again, ready to wear can serve as an inspiration for your own design as well as give you ideas that you may not have thought of before!

Types of Mastectomy Bras

Prosthesis: Bras that have cups with fabric pockets that can hold a prosthesis. They can be unilaterally pocketed (prosthesis only one side) or bilaterally pocketed (prosthesis on both sides).

Pre-and-post Surgery: Bras that are designed with special features for a person who is undergoing surgery, including pockets to hold drains, soft fabrics for ultimate comfort, and/or snap or front closures to make getting a bra on/off easy.

Radiation: Bras that are made with soft fabric and the elastics encased inside the seams since a person's skin is usually very sensitive while undergoing radiation.

Front Closure: Bras that have a hook and eye or other type of closure in the front instead of the back.

Reconstructive (Bras for Implants): Bras that are designed with comfort, not support, in mind since breast implants are not heavy. These bras aren't heavily structured and are usually wire free.

ABOUT THE AUTHOR

South Florida native Maddie Kulig is the founder, designer, sewist, and driving force behind Madalynne Intimates. Maddie learned to sew at the age of 18, discovering her mom's sewing machine shortly after she passed away from a six year battle with breast cancer. Maddie took it to her local tailor, and one lesson turned into a two year apprenticeship with a tailor, Myshka, who once worked for Christian Dior.

Maddie's priorities changed when she saw how cancer and chemotherapy destroyed her mother's body and took her life. She decided to only surround herself with the people and the things that mattered to her. Sewing was one of them.

Maddie spent most of her later teenage years at the shop with Myshka. One day, Myshka turned to Maddie and asked what she wanted to do with sewing. It was a simple question that was the incentive for Maddie to apply for her dream job.

At the age of 21, Maddie landed that dream job—a summer internship at URBN (parent brand for Anthropologie, BHLDN, Free People, Terrain, Urban Outfitters) in technical design. Only intending to stay for 10 weeks, Maddie ended up staying 7.5 years. It was during this stint that she discovered DIY lingerie. She found her calling. Hungry to learn more, Maddie continued to make more bras, then panties, then bodysuits, and so on. Maddie started making her own lingerie in a fast fashion world.

In the summer and fall of 2016, Urban Outfitters launched two exclusive Madalynne collections in 50 stores and online. That same summer, Simplicity launched the first two Madalynne patterns, #S8228 and #S8229. Then, Maddie took Madalynne full time.

Since then, Madalynne has grown into a lingerie brand for a new generation. Madalynne continues to offer DIY lingerie kits, tutorials, workshops, and sewing patterns. For people who don't sew, Madalynne offers ready made lingerie that is hand-crafted by a small team of sewists out of their Brewerytown studio in Philadelphia. Madalynne also wholesales DIY kits and ready made lingerie to sew shops and lingerie boutiques around the world. She has taught more than 100 classes worldwide.

Combining an attention to sewing and fit with exclusive fabrics, Madalynne creates customized me-made and ready made lingerie for all sizes, races, genders, and styles.

> "What really knocks me out is a book that, when you're all done reading it, you wish the author that wrote it was a terrific friend of yours and you could call him up on the phone whenever you felt like it."
>
> —J.D. Salinger, The Catcher in the Rye—

SEW LINGERIE

INDEX

activewear fabrics 29–30
adhesive 36, 50
#AerieREAL 7
babydoll 12
back band (wing) types 22
balconette bra 14
ballpoint needles 36
bamboo fabric 26
bandeau bra 15
Barker panty 78–81
bikini, Hallie 150–157
bikini panty 16
body neutrality 9
bodysuit 11, 159–167
boning 34
boutique straps 103
boyshort panty 16
bra
    component terms 18–22
    evaluating fit 48–49
    projects 94–143
    sizing 41–44, 47
    types 13–15
    underwire channeling 23, 60
    underwires 18, 23, 35, 68–69, 124–135
bra alterations
    back band 58
    cup 66–69
    frame (gore) 59–63
    strap 64–66
    test fit (toile) 47
    underarm 64
bralette .. 13, 96–103, 114–123, 134–143
breast terms 14
brief panty 16, 78–81
Brooklyn bralette 96–103

bustier bra 14
channeling underwires 23, 60
cheeky panty 17
chemise 12
clear elastic 33
closures 22, 34, 111, 133
contour bra 14
corset 7, 8, 11, 22, 35
cotton 26
cup sizing 41–44, 49
darted cup 13
demi bra 14
DOGS (direction of greatest stretch) 31–32
Dri-Fit fabric 29
duck-billed scissors 36
duoplex 26
Econyl 30
elastic 32–33, 52, 100
fabrics
    buying 39
    cutting 50
    delicate fabrics 45
    directional vs non-directional 46
    lining 27–28
    main fabrics 25–26
    vs needle size 36
    stretch direction 31–32
15 Denier tricot (lining) 28
foam (polylaminate) 34, 170–171
FOE (fold over elastic) 100
frame (cradle) 21, 49
#freethenipple 8
French curve ruler 36
French cut panty 16, 86–93
front closure bra 111
full-band bra 15

full cup bra 13
galloon lace 25, 39, 55
    See also Ross Panty
garter 12
G hooks 34
girdle 12
Godiva underwire bodysuit 159–167
gore (bridge) 21
GSM 27
G-string 17
gusset width 71
Hallie bikini 150–157
halter bra 14
hashtags 7, 8, 9, 39
Helenca lining 147, 151
Henrietta one-piece swimsuit .. 146–149
high-rise panty 16
hip hugger (hipster) panty 16
hook and eye closure 22
ironing delicate fabrics 46
jersey fabric 26
Kennedy sports bralette 134–143
lace 25, 45, 55
lingerie
    bra types 13–15
    component terms 18–23
    elastic, notions, and underwire 32–35
    fabrics for 25–32
    history of 6–7
    panty types 16–17
    sewing techniques 40–55
    types of 11–12
    See also sewing; tools
lining fabrics 27–28
longline bra 13
lounge bra 15
LYCRA 25, 28

Margo bralette ... 104–113
mastectomy bras, about ... 173
mesh, stretch ... 26, 27
microtex (sharp) needles ... 36
Millie panty ... 82–85
needles ... 36
neoprene ... 29
notions ... 32–35
nursing bra ... 168–173
nylon vs polyester ... 29
panty
    component terms ... 23
    pattern alterations ... 70–75
    projects ... 76–93
    types ... 16–17
    VPL (visible panty line) ... 12, 17
partial-band bra ... 15
patterns
    bra alterations ... 58–69
    dotted pattern paper ... 36
    how to access ... 76
    panty alterations ... 70–75
    pattern-making terms ... 57
    pattern weights ... 50
PBT ... 29
peek-a-boo bra ... 15
picot elastic ... 32, 108
pins ... 36
plunge bra ... 13
polyester vs nylon ... 29
power bar ... 19
power net ... 27
push-up bra ... 14
racerback-style bralette ... 114–123
Rey underwire bra ... 124–135
rings and sliders ... 18, 22
Ross panty ... 86–93
rotary cutter ... 36, 51
rubber elastic ... 33
rulers ... 36
Ryann bralette ... 114–123

Savage X Fenty ... 7
scissors ... 36, 51
seams, finishing ... 53–54
serger ... 53
sewing
    backstitching ... 45
    finishing seams ... 53–54
    foam cups ... 170–171
    lace ... 55
    needles and thread ... 36
    sewing elastic ... 52
    sewing machine ... 37–38
    stitch length ... 53
    straight stitch or zigzag ... 46
sharp (microtex) needles ... 36
sheer cup lining ... 28
silk ... 25
"sister sizing" ... 43
snap closure ... 34
social media ... 39
space dye ... 29
spandex ... 25
sports bra ... 7, 15, 134–143
stabilizers ... 45
stitch length ... 53
strapless bra ... 13
straps
    boutique ... 103
    shoulder ... 22, 33, 134
    strap fit ... 49, 65–66
stretch fabrics
    stretch direction ... 31–32
    types of ... 26
stretch needles ... 36
swimwear
    fabrics ... 28–29
    projects ... 144–157
Tactel fabric ... 29
tanga panty ... 17
teddy ... 12
TENCEL ... 30

thong ... 17, 82–85
thong bodysuit ... 159–167
thread ... 36, 47
toile (test fit) ... 47
tools ... 36–37
triangle bra ... 15
tulle lace ... 25
twill tape ... 34
underwire bra ... 15, 23, 35, 60, 68–69, 124–135
universal needles ... 36
velvet, stretch ... 26
"V" opening ... 153–154
VPL (visible panty line) ... 12, 17
wash away thread ... 47
wedgies (fixing) ... 74
wool ... 30
zigzag stitching ... 53